AF305030

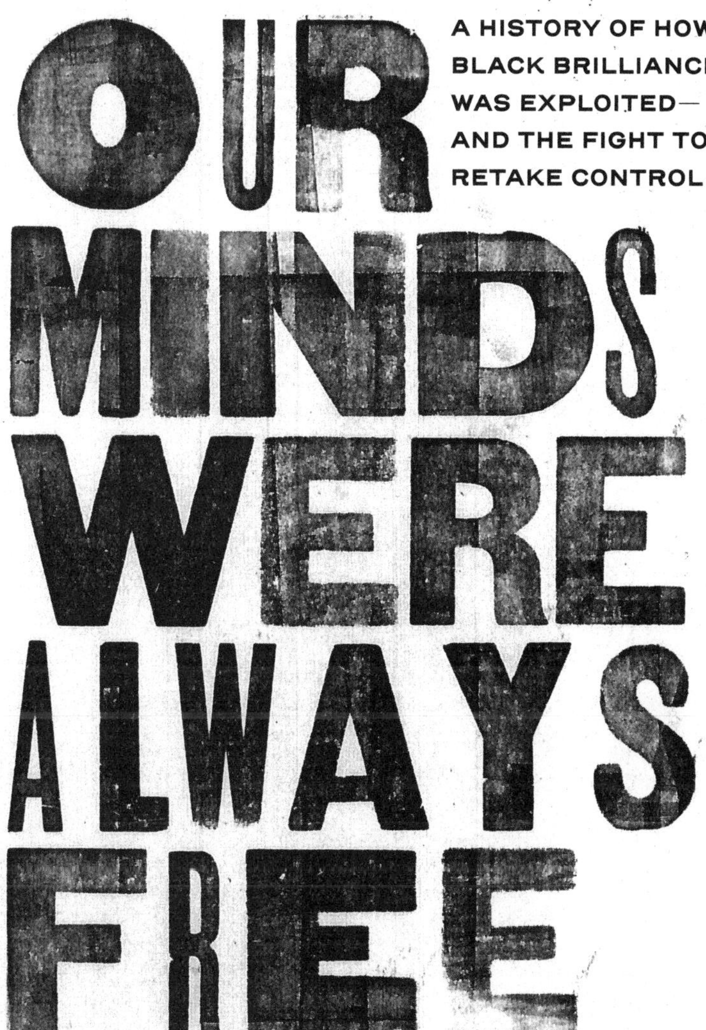

A HISTORY OF HOW
BLACK BRILLIANCE
WAS EXPLOITED—
AND THE FIGHT TO
RETAKE CONTROL

LISA E. DAVIS

SIMON & SCHUSTER

NEW YORK AMSTERDAM/ANTWERP LONDON
TORONTO SYDNEY/MELBOURNE NEW DELHI

Simon & Schuster
1230 Avenue of the Americas
New York, NY 10020

For my mother, Gwen T. Webb,

who taught me to love and

have pride in Black people

Contents

When FN Meka arrived on the music scene, it seemed to be out of nowhere—because it was. Factory New, a digital record company that specialized in "virtual beings," created this musical artist character in 2021. The avatar for FN Meka sported green dreadlocks atop a partially shaved head, face tattoos, an ostentatious gold grill covering half his face, and an olive complexion, rendering him deliberately racially ambiguous.

FN Meka quickly amassed ten million followers on TikTok, and in August 2022, Factory New announced to much fanfare that it had signed FN Meka to Capitol Records. The deal was likely based on the size of the artist's social media following and a debut single, "Florida Water," that boasted features by established Black Hip Hop artist Gunna and professional Fortnite player Clix and was produced by Turbo, a prominent Hip Hop producer. The presence of these established figures lent the newcomer credibility with the Hip Hop audience.

FN Meka "rapped" about being the victim of police brutality and liberally used the N-word. Created by non-Black music executives, FN Meka was an example of modern digital blackface. As soon as the deal was announced, the music industry advocacy group Industry

Blackout said that "FN Meka insulted Black culture and leeched off of the sounds, looks, and life experiences of real Black artists." The blowback was heavily covered in *The New York Times*, and Capitol Records quickly reversed course, canceling the deal and apologizing to the "Black community" for its insensitivity. Perhaps Capitol belatedly realized that it was a bad look for a record company with no Black people at the helm to sign a virtual "Black artist" that trafficked in stereotypes and Black pain and gained an audience by leaning on established Black artists, with all profits going to the record label.

Factory New label head Anthony Martini boasted that FN Meka represented a new frontier, "an artist created using thousands of data points compiled from video games and social media . . . voiced by a human," but otherwise completely powered by AI. Martini's characterization conjured up a dystopian future where Black people's words and actions on social media and in video games would be harvested without credit or compensation to create a completely digital, fictional "Black" artist whose performance could be endlessly monetized by white-owned labels without the pesky need for advances, royalties, or basic human consideration. Martini appeared to lean into this vision, calling "the biggest stars in the world . . . just vessels for commercial endeavors," blithely dismissing the towering talent of very human artists like Beyoncé and Taylor Swift.

Despite all its crowing about the technological advances that FN Meka represented, it appears that Factory New might have engaged in old-fashioned human exploitation that has a long, ignominious history in the music business. Once the deal imploded, Black Houston-based rapper Kyle The Hooligan said that he had written FN Meka's first three songs and hadn't been paid.

FN Meka's brief career unfolded like a parody of a dystopian sci-fi tale, where the messy, sweaty business of composing hit music and delivering iconic performances was offloaded to digital and robotic creations. In truth, FN Meka is merely the logical outgrowth of an entertainment business built on a foundation of underpaying or *not* paying those creators and performers who made an outsized impact on the culture.

America has a long and sordid history of mining the value of the art and inventions of Black people for its own benefit and erasing evidence of Black authorship to prop up the myth of white superiority. Our country is built on the creativity, innovation, and resilience of thousands of Black people whose names have been buried. The refusal to acknowledge them and learn their stories is a refusal to acknowledge the scope of what this country owes its Black citizens.

Just as structural racism is embedded in our criminal justice system, over the course of American history, the laws governing intellectual property have operated in ways to deprive Black people of the value of their mental labor as much as their physical labor.

Throughout the twentieth century, the development and distribution of film, television, music, books, and theater involved an uneasy marriage between capital and creators. The law addressed this tension in part by giving creators nearly exclusive control over the exploitation of their creations or inventions. The problem, of course, is that in a capitalist country, the companies with money were always going to have more leverage than their workers—even if those workers were beloved artists.

The fact that the law has always lagged behind technology has only exacerbated this imbalance. Almost seventy years elapsed between the Copyright Act of 1909 and the January 1, 1978, effective date of the Copyright Act of 1976. Those seven decades saw many changes in how we consumed entertainment: player piano technology was supplanted by radio, then vinyl records, then by cassette audio tape that empowered consumers to create their own compilations. It saw film evolve from silent shorts viewed in nickelodeons to silent feature-length films viewed in movie palaces to black-and-white talkies to glorious Technicolor to Dolby Stereo.

During this time, despite outmoded intellectual property law, creators maintained a fragile equilibrium between control of their work and the ability to profit from it because of three factors: (1) the pace of adoption of new technologies for the consumption of content was slower than it would later become in the last quarter of the century; (2) labor organizing by writers and musicians moderated some of the excesses of studios and record companies; and (3) the US Department of Justice broke up the monopoly that the studios held over the development, production, and distribution of movies in the antitrust case that led to the Paramount consent decree in 1948.

Take, for example, the invention of the phonograph in 1877 by Thomas Edison. It would become a vehicle for recording everything from "artistic whistling" to vaudeville skits, but not until Black blues singer Mamie Smith sold one million copies of her 1920 song "Crazy Blues" did the record player take off and become the widely adopted way that Americans consumed music. It was also an early example of Black creativity spurring demand for nascent technology, a pattern that would be repeated in the twenty-first century.

In fact, the twentieth and twenty-first centuries were a struggle, built on an even longer history we'll soon see, between those who seek to make a living from their intellectual property and those who seek to wring every cent of value from those creations while leaving creators impoverished. Like most inexplicable policy choices and societal phenomena in America, race is at the core.

With film, as the technology progressed from silent shorts to full-length features with sound, it became a vehicle for selling American audiences a vision on a mass scale of who could be the main characters in American life and who existed just to be servants or comic foils. Many people contributed to the development of early motion picture technology, such as English photographer Eadweard Muybridge and French physiologist Étienne-Jules Marey, who in 1878 each independently invented devices that could capture moving images. In the United States, prolific inventor Thomas Edison worried that someone else would beat him to market and began working with his assistant to develop a motion picture camera. By the 1890s he had announced the invention of a projector and then opened kinetograph parlors where the public could pay a small admission fee to see moving pictures. The emergence of the narrative film, starting with *The Great Train Robbery* in 1903, is what sparked the wildly popular nickelodeon boom of single-reel films that the public could view for a 5-cent admission fee. Once the modern film business was born in 1910 with the development of multiple reel "feature" films, consumers and the market responded quickly. By 1916, there were twenty-one thousand movie theaters in the United States.

What followed less than two decades later was the formation of the modern Writers Guild of America (WGA) to protect screenwriters. At the height of the Great Depression, MGM founder Louis B. Mayer proposed to slash screenwriters' pay by 50 percent when FDR declared a bank holiday in March 1933 to address the panicked mass withdrawals, or "bank runs," that led several banks to collapse during the Great Depression. Notably, Mayer did not propose any reduction in executives' pay, or in the pay of unionized film production crews. Screenwriters fought back and prepared a union constitution and by-laws that were ratified one month later. Still, it took nearly ten years for the WGA to secure a Minimum Basic Agreement with the studios in 1942.

The defining moment for the musicians' union, the American Federation of Musicians (AFM), was the recording ban it initiated in 1942. The ban's purpose was to combat the devastating effect that widespread adoption of phonograph records had on the employment opportunities of musicians. Radio stations increasingly preferred to play recordings of big bands, rather than broadcast their live performances. This practice drastically reduced the employment of AFM's members, with the added irony that musicians' own performances at recording sessions were putting them out of work. Union leader James Petrillo believed that a boycott of recording would stave off the collapse in the employment market for his members. Yet it was twenty-seven months before the union could end the ban, because recording companies anticipated it and simply stockpiled recordings. At the end of their labor action, the union secured the establishment of a trust fund to offset their members' earning loss.

We can see echoes of the twentieth-century struggle by creators against technology designed to render them obsolete right now. It is evident in the lawsuits brought by authors to combat the unauthorized use of their copyrighted work to train artificial intelligence systems, in the demands by the WGA and SAG-AFTRA for guardrails around the use of AI, or for increases to the residual payments that nosedived after the film and television industry adopted streaming as the principal method of distribution.

The battles being waged by writers, actors, and musicians today echo the fight that Black people have been waging since human traffickers brought them here four centuries ago. Black people have long been the canaries in the coal mine with respect to policy decisions around issues such as the social safety net and reproductive rights. It is all too common for policies designed to explicitly harm Black Americans to end up ensnaring countless white people as well, from work requirements for food stamps to voter ID laws. With each of these policy decisions, many white people look away until personally affected. This is equally true of the operation of American intellectual property law and the business models that emerged in the twentieth and twenty-first centuries to exploit it.

The extent to which American exceptionalism was powered not only by Black bodies but Black brains is a significant part of our history we must face, despite the desire of racists to erase it. From the carbon filament that allows light bulbs to last longer than a few days, invented by Lewis Latimer in 1881, to the ironing board design improvement patented by Sarah Boone in 1892, to countless other inventions and creations, Black Americans' creativity and genius helped power this country's global preeminence. Some want this history buried because it flies in the face of the lie of white superiority. Others want to bury it because confronting the myriad ways in which Black intellectual capital was stolen and Black authorship and invention erased sullies the myth of America's essential goodness.

Numerous historians have written about the inherent contradiction between America's stated veneration of human freedom and its institutionalization of racialized slavery. There has been little focus yet on the contradiction embedded in the legal framework governing intellectual property and the racial caste system. While slavery gave slaveholders the right to profit from the physical labor of the people they "owned," American intellectual property law reserved the limited monopolies of patents and copyrights to the actual human inventors or authors, *not* to those claiming ownership of the inventor or author. This meant that while slaveholders could physically torture people to pick more cotton, they could not own the poems that they wrote or patent the inventions that enslaved Africans devised.

That paradox is embedded in our founding documents, our secular bible—the Constitution. The Founders believed that both the ability of white men to profit from their creation and invention *and* the ability of those same white men to *own* other human beings and profit from *their* labor were required for the fledgling republic to thrive. They drafted the Constitution accordingly.

The legal protections afforded to creators and inventors and to slaveholders both appear early in the document. The Three-Fifths Compromise, a 1787 agreement articulated in Article 1, Section 2, used the numbers of Black people held in bondage to bolster the political power of their oppressors. Article 1, Section 8, states that Congress shall have the power "to promote the progress of science and useful arts, by securing for limited times to authors and inventors the exclusive right to their respective writings and discoveries." The very next section, Article 1, Section 9, prohibits Congress from passing laws relating to the "migration or importation of such persons as any states now existing shall think proper to admit," prior to 1808. Though the word *slave* is absent from this provision, its explicit purpose was to prohibit Congress from outlawing the slave trade for a period of twenty years after the signing of the Constitution. While some signers of the Constitution expressed their opposition to slavery, given that twenty-five of the fifty-five signers of the Constitution owned other human beings, all signers clearly believed that permitting slavery was necessary to forge the fledgling union among the states.

Since the first enslaved Africans arrived on these shores in 1619, history has been replete with stories of Black people, both during slavery and afterward, whose brilliance was exploited to create wealth for others. Even before the founding of the republic, white colonists relied on the superior skills and scientific knowledge of enslaved Africans to forge their lives on a new continent. The story of Onesimus, a West African enslaved by fire-and-brimstone Boston preacher Cotton Mather, is one prominent example.

In the early eighteenth century, smallpox was a recurring threat in the colonies, often arriving with kidnapped Africans on slave ships. Mather asked Onesimus if he had ever had smallpox. Onesimus explained that he had been inoculated against the disease prior to his capture. Onesimus detailed the procedure, by which a doctor took a drop of live virus and purposely infected people through a small incision on the arm. Onesimus explained that the inoculation typically resulted in a mild case of smallpox but conferred immunity to the disease.

When Mather attempted to convince his fellow Bostonians to implement inoculations to fight smallpox, he was met with hostile resistance. White Bostonians either believed that their enslaved captives wanted to poison them or that it was not conceivable that the Africans' medical knowledge was superior to theirs.

In 1721, when another smallpox epidemic was ravaging Boston, Mather finally convinced local doctor Zabdiel Boylston to try inoculating Bostonians against smallpox. Boylston inoculated 242 people, and only six died—a rate of one in forty. Conversely, among the uninoculated, the death rate of those who contracted smallpox was one in seven.

Although Onesimus was clearly responsible for teaching Cotton Mather about inoculation, his role was erased until three centuries later, when *Boston Magazine* named Onesimus as #52 on its list of the 100 Best Bostonians of All Time, along with people like JFK, Bill Russell, and Leonard Bernstein.

This pattern of appropriating Black knowledge or skill while erasing Black authorship was rampant during slavery to prop up the myth of Black inferiority. During slavery, human traffickers persistently tried to own not only the fruits of Black people's physical labor but their intellectual labor as well. The structure of American intellectual property law prevented that, so white people often simply lied about Black authorship to profit directly from Black brilliance.

Throughout the antebellum period, the American economy depended on extracting as much as possible from the physical and intellectual labor of enslaved Black people through violent repression to maximize efficiencies in methods of cultivating, harvesting, and processing the cotton that was the lifeblood of the Southern economy.

Although Eli Whitney received a patent for the invention of the cotton gin in 1794, he "got the idea from [an enslaved man] only known to history as Sam, whose father developed a comb which separated cotton seeds from the boll." As author Clay Thompson details, Whitney learned about the device and "simply mechanized it."

Once Black people were freed after the Civil War, there was an "explosion of patents awarded to Black people," evidence that legal barriers were the main obstacle preventing Black people from being recognized for and profiting from their inventions. As Portia P. James details in her book *The Real McCoy: African-American Invention and Innovation, 1619–1930,* in the period commencing with

Reconstruction and continuing until the imposition of Jim Crow, free Black people were responsible for many seminal inventions.

Black innovators played a key role in the technological advances that powered urban life in the early twentieth century. A Black person invented the traffic light, thereby regulating the flow of pedestrian and vehicular traffic; a lubrication mechanism for train engines so essential that the inventor's name became synonymous with authenticity and quality; and a mechanism to automate the opening and closing of elevator doors, vastly improving elevator safety.

Yet outbreaks of racial violence and the imposition of Jim Crow laws in the early twentieth century led to a dramatic drop in Black patent ownership. According to economist Lisa D. Cook, those factors led to a decline in Black patent ownership at a rate of 1 percent per year. To cite one example of what Black inventors were up against: The Illinois home of pioneering Black chemist Dr. Percy Julian, whose research laid the foundations for steroids and birth control pills, was firebombed twice.

State-mandated school and employment segregation in the twentieth century created knowledge and opportunity gaps between Black and white Americans, further contributing to the decline in Black patent applications. Yet Black people's resourcefulness and capacity for innovation did not disappear; it merely found another outlet. In the twentieth century, Black people channeled those gifts into the creative arts—inventing musical genres from blues to jazz, rock and roll to Hip Hop.

While intellectual property laws governing copyrights did not present the rigid barrier to entry that patent law did, knowledge or ignorance of those laws, along with ownership of the means of producing and distributing copyrighted work, made the difference between monetizing or even being credited with authorship of one's creative works.

Black people's work is inextricably bound to what makes America *America*, from the stolen physical labor that enabled the young republic to become an economic superpower to the technological innovation that drove the Industrial Revolution to the creative genius that made American culture our most dominant twentieth-century export.

Many of the names of the Black people responsible for critical inventions or seminal musical genres, like Sister Rosetta Tharpe, were deliberately erased. Others became famous, like Billie Holiday, while enriching everyone but themselves. A savvy few, like Thomas Jennings and Berry Gordy, combined creative or inventive skills with knowledge of intellectual property law to build a fortune for themselves and their families.

All their stories are worth telling—to correct and expand the historical record, and to show the depth, breadth, and persistence of Black invention and creation. This book is a work of excavation and reclamation, hoping to show that no matter how much America denied Black humanity, no matter how much America treated Black people as property or as inferior beings unworthy of citizenship, Black brilliance could not be contained. No matter what the letter of American law said—our minds were always free.

ONE

THE INTELLECTUAL PROPERTY OF PROPERTY

What do you see when you picture slavery? Technicolor images out of *Gone with the Wind* of industrious, childlike Black people with no higher goal than serving their white "masters"? A mammy figure played by Hattie McDaniel, the Oscar-winning performance that crystallized the stereotype of the sturdy, sexless Black woman, short on intellect but long on mother wit?

Or maybe your mental picture of slavery is inspired instead by scenes from *12 Years a Slave*, with noble Black folks subjected to the cruel whims of sadistic slavers, raped and brutalized at will. Even if that picture is more realistic than others, does it allow you to imagine that Black people in nineteenth-century America, whether free in the North or enslaved in the South, had the capacity to create and innovate?

Decades of scholarship produced by historians, from John Henrik Clarke to Ibram X. Kendi, have established the truism that the wealth of America was built on the bloodied backs of Black bodies. But that truism lends itself too easily to a notion of an undifferentiated mass of people reduced to what their bodies could produce. It offers no insight into the interior lives of Black people, much less their astonishing capacity for ingenuity and invention.

A critical component of American exceptionalism is our culture of innovation and creativity, a culture deemed important enough to be enshrined in our Constitution. Article I, Section 8, Clause 8 of the Constitution directs Congress to make laws promoting "Science and useful Arts, by securing for limited Times to Authors and Inventors the exclusive Right to their respective Writings and Discoveries." American laws made the acquisition of intellectual property rights more accessible than their British antecedents, with early US patent law granting rights to the actual inventor rather than his employer.

This provision spurred the development of intellectual property laws that gave a limited monopoly to inventors and creators. Patent law incentivized citizens of the young nation to develop methods, machines, and devices to facilitate agriculture and commerce. Copyright law encouraged the creation of American literature, art, and music. The Founding Fathers understood that a legal system enabling individuals to profit from their own intellectual production would spur innovation and give the burgeoning republic a competitive advantage in trade with other countries. In a country governed "by the people," patents and copyrights would benefit the individual creator or inventor, democratizing art and industry. The reference to intellectual property rights in the Constitution predating the Bill of Rights shows that the Founders viewed these rights as an essential building block in the economy of a young nation.

An economy is built by what a country can buy and sell, but a nation is built by what its people create. In the American popular imagination, the great inventors who powered the country's rise have for centuries been thought of as ingenious, solitary white men, from Eli Whitney to Thomas Edison. The truth is messier and more complicated.

Enslaved African people were not animate raw material whose sole purpose was to contribute their unskilled physical labor to the construction of the American empire. Those kidnapped from Africa came from diverse peoples with rich histories of achievement and innovation in science, industry, and agriculture. Evidence exists of steel being produced as far back as two millennia ago in what is now Tanzania, and of an astronomical observatory in what is now Kenya hundreds of years before that.

The African people kidnapped to serve as free labor in the Americas brought their knowledge with them. Their legal status as noncitizens who were considered less than human by their captors, along with the prohibition against teaching them to read and write, should have put America's complex laws about invention and creation beyond their reach. We have long presumed that enslaved Africans had no means of recording and protecting their innovations, erasing any memory of their brilliance and allowing a greedy and exploitative class to shore up the myth of white supremacy. A closer examination of history reveals that, despite formidable obstacles, Black people in America, both enslaved and free, have a history of innovation and creativity that is as old as the republic.

Although there are earlier recorded examples of Black innovation, the first Black person to successfully avail himself of the country's fledgling intellectual property law was a Black New Yorker named Thomas L. Jennings. In the colonial era, New York City was already a teeming metropolis with a diverse population of Dutch, British, French, and German immigrants and enslaved Africans. It hosted a bustling slave market on Wall Street from 1711 to 1762, when Black people comprised between 14–21 percent of colonial New York's population. Many enslaved Black people were skilled artisans who earned money for their owners by being hired out for work in the trades.

After the Revolutionary War, New York City became the nation's first capital and one of the country's most important trading ports. Cotton cultivated by enslaved Africans on Southern plantations was shipped to New York to be sent on for processing in English mill cities such as Manchester. Although New York outlawed slavery in 1799, the law provided for "gradual emancipation" and didn't actually free enslaved people until 1827. Even after the effective date of emancipation in New York State, New York City remained a center of the illegal slave trade, dominating it by the 1850s.

Thomas L. Jennings was a free Black man born into this complicated city in 1791. In his boyhood, Jennings apprenticed to a successful tailor. When he was twenty-one, Jennings dug trenches on Long Island during the War of 1812. Like many other Black men serving in the military in American wars across the centuries, Jennings probably viewed military service as a way of proving his citizenship and "earning" the right to be treated accordingly. According to Frederick Douglass's obituary of Jennings, as a young man he "paraded the streets of [New York City] with a banner inscribed with the figure of a Black man and the words, 'Am I not a man and brother?'" Jennings's protest prefigures the I AM A MAN placards held by Black Memphis sanitation workers more than a century later in 1968.

Later, Jennings opened his own tailor shop on the corner of Nassau Street and what is now Park Row in Lower Manhattan. Jennings's shop was extremely successful. He soon recognized that his customers needed a way to remove stains and soil from fine fabrics that could not be laundered. Jennings developed a method called dry scouring, the precursor to the modern-day dry-cleaning process. Jennings applied for and received a patent for his invention in 1821.

The significance of Jennings's patent cannot be overstated. After all, the Founders considered patent rights so essential to the economic development of the fledgling republic that they were included in the Constitution. These laws granted the inventor a monopoly over the rights to any machine, method, or material that was both useful and new. The first patent law in the country, enacted in 1790, limited eligibility for patent grants to US citizens; the law was amended in 1800 to permit foreigners who had lived in the country for two years to obtain patent rights, but the grant of a patent to Thomas Jennings in 1821, a Black man born and raised in the United States, was prima facie evidence of his citizenship as a free Black man. Historian Martha Jones has argued that grants of patents were evidence of Black citizenship. The attendees at the 1858 National Convention of People of Color cataloged the inventions of Black men to bolster the case for abolition. Jennings hung his letters patent, signed by then Secretary of State John Quincy Adams, in a gilded frame over his bed.

Jennings's timing in securing his patent was fortuitous. The patent laws in effect in the United States between 1793 and 1836 made no distinction between enslaved and free persons in their ability to hold a patent. The mere fact that Jennings obtained a patent is one of many examples that belied the noxious myth of Black intellectual inferiority used to justify the peculiar institution.

Jennings was not content to be a symbolic token for advocates and activists to deploy in antislavery campaigns. With the income generated from his invention, he bought his wife's freedom. He plowed his wealth and spare time into the causes of abolition and civil rights for Black people. He led celebrations of New York's abolition of slavery in 1827 and was a leading figure at the first four Colored Conventions from 1831 to 1834. At the national conventions, those assembled contemplated buying land in Canada to serve as a refuge for Black people and establishing a college for Black men in New Haven, Connecticut. Jennings was one of the founding subscribers to William Lloyd Garrison's abolitionist newspaper *The Liberator* as well as a founder of the storied Abyssinian Baptist Church in New York City. Little more than a century later, Abyssinian served as the springboard for the career of Rep. Adam Clayton Powell Jr.

Jennings and his wife, Elizabeth, had five children, all of whom were able to secure the skills and education for careers of their own, thanks to their status as free Black people with the material wealth earned from Thomas Jennings's invention. One of Jennings's daughters, Matilda, became a dressmaker, and his sons, William and Thomas, found success as a businessman and a dentist, respectively. None of Jennings's children followed his path as an activist as much as his daughter, Elizabeth, a New York City schoolteacher. One hundred years before Rosa Parks's famous refusal to give up her seat on a bus in Montgomery, Alabama, Elizabeth Jennings challenged segregation in New York City public transportation and won.

On July 16, 1854, Elizabeth Jennings was rushing to the First Colored American Congregational Church, where she served as the church organist. To get there, Elizabeth took the Third Avenue street-car. In New York City in 1854, streetcars had an official policy of seg-regation. Streetcars for Black passengers bore a sign that read COLORED PEOPLE ALLOWED IN THE CAR.

Since she was in a hurry, Elizabeth boarded the first streetcar to arrive, even though it was not one designated for Black passengers. The conductor immediately challenged her presence and told her to get off the car. When Elizabeth refused, the conductor tried to forc-ibly eject her, but she resisted and stayed on the car. At the next stop, the conductor flagged down a police officer, and the two white men physically dragged Elizabeth off the car, assaulting her in the process. Elizabeth's clothes were torn, and she suffered bruises and broken bones. What happened to Elizabeth Jennings was proof, then as now, that a Black person's wealth and privilege could not insulate them from racist violence. The difference was that Thomas Jennings, as a wealthy and prominent Black person, had the means to make the streetcar company pay for their casual brutality. He had the means to effect systemic change.

The day after Elizabeth was assaulted, her father convened an emergency meeting of Black New Yorkers at the First Colored American Congregational Church. The group took up a collection and decided to hire a lawyer to press Elizabeth's case against the Third Avenue Railroad Company. The Black New Yorkers decided to hire a prominent lawyer named Erastus Culver, but Culver was unavailable due to his recent appointment to the bench. Culver recommended his protégé, a twenty-four-year-old lawyer named Chester Arthur. Arthur, who would go on to become the twenty-first president of the United States, won the civil case on behalf of Elizabeth Jennings in March 1855. The decision resulted in the desegregation of public transportation in New York State, one hundred years before Rosa Parks would spark the Montgomery bus boycott.

Jennings's success in antebellum America was anomalous for several reasons. First, he was able to harness intellectual property law to generate the resources to secure a patent grant. Second, he was able to wield that patent to secure significant wealth for himself and his family. Third, Thomas Jennings was both a successful businessperson and a staunch and vocal advocate for abolition and the rights of Black people. That he was able to accomplish all this without a white patron or partner is a testament to the fact that Thomas Jennings was indeed an extraordinary person. Jennings was an early example of a pattern that repeats throughout American history: Time and again, Black people leveraged the wealth and/or fame earned through their intellectual property to benefit the broader Black community.

We must be careful not to fall into the "great man" trap of history. Jennings's success owes as much to when and where he lived as it does to his admittedly extraordinary character. Jennings was born in the late eighteenth century, into a fledgling republic that had yet to solidify the legal structure that consigned Black people to a lower caste. By virtue of when and where he was born, Jennings outwitted America's racial caste system, a system designed to deny Black folks the protections and privileges of American laws.

For example, in the period after the Revolutionary War, federal law allowed individual states to determine the composition of their militias. Policy regarding the possibility of Black men serving in the military varied from state to state. By the War of 1812, New Jersey, Vermont, and New Hampshire laws were silent on whether Blacks could serve in militias, while North Carolina and Virginia allowed Black men to serve alongside whites, and Connecticut,

Massachusetts, and South Carolina prohibited Black people from serving altogether.

This porous legal structure began to change radically when the plantation economy switched from cultivating tobacco and rice to producing cotton. After the War of 1812, demand for cotton began to grow exponentially, thanks to the soaring British demand for cotton to feed its textile industry, and with it grew a concomitant need for an increasing number of enslaved people to cultivate the crop. The fifteen slaveholding states began aggressively fighting for their "right" to traffic and exploit human beings, pushing for enforcement of the first Fugitive Slave Act of 1793. These draconian laws led to the persecution of all Black people in many free states, as Northern businessmen were loath to alienate their Southern trading partners.

As a result, less than twenty years after Jennings obtained his patent, Black inventors seeking the protection of the country's intellectual property laws confronted many more obstacles. They had to resort to subterfuge to profit from their inventions. One example is Henry Boyd, a carpenter who was born enslaved in Kentucky in 1802. After purchasing his freedom, he fled to Cincinnati in search of work as a skilled artisan. Boyd remained unemployed due to widespread de facto discrimination but remained focused on his inventiveness. He developed his own product, a corded bedframe he dubbed the "Boyd Bedstead." Noted historian Carter G. Woodson reported that Boyd's invention was lauded as "the most comfortable bed prior to the use of springs." Still, Boyd felt compelled to recruit a white partner to apply for the patent for his invention in 1835.

Armed with legal protection, Boyd built up a manufacturing business that employed an integrated workforce of twenty-five, and the Boyd Bedstead became popular throughout the Ohio and Mississippi

Valleys. White envy of Boyd's economic success was so severe that his factory was burned down several times. Insurance carriers then refused to cover Boyd's business and forced him to close permanently in 1863. Boyd's predicament is early evidence of the violent white opposition that frequently greets Black success.

The increasing hostility to the mere existence of free Black people was driven by the Southern economy's increasing reliance on King Cotton. In 1830, the US passed the Indian Removal Act, a law that drove Indigenous people from their lands. Between 1833 and 1837, after the Choctaw and Chickasaw people were evicted from Mississippi, the state sold seven million acres of land to white planters eager to profit from the cotton boom. By 1839, cotton production in the state, which stood at twenty million pounds per year in 1820, had ballooned to 193 million pounds annually. During the 1830s, Mississippi's population of enslaved people increased by 200 percent, and by the start of the Civil War, Mississippi was the South's undisputed cotton king, producing more than half a *billion* pounds of cotton annually from the unpaid labor of enslaved Black people.

The crushing demands of plantation cotton production pushed Black people to produce increasing amounts of cotton under punishing conditions. It makes sense that they would invent labor-saving devices and processes to lighten their load, if only slightly.

American law considered the physical labor of enslaved Black people to be the property of their enslavers and could not conceive that the enslaved had the capacity for intellectual labor. This created a conundrum under intellectual property law, and patent law specifically, that limited patent protection to the actual inventors. Inventors were required to swear an oath that they had created the device or method for which they were seeking patent protection. Many slaveholders got around this requirement by simply lying and claiming credit for the inventions of those they enslaved. In this way, intellectual property law was another example of the paradox between American ideals and American reality. Intellectual property law empowered the individual, but slavery required that Black people be considered something other than humans to justify the extraction and exploitation of our intellectual labor. The inventions and creations of Black people exposed the lie.

The long history of Oscar J. E. Stuart's repeated efforts to obtain a patent on the double-bladed plow, invented by an enslaved man named Ned, reveals the paradox inherent in laws predicated on the self-serving lie that Black people were inherently inferior and incapable of invention or creation.

Oscar J. E. Stuart was a lawyer and plantation owner in Holmesville, Mississippi. On November 15, 1857, Stuart applied for a patent for a double-bladed plow that would allow one (presumably enslaved) person and two horses to perform the work of two plows and four horses, thereby wringing even more labor out of those who worked for free. On November 24, 1857, Patent Commissioner Joseph Holt denied Stuart's application because Stuart was not the inventor, and in the commissioner's view, enslaved people were ineligible for patent protection. Holt employed the reasoning of the recent, notorious *Dred Scott* decision, where Chief Justice Roger Taney had written for the 7–2 majority of the Supreme Court that Black people "were beings of an inferior order . . . [with] no rights which the white man was bound to respect."

Perhaps Stuart had anticipated this result, as he wrote preemptively to the secretary of the interior as a "fellow Mississippian" and to his US senator John Quitman, to explicitly request that slaveholders be permitted to obtain patents on the inventions of their human property. Stuart asserted that the refusal of the law to grant slave-holders a monopoly on the intellectual labor of those they enslaved constituted "unjust discrimination [which] subverts the principle of equality between the citizens of the country." This contention might be laughable if it weren't so tragic. Stuart completely absorbed the idea that enslaved human beings were possessions, not people. He had to, in order to make the internally inconsistent argument that his inability to profit from the mental productivity of the enslaved deprived *him* of equal protection under the law!

Despite Stuart's extensive lobbying, in June 1858, the attorney general issued an opinion adopting Commissioner Holt's extension of the noxious *Dred Scott* reasoning to patent law. By implication, this meant that no Black person, enslaved or free, could avail themselves of patent law protection.

Stuart used this opening to continue to push for his "right" to wring every ounce of value out of the people he enslaved, including the fruits of their mental labor. Stuart's letter to Senator John Quit-man provided insight into his thinking, detailing precisely how he came to claim title in the invention of the double-bladed plow, as executor of his deceased wife's estate. Stuart offered no details about the inventor himself, with nothing more than his name, Ned, men-tioned. Nowhere in the record was there any indication that Stuart saw a contradiction in claiming that an entire group of people were ordained to "serve" white people by dint of their "general stupidity," yet were capable of inventing devices so unique and useful that they were deserving of patent protection.

In January 1859, six months after the attorney general's opinion upheld the denial of Stuart's patent, Senator David Reid of North

Carolina introduced a bill that would amend patent law to allow enslavers to obtain patents on the inventions of their slaves. There is no evidence that Stuart lobbied Reid, which suggests that this issue was a concern among slaveholders, who were not content with exploiting the free physical labor of Black people. They believed in their right to extract the ingenuity and intellectual labor from the enslaved to further increase their own wealth as well. It was proof of the grim determination of these human traffickers. They erased any trace of agency or humanity in those they enslaved by attempting to capture their liberty, their labor, and their minds.

Senator Reid's bill went nowhere, but one year later, in January 1860, Mississippi Senator Albert Gallatin Brown reintroduced it. Again, no action was taken. After three years of lobbying, Stuart finally abandoned his effort to secure a patent, but *not* his effort to profit from Ned's invention. Stuart began manufacturing and selling the plow, publishing ads that proudly trumpeted the fact that it had been invented by an enslaved person. Stuart's ads contained an endorsement from Senator Brown, who stated that he was "glad to know that your implement is the invention of a negro slave, thus giving lie to the abolition cry that slavery dwarfs the mind of the negro. When did a free negro ever invent anything?" As white people have done since the dawn of the republic, Brown mistook his ignorance of Black invention for its absence, making the paradoxical claim that the invention proved that slavery *benefited* Black people by improving their minds! In the North, abolitionists published editorials and cartoons widely mocking the absurdity of slave owners trying to patent their slaves' inventions.

Given Mississippi's centrality to the plantation economy, it is no wonder that Oscar Stuart was not the only slaveholder who sought to use patent law to profit from the labor-saving inventions of those he enslaved. Benjamin Thornton Montgomery's story is another fascinating tale that illuminates both the brilliance of many enslaved Black people and how the contorted logic of America's racial caste system had unintended consequences in the economy of intellectual property.

Montgomery was born enslaved in Loudoun County, Virginia, in 1819. He was the same age as his enslaver's son and learned to read and write alongside him. In 1836, when Montgomery was seventeen years old, he was sold down the river and ended up at a slave market in Natchez, Mississippi. There, he was purchased by Joseph Davis, the eldest brother of Jefferson Davis, who would go on to become the president of the Confederacy. Unlike his youngest brother, Joseph Davis had an unusual approach to the management of his enslaved workforce, treating his enslaved people with more benevolent paternalism than was common at other plantations. The older Davis had been influenced by the ideas of British industrialist Robert Owen, who had attempted to establish utopian manufacturing communities in New Lanark, Scotland, and New Harmony, Indiana.

Inspired by Owen, Davis tried to establish a "utopian community" at Davis Bend, Mississippi. He believed that enslaved people should cultivate their skills and permitted them to retain any profits derived from those skills that *exceeded the value of their labor as field hands*. Davis appeared to have been blissfully unaware of the contradiction inherent in imagining that a utopia could be built in a system where human beings *owned* other human beings, wherein the "workers" had no ability to profit from their physical labor and no agency over the jobs that they did or for whom they worked. This paradox is best illustrated by the fact that there is no evidence that Davis ever freed any of his slaves, despite his alleged beneficence.

Nonetheless, Montgomery made the most of this system. In 1842, Joseph Davis permitted Montgomery to open a general store on the premises that sold textiles and groceries. In his second year of operation, Montgomery established his own line of credit with wholesalers in New Orleans and expanded his product offerings, attracting white customers, including some of the residents on the plantation. He also sold supplies to steamboat captains. Montgomery made so much money from the store that he was able to build a larger store and adjoining home for himself and his family. Most important, he was able to purchase his wife's freedom.

Montgomery and his wife, Mary Lewis Montgomery, were determined to educate their four children. Although they initially assumed this job themselves, when their oldest son, Isaiah, was seven, Benjamin Montgomery hired a white teacher, George Metcalf, to teach his children.

Montgomery's talents were not limited to his skills as an entrepreneur. Taking full advantage of his enslaver's paradoxical philosophy of encouraging those he enslaved to develop their talents, Montgomery acquired skills as an engineer, a land surveyor, and an architectural draftsman. In the late 1850s, Montgomery invented a lightweight steamboat propeller that would prevent the boats from getting stuck in the mud, thereby speeding the flow of cargo down the Mississippi River. Jefferson Davis applied for a patent in Montgomery's name in February 1859, but the application was denied because of the patent office policy that, as noncitizens, enslaved people were ineligible for patent protection. The following year, Davis applied again, this time in his brother Joseph Davis's name, but was rejected because Davis was admittedly not the inventor.

The Davis brothers abandoned any further effort to secure the monopoly protection that a patent would provide. After the outbreak of the Civil War, Joseph Davis fled Mississippi, and the federal government confiscated his property. Benjamin Montgomery moved to Cincinnati and found work as a shipyard carpenter. In November 1862, Attorney General Edward Bates issued an opinion that free Black people were citizens. That, combined with a Senate resolution sponsored by Senator Charles Sumner explicitly providing that Black people were eligible for patent protection and the Emancipation Proclamation in 1863, changed the legal landscape. In 1864, Montgomery, who clearly understood the importance of patent protection and believed in the importance of his invention, filed for patent protection on his own behalf.

Although the patent office did not grant Montgomery's application, his ambition was undimmed. Montgomery had a vision of building a self-sufficient community of free Black people who could thrive by controlling their own labor, and therefore their own destiny.

After the Civil War ended in 1865, Benjamin Montgomery and his family returned to Davis Bend. They reopened two general stores and operated a sawmill on the property, servicing the community of newly freed Black people who had leases on the former plantation.

After the Civil War, the Bureau of Refugees, Freedmen, and Abandoned Lands, known as the Freedmen's Bureau, was established by Congress on March 3, 1865. The purpose of the Freedmen's Bureau was to help formerly enslaved people become self-sufficient. The bureau took titles of former plantations and leased land to the formerly enslaved who had previously worked it for free. As part of that program, the bureau took over Davis Bend. Joseph Davis was initially ineligible to reclaim his property, as it required that he complete a lengthy legal process. He took an oath of loyalty to the United States and eventually received a pardon from President Andrew Johnson in 1866. But rather than return to Davis Bend, he elected to sell his property to Benjamin Montgomery for the sum of $300,000 in November 1866. Davis sold the land to Montgomery before he had regained title to it, which was not prudent, because the Freedmen's Bureau leases had not yet expired. The sale also violated Mississippi's black codes, which prohibited Black people from owning property. Under the terms of the sale, Montgomery made no down payment and secured a nine-year mortgage from Joseph Davis.

Although chroniclers like historian Janet Sharp Hermann cite this as evidence of Joseph Davis's enlightened attitude toward Black people in general, or Benjamin Montgomery in particular, the likelihood is that Davis's decision to sell to Montgomery was probably equal parts beneficence and calculation. By the end of the Civil War, Joseph Davis was eighty-one years old and in no position to manage his sprawling property himself. His younger brother, Jefferson, was in prison for treason against the United States. By selling to Montgomery and holding the mortgage, Davis may have been gambling that Montgomery would eventually default, which would allow him to foreclose and regain his property once the heightened government scrutiny of former Confederates had passed.

Once Mississippi law was amended in 1867 to allow Black people to own property, Benjamin Montgomery formally closed on his purchase of Davis Bend. Montgomery immediately placed an ad in *The Vicksburg Times* announcing his intention to "create a community composed exclusively of colored people." Montgomery's ad included an endorsement from Freedmen's Bureau General T. J. Wood, signaling to any disgruntled whites in the area that his planned community would have the full protection of federal troops.

Although massive flooding of the Mississippi River made Montgomery's first year as owner of Davis Bend extremely challenging, he rebounded the next year and prospered for several years thereafter. Montgomery successfully petitioned to have the US Postal Service reopen the post office at his general store, arguing that his store was the proper location for a post office because most of the mail was sent and received by newly freed Black people who were trying to track down family members. In 1868, Montgomery was appointed justice of the peace, making him the first Black public official in Mississippi.

Montgomery's success was due both to his managerial skills and his innovative abilities. From the late 1860s on, Montgomery developed a steam-powered cotton press, mechanical improvements for a steam pump, and a cotton gin of his own design. He was an agricultural innovator as well and cultivated a superior strain of cotton seed. His agricultural innovations garnered prizes at the 1870 St. Louis Fair and the 1876 Centennial Exposition in Philadelphia.

There is no evidence that Montgomery attempted to patent any of his other inventions. He may have become disillusioned from his experience in trying to patent his steamboat propeller, or it may have been that he saw his inventions as a way to gain a competitive advantage for Davis Bend, rather than an independent source of revenue.

Joseph Davis died in 1870, and his heirs, who did not share their patriarch's investment in Benjamin Montgomery's success, inherited the mortgage on Davis Bend. Despite that vulnerability, Benjamin Montgomery prospered for several years. In 1871, he was able to buy Ursino, a neighboring plantation. By 1872, Benjamin Montgomery had the highest possible credit rating and was the third wealthiest planter in the state of Mississippi.

Benjamin Montgomery lived at Brierfield, the former home of

Jefferson Davis, with his wife and daughters, while his two adult sons had homes of their own on other parts of the family's vast land holdings. In addition to a plantation that produced cotton, corn, and sweet potatoes, Montgomery presided over a general store that housed the post office and provided banking services to the newly freed Black people in the community. At a time when a successful general store was earning $10,000 in annual revenues, Montgomery & Sons was generating $50,000 a year.

Montgomery's ability to succeed, however, owed as much to the protection of federal troops and Republican elected officials as it did to his acumen and industry. The erosion of that protection began as early as 1870, when Hiram Revels, a Republican, was appointed the first Black US senator by the Mississippi state legislature over the vociferous objections of white Democrats. By 1874, white opposition to Republican governance was gathering steam and would ultimately radically alter Benjamin Montgomery's fortunes.

In 1874, former Confederate president Jefferson Davis was broke. After being released from prison, Davis had an unsuccessful run as head of an insurance company. He was unwilling and unable to support himself through honest work. Davis sued his relatives for ownership of Brierfield, one of the two plantations that Joseph Davis had sold to Benjamin Montgomery on which his heirs held the mortgage.

As if the challenges of resurgent former Confederates and a legal action from the former president of the Confederacy were not enough, in December 1874, Benjamin Montgomery suffered a debilitating injury from a demolition accident. Montgomery never fully recovered and died in May 1877.

His sons, Isaiah and Thornton, tried to continue running the family's formerly thriving empire, but they were buffeted by forces beyond their control. Cotton prices were declining, and poor farm conditions resulted in a lower yield. The end of Reconstruction and the discrimination and terror it unleashed caused many of their Black borrowers to default on their debts, precipitating mounting losses for the Montgomerys.

In 1878, a Mississippi Supreme Court now dominated by two former Confederate judges reversed a lower court decision and awarded ownership of Brierfield to Jefferson Davis. Joseph Davis's heirs then foreclosed on the Hurricane plantation, leaving Benjamin Montgomery's family with its land at Ursino and one general store.

Like his father, Isaiah Montgomery yearned to build a community where Black people could thrive. In Isaiah's view, the way to accomplish that was to create an all-Black town, where labor, capital, and law were exclusively controlled by Black people. In 1887, Isaiah and his cousin Ben Green took advantage of the cheap land prices being offered by the Louisville, New Orleans and Texas Railway and purchased 840 acres in Mississippi's Yazoo Delta, halfway between Vicksburg and Memphis. Isaiah named the town Mound Bayou. Montgomery urged Black freedmen from Davis Bend to join him and told the first settlers to "buy land and own it and do for themselves what they had been doing for other folks for 250 years." Mound Bayou prospered as a successful example of Black self-sufficiency for another fifty years.

The stories of men like Thomas Jennings and Benjamin Montgomery provide proof that Black people in America were creative and forward-thinking, despite being deprived of civil or human rights by the institution of slavery. After emancipation and Reconstruction Era constitutional amendments provided Black people with some measure of legal rights, the record is replete with examples of Black innovation.

In our acceptance of the myth of the genius lone inventor, we have not stopped to think about who that myth serves and who it excludes. The idea that individual white men were responsible for most important advances of the Industrial Age fuels both white supremacy and the rugged individualism that undergirds capitalism. In truth, we have simply erased the fact that many of those we laud as solitary geniuses were merely using their knowledge of the law to document and obtain intellectual property rights for the inventions of the enslaved. Eli Whitney's famous cotton gin, for example, may have been a refinement of a comblike device developed by an enslaved man named Sam, who in turn got the idea from *his* father. It stands to reason that those closest to the backbreaking labor of cotton cultivation would be the ones to develop a key labor-saving device. Ironically, historians speculate that the invention of the cotton gin, by "remov[ing] inefficiencies . . . may have delayed slavery's . . . decline for at least two decades."

Thomas Edison, whom history credits with the invention of the electric light bulb, could not have accomplished electrification on a mass scale without the key contribution of Lewis Latimer, the Black inventor who developed the production method for the carbon filaments inside of the bulbs that Edison used. Latimer, who worked in New York for the Edison Electric Light Company, wrote the first book on electric lighting (titled *Incandescent Electric Lighting*) in 1890 and supervised the installation of electric streetlamps in Montreal, New York, and London.

Throughout the late nineteenth and early twentieth centuries, examples abound of Black inventors whose fertile imaginations fueled the Industrial Revolution. In 1887, Granville T. Woods invented the induction telegraph, a device that enabled voice communication over telegraph wires, contributing to railroad safety. Woods also invented the precursor to the third rail, powering mass transit. Granville T. Woods obtained sixty patents over the course of his life, earning the nickname the "Black Edison." Elijah McCoy invented the automatic rail engine lubricator, empowering trains to travel long distances nonstop. McCoy's invention was so successful that it spawned many imitators, prompting rail engineers to request the "real McCoy."

Black people did not view these inventors as "lone geniuses" but rather as powerful rebuttals to the pervasive myth of Black inferiority. From the slavery-era Colored Conventions to W. E. B. Du Bois's *The Crisis* magazine, Black organizations painstakingly cataloged the intellectual labor of Black inventors. Black inventors in turn did not view their innovations solely as a means of increasing their personal wealth, often reinvesting their resources into the fight for human rights for Black people. Jennings and Montgomery are just two examples of a pattern that recurs across the decades. For Black artists and inventors, their creativity and innovation are indivisible from their quest for recognition of their shared humanity.

TWO

GOD AND THE DEVIL: GOSPEL MUSIC VERSUS THE BLUES

Most people have never heard of Harry T. Burleigh. He suffers from a special version of Black fame: He is better known for the people he worked with than for the work that he did himself. On the other hand, everybody knows who Bessie Smith is. Also known as the "Empress of the Blues," Smith was the highest-paid Black performer of her day. She was the biggest-selling recording artist of any color for Columbia Records during her peak years of 1923 to 1929. Three of her songs are in the Grammy Hall of Fame: "Empty Bed Blues," "St. Louis Blues," and "Down Hearted Blues."

Burleigh, to the extent he is known at all, is known as the Black man who introduced Czech composer Antonín Dvořák to the harmonies, melodies, and rhythms of African American spirituals. That introduction formed the foundation for Dvořák's groundbreaking *New World* Symphony. Burleigh may also be known as a mentor to the renowned tenor vocalist Roland Hayes and a friend and mentor to the inimitable activist, singer, and actor Paul Robeson. But Harry T. Burleigh was a groundbreaking African American composer, performer, and arranger, credited with popularizing African American spirituals. Burleigh's work made Black spirituals accessible to the broader American public in the early twentieth century. His arrangements of "Swing Low, Sweet Chariot" and the Black national anthem "Lift Every Voice and Sing" were widely known and performed for decades.

Burleigh's name has mostly been lost to history, while Bessie Smith has been immortalized in books and films since her untimely death in 1937. Both were instrumental in popularizing two seminal Black musical genres—gospel and the blues. In the process, they had a profound impact on American music and culture. Yet only Burleigh, using a sophisticated understanding of copyright law and the assistance of white patrons and mentors, was able to build a foundation for a long, comfortable life and multigenerational wealth. Smith, on the other hand, died in a tragic accident that was mythologized for years. She was treated like a workhorse by the Black men in her life and ruthlessly exploited by the white ones. Bessie Smith was denied ownership of her art and the royalties from her recordings. Her ability to generate wealth for her family died with her. An examination of the inverse relationship between Burleigh's and Smith's fame and the control each had over the fruits of their creativity shows the centrality of intellectual property law in the exploitation of Black genius.

Harry T. Burleigh was born with every privilege available to a

Black person in the late nineteenth century. He was middle-class at a time when most Black people were impoverished. Poverty was one of the many consequential outcomes reinforced by the rigid racial caste system that replaced slavery after Reconstruction. As a man, Burleigh had some agency in a country that had yet to give women of any race the right to vote. Burleigh was light-skinned and benefited from the inter- and intra-racial prejudice of colorism. His lighter complexion afforded him more opportunities than his darker brethren. In addition, Burleigh was fortunate to be born in the North. In the Jim Crow South, Black people's position at the bottom of America's racialized hierarchy was enforced through vicious and barbaric violence.

In the mid-1800s, Erie, Pennsylvania, was a bustling transportation hub located halfway between Cleveland and Buffalo. Although its Black population was small, several members of Erie's Black community ran successful businesses. Some were staunch advocates for abolition and Black advancement. Henry Burleigh Sr. was one such leader. Burleigh Sr. cofounded the Erie Colored Free School and married Elizabeth Waters, one of the teachers there. The couple gave birth to son Harry in 1866. While Burleigh's family was by no means wealthy, his parents enjoyed stable employment that afforded them a comfortable living. They saw education as a critical tool for social mobility, and young Burleigh and his siblings were among the first Black students to attend Erie's public schools. Music was central in the Burleigh household, and Harry received piano and vocal lessons as a young boy. Burleigh's grandfather Hamilton Waters, a former slave who had purchased his freedom, sang spirituals regularly in the Baptist church that he attended every Sunday. As a young boy, Burleigh accompanied his blind grandfather everywhere, absorbing

Waters's knowledge and love of Black spirituals. Burleigh's interest in music was nurtured and encouraged from an early age, not only by his parents but by his extended family as well. Burleigh's Aunt Louisa arranged for his first voice and piano lessons.

It may be difficult to imagine now, but most upwardly mobile Black families of the time disdained spirituals. In spite of this, Burleigh was taught to cherish "plantation songs" and spirituals. It was the music that had been passed down to Black people through a powerful and aesthetically innovative oral tradition. Throughout his childhood in Erie, Burleigh heard African American spirituals performed in churches and by touring groups, such as the Fisk Jubilee Singers and the Hampton Institute Jubilee Singers. Burleigh was also steeped in the study and performance of European classical music and the American "art song." Art songs are musical compositions written for solo voice with piano accompaniment that had their origin during the European baroque period of classical music.

In 1891, Burleigh graduated from Erie High School, during which he had simultaneously taken courses in accounting and stenography at Clark Business College. After high school, he attended the National Conservatory of Music of America in New York City. Founded by philanthropist Jeannette Thurber, the National Conservatory was ahead of its time in offering admission to African Americans, women, and disabled people. Burleigh arrived at a propitious moment. At the start of his second year, the conservatory hired celebrated Czech composer Antonín Dvořák as its director.

In his native Czechoslovakia, Dvořák had been a strong proponent of the intrinsic artistic value of traditional folk music. He interpolated Bohemian musical themes into his classical compositions. Dvořák had a keen interest in African American and Indigenous traditional music and believed that it could be the source of a uniquely American form of classical music. According to Burleigh biographer Jean E. Snyder, Dvořák developed a close relationship with Burleigh, inviting him frequently to his home for dinner, where he peppered him with "hundreds of questions about Black life." Dvořák was an avid audience of one as Burleigh sang spirituals, accompanying himself on the piano. Harry Burleigh was Dvořák's "most direct link to African-American traditions," Snyder argues. At the same time, Burleigh understood that Dvořák's imprimatur was an important (i.e., white) validation of the beauty and originality of African American music. His private performances for Dvořák suggest that he pursued the Czech's endorsement with enthusiasm and an abiding understanding of the value that Dvořák's endorsement would bring to his career.

In 1893, Dvořák premiered his *New World* Symphony, a musical composition directly influenced by the African American traditional music introduced to him by Burleigh. In an interview with *The New York Herald* just prior to the opening, Dvořák is quoted as saying that "the future of American music must be founded on what are called the negro melodies. . . . These [are] beautiful and varied themes. . . . They are American." Armed with this validation, Harry Burleigh embarked on a career in which he would become a prominent composer, arranger, and performer of African American spirituals. He was a key figure in preserving, popularizing, and monetizing a foundational African American cultural aesthetic. Burleigh did not accomplish this only for himself. Through his sophisticated understanding of copyright law and his ability to navigate the nascent music publishing business, he helped to create a mechanism through which other Black composers, songwriters, and performers could profit from their creative output.

Shortly after Dvořák's triumphant premiere, Bessie Smith, who would grow up to play a vital role in another seminal African American art form, was born. Smith was America's first Black superstar. When her tragic death at the age of forty-three abruptly ended her career, though she was no longer Columbia Records' bestselling recording artist, her shows still commanded enthusiastic audiences. During the apex of her fame in the 1920s, she commanded as much as $2,000 per week for her live shows, the equivalent of $37,000 per week in 2025. At one point, Smith bought her own railroad car to efficiently transport her entire cast and crew on tour, a brilliant and flashy way of thumbing her nose at racist Southerners who banned Black people from their segregated hotels and restaurants. Fans adored the Empress of the Blues, and Smith sustained a successful career long after the popularity of the blues began to wane in the mid-1920s. When Bessie Smith died in 1937, she left behind a catalog of 160 recordings considered the peak of blues artistry. She was often accompanied by musical legends, including Fletcher Henderson and Sidney Bechet. Her recording of W. C. Handy's "St. Louis Blues" with Louis Armstrong is considered the definitive version of the song.

Although Bessie Smith displayed fierce independence in her lyrics and her life, she remains one of the most exploited artists in the history of the music industry. Shady figures across the industry exploited her ignorance of intellectual property law and the economics of the music business to extract an outsized profit from her during her life and continued to do so long after her death.

Bessie Smith was born in Chattanooga, Tennessee, on April 15, 1894. At the time, Chattanooga was a world away from the relative racial harmony of Harry Burleigh's Erie. Bessie's early life was the opposite of the comfortable and supportive upbringing that Burleigh enjoyed. Chattanooga was incorporated in 1839, one year after members of the Indigenous Cherokee Nation were violently ejected and forced upon the Trail of Tears. In 1850, the railroad arrived, transforming Chattanooga into a transportation hub that connected major supply lines for the Confederate Army during the Civil War.

By the time of Bessie Smith's birth, Chattanooga was 50 percent Black, but the majority of those Black residents were condemned to poverty-stricken lives constrained by Jim Crow laws. When Bessie Smith was eight years old, Chattanooga was the site of a lynching so heinous that it led to the first and only trial in the Supreme Court, the 1906 case of *United States v. Shipp*. Ed Johnson, who had been convicted of raping a white woman by an all-white jury, filed a motion to the United States Supreme Court for a writ of habeas corpus. He argued that he was about to be executed without due process of law. The Supreme Court agreed with Johnson, granted his motion, and sent a telegram to the jail to advise the sheriff of its ruling. Nonetheless, Chattanooga Sheriff Joseph F. Shipp allowed a mob to seize Johnson from the jail and lynch him on Walnut Street Bridge. This blatant disregard of the federal ruling led the Supreme Court to prosecute Sheriff Shipp for contempt of court. In case there was any question about the character of the white community in Chattanooga at that time, after Shipp served nine months in jail for contempt, he received a hero's welcome upon his return.

Turn-of-the-century Chattanooga was not the kind of place that would embrace a talented young Black woman under the best of circumstances, but even by the standards of the time, Bessie's early life was particularly harsh. Orphaned by the age of eight, Bessie and her siblings were raised by her eldest sister, Viola, a bitter and resentful woman who punished Bessie's perceived misbehavior by locking her in the outhouse. As a young girl, Bessie began singing and dancing on the street with her brother Bennie to supplement the family's meager earnings. Her older brother Clarence was also beginning to stake out a career in show business. In 1911, Clarence left Chattanooga to join Moses Stokes's touring vaudeville company as a comedian and MC. One year later, when the company came back through town, he arranged for Bessie to audition, and she too joined the company as a fledgling dancer.

In the early twentieth century, Black musicians looking for material success had two paths, through the church or the vaudeville circuit—the sacred or the profane. Although former circus clown Tony Pastor had produced "polite vaudeville" performances in New York theaters in the mid-nineteenth century, Boston businessmen Benjamin Keith and Edward F. Albee (grandfather of playwright Edward Albee) are credited with pioneering and popularizing the daylong variety shows dubbed *vaudeville* in the late nineteenth century. Keith and Albee began producing these shows at the Bijou Theatre, their Boston venue. When vaudeville proved successful, Keith and Albee expanded the shows into their circuit of theaters, and by 1900, vaudeville was the most popular live entertainment in the United States.

Of course, Black performers did not have access to the opulent theaters on the circuit owned by Keith and Albee. Instead, they were consigned to the smaller Theatre Owners Booking Association (TOBA) circuit, a group of theaters in the South and Midwest owned and operated by a mix of Black and white theater owners. Black performers joked that TOBA, the first iteration of the "chitlin circuit," stood for "Tough on Black Asses," thanks to the cramped and dilapidated conditions that characterized most venues. Still, the

TOBA circuit provided Black musicians the opportunity to perform in front of appreciative Black audiences.

Although Bessie Smith began performing professionally as a dancer, she was fortunate to have joined the company that boasted the legendary "Mother of the Blues," Ma Rainey. Ma Rainey took the young Bessie Smith under her wing, and by 1913 Bessie was headlining venues as a blues singer.

PARALLEL PATHS

During the 1910s, as Bessie's star was rising on the grueling TOBA circuit, Harry Burleigh was establishing himself as a premiere composer, arranger, and performer. Burleigh was a staunch advocate for the artistic merit of African American spirituals, performing them alongside classical art songs in concert halls and in private recitals for wealthy white patrons such as J. P. Morgan. The gulf between the venues where Smith and Burleigh performed mirrored the divergent reception that the two emergent forms of Black music received in the aftermath of emancipation. Spirituals, dating back to slavery, documented the "collective desire of Black people for freedom" and were "performed collectively." The blues, by contrast, embraced themes relevant to newly liberated Black people—sex and love, travel and labor. Burleigh's work of transcribing, arranging, and publishing spirituals made them available to a broader audience, both Black and white. Burleigh made Black spirituals accessible to and for those who couldn't make it to Carnegie Hall. In the process, thanks to his savvy understanding of copyright law and the attendant music publishing business, Burleigh generated a consistent stream of passive income for himself through sales of sheet music of this newly popular genre, which also generated royalties for composers and arrangers. The blues, because it reflected the lived experience of working-class Black people, needed no evangelists to increase its appeal.

African American spirituals emerged as popular American music at the moment in musical history when the ways that Americans enjoyed and consumed music were being transformed by technology. In the late nineteenth and early twentieth centuries, many Americans had pianos in their homes, and the principal way they enjoyed music was by purchasing sheet music to accompany themselves and their families while they sang along. The invention of the player piano in 1901 mechanized this function. In a player piano, sheet music is preloaded so that the piano can play tunes automatically, without the need for human performance or manipulation. The piano manufacturers loaded music into their devices at the factory, circumventing the market for sheet music. Player piano companies did not make any payments to songwriters or publishers. Manufacturers took the position that the reproduction of the music on piano player rolls was merely part of their own production process.

When the Supreme Court agreed with piano manufacturers in the 1908 case of *White-Smith Music Publishing Co. v. Apollo Co.*, it was proof that the law was woefully out of touch with technological advances. This case was a legal harbinger of the technological disruption yet to come in subsequent decades. Congress responded the next year by passing the Copyright Act of 1909, which introduced the concept of a "mechanical license" and the "compulsory mechanical license." The mechanical license provision made clear that any physical reproduction of an original composition, whether for a player piano roll or a vinyl record (or decades later, for a CD), required that the manufacturer secure a license permitting the physical reproduction of the composition. Thereafter, once a song had been reproduced and released, the 1909 law allowed for a compulsory license, meaning that any artist could record a "cover" of a song, as long as they paid the owner of the copyrighted composition a mechanical license fee that was set by statute. This meant that those who owned the copyright in a song stood to profit every time it was rerecorded.

Harry Burleigh's stepfather was the trusted key employee of the wealthiest white man in Erie, which contributed concretely to his family's stature in the community. As a result, Harry Burleigh understood the importance of relationships with prominent white people from an early age. He knew that cultivating relationships with white faculty members would advance his musical career. His ability to profit from his creative output was the direct result of being mentored by some of the most prominent white musicians of his time as a student at the National Conservatory. Max Spicker, Burleigh's counterpoint professor at the conservatory, was responsible for hiring Burleigh as a member of the choir at Temple Emanu-El in New York City, and may have facilitated getting him signed to the prominent music publisher G. Schirmer & Co. G. Schirmer published Burleigh from 1898 to 1902. Burleigh later moved on to G. Ricordi & Co., the European publisher of Verdi and Puccini. Burleigh then paid these favors forward and served as a mentor to other Black singers such as Abbie Mitchell (who originated the role of Clara in *Porgy and Bess*), celebrated contralto Marian Anderson, and emerging composers such as Jester Hairston and Florence Price.

Burleigh's relationship with conservatory faculty member Victor Herbert may have been the most significant for him early in his career. Burleigh's relationship with Herbert led to his inclusion as one of the original founding members of the American Society of

Composers and Publishers (ASCAP), an organization that would dramatically increase the profits of those who owned the copyright in musical compositions. One day, Herbert, the composer of *Babes in Toyland* and *Naughty Marietta*, was strolling through a hotel lobby when he heard one of his compositions being played on a piano. He had not licensed the song. At that moment, Herbert recognized that the only way to ensure that composers and publishers would be paid for public performances of their work was for composers and publishers to form a trade association that could monitor the public performances of their work and collect royalties on their behalf. Herbert, along with Irving Berlin and others, founded ASCAP on February 13, 1914. Restaurants and hotels balked at the prospect of paying royalties and resisted the novel concept of "public performance payments." The dispute landed in court, culminating in the Supreme Court case *Herbert v. Shanley Co.* This case held that the incidental performance of music in a place of business was a public performance for profit, legitimizing ASCAP. This opened up an entire new revenue stream for Black founding members like Harry Burleigh, James Weldon Johnson, W. C. Handy, and those they recruited to join.

While Harry Burleigh was reaping the benefits of a legal system that protected the rights of musical composers, Bessie Smith was a vehicle for record executives to use as a cash cow, filling their own bank accounts at her expense. Bessie Smith's career was emblematic of the fate that awaited other Black artists whose musical genius was matched by an equal lack of legal and business savvy, making them easy targets for an unscrupulous industry.

The popularity of the blues exploded when the record player replaced the player piano as the principal means for Americans to enjoy music in their homes. Prior to 1920, record companies had not focused on Black audiences, assuming that Black people could not afford to buy record players. As always, racism and ignorance caused them to leave money on the table. But in 1920, the Okeh Records release of the first blues record, "Crazy Blues" by Mamie Smith, was a huge hit. "Crazy Blues" sold one hundred thousand copies in its first month and led other record companies to rush to capitalize on the new craze.

W. C. Handy was a songwriter, arranger, and bandleader active at that time, known as the "Father of the Blues." Handy is credited with popularizing the blues by writing down well-known blues melodies and publishing them in sheet music form. In 1921, Handy went one step further and founded Black Swan Records. Paramount Records, founded in 1917, launched its "race records" division (the limiting, pejorative name given to records by Black artists) in 1922. That same year, Columbia Records was on the verge of bankruptcy. Frank Walker became head of the fledgling race records department of Columbia the next year and believed that the blues might be the answer to the company's precarious financial state.

Nothing in Frank Walker's background suggested an affinity for Black people in general or the blues in particular. Walker, born in Fly Summit, New York, in 1889, had done a stint in the navy and started off in banking before pivoting to the music business. Walker's first music business job was as promoter of opera singer Enrico Caruso. Nonetheless, Walker claimed that he had heard Bessie Smith sing in a Southern juke joint. He then told his talent scout, Black musician and composer Clarence Williams, to "go get Bessie Smith." Williams was already serving as Bessie's accompanist and her manager, so it was easy for him to "get" her. On February 15, 1923, Smith had her first recording session at Columbia Records. Although Columbia had agreed to pay Bessie Smith $125 per song, she had signed a contract with Clarence Williams that enabled him to pocket half of her fee. When she discovered this, she and her boyfriend (later husband), Jack Gee, stormed into Williams's New York office and threatened Williams with an old-fashioned beatdown unless he released her from the one-sided contract.

Unfortunately, Smith merely traded a small-time hustler for a bigger one. Armed with the release, Bessie Smith marched into the office of Frank Walker and showed him proof that Williams no longer controlled the rights to her recording services. Sensing an opportunity, Walker signed Smith to a one-year contract for twelve songs at a flat rate of $125 per song. He also paid her $500 for four songs that she had recorded earlier that month. Smith was impressed by what she perceived as Walker's "generosity" and asked him to be her manager on the spot. Walker accepted. He did not point out the obvious conflict of interest posed by having an executive of her record company serve as her manager. Bessie Smith did not notice, and Walker did not point out, that he had crossed out the provision for royalty payments in the contract, meaning that $1,500 was the only money she would receive from the twelve songs she had contracted to record.

If Walker's one-sided, ruthless business dealings were not proof that he was motivated by profit, not passion, his next business moves were. On the heels of signing Smith, Walker looked to replicate the success of rival label Okeh in country music. He signed Gid Tanner and Riley Puckett in 1924 and created the first country music supergroup, the Skillet Lickers. These white artists were similarly exploited and underpaid, only receiving flat session fees on records that generated thousands of dollars for Columbia. Later in Walker's career, he came out of retirement to start a label for MGM and signed country star Hank Williams in 1947.

In the spring of 1923, Columbia released "Down Hearted Blues," Bessie Smith's first recording for the label. "Down Hearted Blues" was a cover of a song that had been written and recorded by Black blues singer Alberta Hunter. The B-side was a song called "Gulf Coast Blues," written by Bessie's former exploiter Clarence Williams. The record was a smash, selling 780,000 copies. Hunter, the songwriter of "Down Hearted Blues," stood to earn $15,600 in mechanical royalties on those sales figures. Clarence Williams, as the songwriter of the B-side, earned the same amount, because mechanical royalties were payable (at a rate of 2 cents per song) on physical copies embodying a composition, regardless of whether it was the hit or the B-side prompting sales.

At least Hunter and Williams were being paid for their creative output. Bessie Smith, the artist performing the songs that they wrote, was not. Columbia Records, which had been on the brink of bankruptcy the year before, reaped an outsized windfall. In 1923, the average price of a 78 rpm record ranged from $0.85 to $1.25. Using back-of-the-napkin math, if we assume a $1 sale price and a deduction of 20 percent retained by retailers, Columbia would have stood to garner $624,000 from one record—the equivalent of approximately $11.8 million in 2025—in that year alone. Columbia never paid Smith a dime more than the $250 Frank Walker contracted her for in 1923.

Bessie Smith was also a talented songwriter who wrote 25 percent of the songs she recorded. Another predatory Columbia Records executive, Jack Kapp, signed Smith to a music publishing company that he had established and copyrighted her compositions in his company's name; she never received any mechanical royalties for her compositions. During her lifetime, she sold between eight and ten million records but never received more than a total of $28,575. During that same period, Columbia Records netted between $6.8 and $8.5 *million* (the equivalent of between $128 million and $160 million in 2025 dollars). If we assume that Bessie Smith wrote forty of the 160 songs that she recorded, and they sold the same amount, on average, Jack Kapp stole between $20,000 and $25,000 in mechanical royalties from Smith, or the equivalent of between $377,800 and $472,250 in 2025 dollars.

After her smash-hit record, Bessie Smith was in even higher demand around the country. On the grueling TOBA circuit, her shows commanded top dollar. Smith was every inch the star, with a lifestyle to match. She bought fancy cars at the drop of a hat for her husband, Jack. She had affairs with men and women and didn't let Prohibition get in the way of enjoying a good party in every town she toured. Given that she was born dirt-poor in the Jim Crow South, the freedom and agency that Bessie Smith enjoyed was remarkable. Like most other blues women, Bessie Smith couldn't be bothered with the respectability politics promoted by the "New Negroes" of the Harlem Renaissance or concerned with patriarchal notions of acceptable femininity. Bessie never packaged herself to be palatable to white audiences, and Black (and white) people loved her for it.

Still, any close examination of her career shows the limits of Bessie Smith's agency. She was a larger-than-life figure who dominated popular music during the 1920s, but the emergence of talkies and the onset of the Depression decimated the audience for the blues. Undaunted, Smith continued touring on a smaller scale and even tried her hand at movies, costarring with Black actress Isabel Washington Powell (sister of Fredi Washington and first wife of Adam Clayton Powell Jr.) in the W. C. Handy–produced 1929 short film *St. Louis*

Blues. Nonetheless, Columbia Records dropped Bessie Smith from its roster in 1931. After eight years with the label, Columbia had paid her a grand total of $28,575, the equivalent of a salary of $76,253 a year in 2025 dollars.

Bessie Smith died in a tragic car accident in Clarksdale, Mississippi, on September 26, 1937. Though the apocryphal tale that she died because a white hospital refused to admit her has been debunked, that does not mean that racism did not contribute to her untimely death. How else can we explain the fact that the white doctor who arrived at the scene of the accident called an ambulance, rather than immediately driving Bessie Smith to the hospital? How can we deny the likelihood that the segregated hospital that treated Bessie had inadequate facilities and equipment? The severity of her injuries was such that she probably would not have survived, but it is devastating to think that she endured unnecessary suffering because of race.

While her family ceased to profit from Bessie Smith's talent upon her death, Columbia Records continued to profit from Smith's talent long after, as explained in heartbreaking detail in the opinion in the case brought in the Eastern District of Pennsylvania federal court by Bessie Smith's adopted son against her record label, *Gee v. CBS.* Bessie Smith adopted Jack Jr. in 1926, when he was six years old. Bessie doted on him, but when she died early in 1937, he was at the mercy of his neglectful father, Jack Gee Sr. At the time of her death, Bessie had long been separated from Jack Sr. and was in a committed relationship with Lionel Hampton's uncle, former bootlegger Richard Morgan. Nonetheless, Jack Gee Sr., who had always been obsessed with money, had no problem capitalizing on his role as the widower of Bessie Smith.

Although he made a great display of grief at her funeral, Jack

Gee Sr. pocketed the funds that were raised for Bessie's headstone, leaving her in an unmarked grave until Janis Joplin and a Black Philadelphia nurse who had known Bessie Smith in her childhood purchased a headstone in 1970. Yet, as an illiterate and unsophisticated man, Jack Gee Sr. was in no position to penetrate the black box of his deceased wife's contractual arrangements with Columbia, even as they remastered and reissued Bessie Smith's recordings from the 1950s through the 1970s.

The full extent of Columbia Records' exploitation of Bessie Smith only became clear after jazz journalist Chris Albertson published a biography of her in 1972. Albertson unearthed decades-old recording contracts and payment ledgers that showed how little Bessie was paid. They became the foundation of a lawsuit brought by Jack Gee Jr. in 1975 in federal court in Philadelphia. Jack Jr.'s complaint alleged that CBS Records (the new name for Columbia Records) had committed fraud and violated the civil rights of Bessie Smith and her heirs, by depriving them of the right to enter contracts on the same basis as white artists, in violation of 42 U.S. Code § 1981, the Reconstruction-era law guaranteeing Black citizens the same right to make and enforce contracts as white citizens.

In a meticulously detailed opinion, Judge Edward Becker acknowledged the myriad ways in which CBS Records exploited Bessie Smith. Judge Becker noted that it was standard business practice at the time to pay royalties to white artists but not Black ones. In addition, Judge Becker wrote that CBS Records failed to produce copies of any agreements actually signed by Bessie Smith during her most lucrative period between 1923 and 1925, and that there was *no* evidence that CBS had ever paid Bessie Smith or her heirs a dime for twenty masters that she recorded that were not released until after her death.

Judge Becker credited plaintiffs' allegations that CBS repeatedly mined Bessie Smith's recordings for profit for decades after her death. After initially rereleasing her records in LP album format in the 1950s, Columbia remastered and rereleased them over a period from 1970 to 1972. According to the plaintiffs, Bessie Smith's reissues were trumpeted in CBS Records' annual report as the "biggest selling reissues in the history of the record industry."

Jack Jr.'s attorneys did not limit themselves to contract and fraud claims but pursued creative arguments that relied on Reconstruction-era civil rights statutes in an effort to show that Columbia's treatment of Bessie Smith could not be divorced from her status as a Black woman. Contemporaneous records show that Columbia's standard contracts contained royalty provisions, which were simply crossed out in Bessie's agreements. The white artists who were Bessie's labelmates, like Bing Crosby and Eddie Cantor, received advances and royalties, despite selling fewer records than Bessie had. Nonetheless, Judge Becker decided the case in favor of Columbia. He based his decision on procedural grounds, finding that because Jack Jr. was unable to produce formal adoption papers, he had not proved that he was Bessie Smith's legal heir. The court also held that the allegations of fraud were insufficient to suspend the expiration of the statute of limitations for nearly forty years. This heartbreaking case shows the limits of the legal system's ability to right moral wrongs.

In 2026, eighty-nine years after her death, Bessie Smith is still recognized as the Empress of the Blues. Her picture is still recognizable, and her artistry remains unmatched. Yet no one in her family has ever profited from the sale or the streaming of her recordings. Although music publishing catalogs have generated prodigious fortunes for songwriters for over a century since the passage of the Copyright

Act of 1909, Bessie Smith never received any royalties from the forty songs she wrote. Her estranged husband, Jack Gee Sr., received some publishing income after her death, but it is not clear that any publishing royalties were paid out after his death in 1973, because by then the compositions may have been in the public domain and not eligible for copyright protection.

Bessie's image has been endlessly commercialized, but thanks to the vagaries of state "right of publicity" statutes, revenues, if any, from some of the most famous images of Bessie Smith would have gone solely to the photographer and copyright holder, such as well-known white writer and literary critic Carl Van Vechten.

In contrast, Harry Burleigh, whose name is largely unknown and whose legacy has been mostly erased, was able to maintain and monetize copyright ownership in his catalog such that, at the time of his death in 1949, Burleigh had amassed a fortune worth $300,000, the equivalent of $4.1 million in 2025.

As the vast gulf between Bessie Smith's and Harry Burleigh's paths shows, racism is one but not the only explanation for their divergent fortunes. Patriarchy and misogyny played a role, given the limited freedom afforded to women of any race in the early twentieth century. Bessie Smith was exploited by Black men like Clarence Williams and white men like Frank Walker and Jack Kapp, who took advantage of her limited education to sign her to shockingly one-sided contracts. Jack Gee Sr. happily spent the money that she earned while trying to police her partying, drinking, and affairs through emotional and physical abuse.

Harry Burleigh's background shaped his worldview, just as Bessie Smith's shaped hers. Burleigh, cosseted by class privilege, became an avatar of respectability politics. His conservative moral rectitude, exemplified by his close association with Booker T. Washington, was rewarded throughout his life with the ability to profit from his intellectual property. Bessie Smith, on the other hand, had no desire to ingratiate herself with upper-class white or Black society. She enjoyed enormous fame and wealth during her life, but had no idea of the outsized fortune that her intellectual property was generating for Columbia Records during the height of her career or that her intellectual property would continue to generate revenue long after her death.

The template of Bessie Smith's career, in which her Black brilliance was simultaneously elevated and abused, has been a rinse-and-repeat process deployed by the music industry for over a hundred years. That exploitation is rooted in an abiding belief in Black inferiority, possibly stemming from thinking that our primary worth comes from performance, another form of physical labor. Remembering the history of slaveholders' attempts to patent the inventions of those they enslaved provides an understanding of the origin of that sense of entitlement.

Harry Burleigh's career has not often been told, omitted by chroniclers who prefer the narrative of the tragic Black artist plagued by substance abuse and preyed upon by exploiters. But Burleigh's model was also replicated time after time by Black people who caught lightning in a bottle—by marrying their creative brilliance with a canny understanding of intellectual property law and the entertainment business to build enduring legacies.

The life and artistic legacies of Harry Burleigh and Bessie Smith demonstrate how race, class, and gender were predictive factors that determined Black artists' capacity to profit from their creations in the vast industry set up to monetize intellectual property. Although both Burleigh and Bessie were talented, Burleigh's status as a middle-class, educated man allowed him to leverage his brilliance to create wealth in the racialized entertainment industry. Smith, conversely, as a systematically undereducated, working-class woman, was easily exploited by that same industry. Across the twentieth century, myriad examples of the naked exploitation of Black artists show that America's creative industries mirrored the racism of the larger society.

THREE

THE POWER OF IMAGE: D. W. GRIFFITH AND OSCAR MICHEAUX AND THE CENSORSHIP FIGHT IN HOLLYWOOD

The camera zooms in on the image of Flora (white actress Mae Marsh), a lovely young woman frolicking in the woods. Although she is seemingly performing the chore of fetching water, her demeanor is carefree. We watch her taking delight in nature, with close-ups of her beatific face as she gambols through the grass. Suddenly, we see Gus, a man in blackface and a Union Army cap, lurking in the bushes behind her.

The director heightens the suspense, showing Flora lovingly trying to entice a squirrel out of its tree with food, while she remains oblivious to the looming threat of the hulking man pursuing her. He cuts between close-ups of Flora and the squirrel. Gus is shot from a middle range, close enough for us to see a crazed, determined look in his eyes as he follows her. The filmmaker's technique invites us to contrast Flora's loving pursuit of the squirrel and Gus's surreptitious hunt for Flora.

When Gus finally catches up to Flora, he announces, "I'm a Captain and I wants to marry," while pointing at her. Horrified, Flora takes off, and the film cuts to her brother, Ben, who has arrived at the family home and found his little sister missing. Ben rushes off in pursuit, and we watch in suspense, praying that Ben finds Flora before Gus catches her. Gus asserts to Flora, "I won't hurt yeh," but his dogged pursuit across a tangled and rocky terrain belies his assertion.

Finally, Flora reaches the summit of a treacherous crag and screams, "Stop or I'll jump!" Undeterred, Gus advances and Flora leaps into the abyss. Ben arrives just in time to cradle his dying sister in his arms. This suspenseful, artfully filmed scene succeeds in getting the audience to share the filmmaker's view of Black men as dehumanized villains and to thoroughly sympathize with the white Southerners who violently resist the political participation of or any notion of equality with Black people. This beautifully shot piece of poisonous propaganda is one of two attempted rape scenes in D. W. Griffith's *The Birth of a Nation.*

The Birth of a Nation has been hailed as a masterpiece for over a century because of the cinematic innovations it introduced that influenced filmmaking for a century afterward. Griffith's film pioneered the use of camera techniques like close-ups, fade-outs, long shots, and panoramic shots. It was the first film to feature a full-length musical score, and its action-packed battle scene (featuring the KKK!) is the blueprint for battle scenes to the present day. Yet all of that artistry was in service of the racist proposition that Black Americans had no place in public life.

When the film was released in 1915, it became the country's first blockbuster, telling the story of two American families—one Union, one Confederate—set during the Civil War and Reconstruction. "The film is one of the most racist films ever made. Maybe the most racist film ever made," says Ellen C. Scott, author of *Cinema Civil Rights*. "This film actually depicts lynching as a positive thing. The politics of the film was essentially to say certain [B]lack people are worthy of being lynched. In that sense, it's extremely racist." Professor Alan Rice finds the Black man who is lynched deeply problematic, noting, "He's the [B]lack rapist figure who is the stereotype of the [B]lack man whose eyes are only for white women," playing into a pervasive fear at the time.

Film critics have paid scant attention to the link between the film's scabrous, ahistorical narrative and increased anti-Black violence. As research by Harvard Kennedy School Professor Desmond Ang documents, in each county where *The Birth of a Nation* had a road show screening, "lynchings increased fivefold." Ang's research revealed that screening locations of *The Birth of a Nation* correlated with an increase in Ku Klux Klan chapters, an effect that persisted eighty-five years after the film's release.

Most Black people understood immediately that the film would lead directly to an increase in racist violence. The National Association for the Advancement of Colored People (NAACP) organized protests at showings in Los Angeles, Boston, and New York in an effort to shut the film down, to no avail. Notwithstanding Black protests, *The Birth of a Nation* became a box office smash. It broke records to become the highest-grossing US motion picture of all time, a record that held until it was dislodged by another revisionist Lost Cause fable, *Gone with the Wind*, in 1939.

Part of *The Birth of a Nation*'s power came from its claim of historical accuracy. After all, President Woodrow Wilson screened the film at the White House, reportedly exclaiming, "It is like writing history with lightning, and my only regret is that it is all so terribly true." D. W. Griffith and Thomas Dixon Jr. (author of the novel *The Clansman,* on which the film was based) defended the film's sensational depictions of Black people as rapacious predators as historically accurate. Griffith was so confident in the veracity of his racist rendering that he bet NAACP cofounder and Harvard-trained civil rights lawyer Moorfield Storey that he would donate $10,000 to charity if Storey found any factual inaccuracies in the film. Although Storey was able to find several, there is no record of Griffith ever making good on his bet.

Five years after the release of *The Birth of a Nation*, Black filmmaker Oscar Micheaux wrote and directed a response to Griffith's distorted portrayal of Black people, releasing *Within Our Gates* in 1920. Like *The Birth of a Nation*, *Within Our Gates* contains scenes of lynching and attempted rape, but the perpetrators are white men exploiting their power rather than bestial Black men.

Within Our Gates centers on Sylvia Landry, a young Black woman in the Deep South who is dedicated to uplifting Black people. Micheaux depicts Landry as angelic but purposeful. When her fiancé is duped into thinking she has been unfaithful, Sylvia harbors no bitterness, and pivots to working at the Piney Woods School, whose mission was the education of impoverished Black Southerners. The film follows Sylvia on a fundraising trip to Boston, where a freak accident connects her with a white philanthropist who comes to the aid of Piney Woods.

In the last reel of the film, a flashback sequence reveals the source of Sylvia's dedication to the cause of Black freedom. Sylvia is shown as a young adult, sitting in the home of her adoptive parents, who are illiterate sharecroppers. Sylvia, who has been educated, goes over her father's accounting of what he is owed for his crops and discovers that he has been shortchanged by the white landowner, Philip Gridlestone. When Jasper Landry goes to confront Gridlestone, a struggle ensues, and Gridlestone tries to shoot him. Meanwhile, unbeknownst to Gridlestone and Landry, an aggrieved white sharecropper is lurking outside his open window and takes advantage of the scuffle between the two. The white man shoots Gridlestone through the window, killing him. Landry, left inside with a dead body and a recently fired gun, is assumed to be the killer.

A lynch mob quickly forms to hunt down Jasper Landry and his family. They are egged on by one of Gridlestone's Black servants, Efrem, an Uncle Tom who accuses Landry of the murder. During a lull in the manhunt, the white mob grows bored and, in a shocking display of casual barbarism, lynches Efrem.

Eventually the mob catches Jasper, his wife, and their young son (but not Sylvia) and prepares to lynch them. The son escapes and rides off on a stolen horse; Jasper and his wife are hanged. As the mob prepares to burn their lifeless bodies, the film cuts to Sylvia Landry hiding in a house nearby. Suddenly a white man, identified as Armand Gridlestone, brother of the murdered landowner, bursts in and attacks Sylvia. He tears at her clothes with a crazed look in his eyes as she fights back. Micheaux cuts back and forth between their struggle and the lynch mob until Armand notices a telltale scar on Sylvia's neck and realizes that she is the daughter he fathered with a Black woman who was given up for adoption. Only then does he relent.

Both *The Birth of a Nation* and *Within Our Gates* depict lynching and attempted rape to make essential points about race in America. D. W. Griffith depicts Black men as uncivilized and predatory, whether they are officers in the Union Army or legislators in the statehouse. Lynching is excused as an appropriate response to barbarism. White women are portrayed as delicate flowers whose innocence must be protected from barbaric Black men by the "white knights" of the KKK.

Conversely, Oscar Micheaux depicts a much more nuanced and realistic picture of both Black and white people. The white Gridlestone brothers cheat Black men and attempt to rape Black women, but the philanthropist who saves the Piney Woods School is white. Sylvia Landry is a selfless Black person dedicated to helping her people, as is the founder of the Piney Woods School, but Efrem is a drunken Uncle Tom, whose craven efforts to curry favor with white people leads directly to the lynching of Jasper Landry and his wife and doesn't save him from his own demise at the hands of an angry white mob.

Despite the pernicious, poisonous stereotypes in *The Birth of a Nation*, the film was lauded for its artistry and uncritically held up as an example of virtuoso filmmaking for nearly seventy years. Despite the important social commentary of *Within Our Gates*, the film was nearly lost to history. The trajectory of these two films, from their production and distribution to the reception they received from censorship boards and their protection, or lack thereof under copyright law, reflects American race relations in a microcosm. Micheaux's film, like much of Black creative achievement, was denigrated and ignored. *The Birth of a Nation* was held up for decades as the apotheosis of cinematic art, allowing its racist propaganda to sway successive generations of cinephiles.

D. W. Griffith's and Oscar Micheaux's life stories strongly influenced the themes they chose to dramatize on film. Griffith was born in a suburb of Louisville, Kentucky, in 1875, during the waning days of Reconstruction. The son of a former colonel in the Confederate Army, Griffith grew up hearing stories that valorized men who fought to keep other humans enslaved. Micheaux was born in the small town of Metropolis, Illinois, in 1884. He was the son of formerly enslaved parents who had moved to Illinois from Kentucky in search of a better life for their children.

Griffith started working as a journalist at a newspaper owned by his brother before moving to New York to become a playwright. Griffith's friend Frank J. Marion was a shareholder in motion picture company Biograph Studios, and he connected Griffith to Biograph in an effort to get his screenplays produced. Biograph had no interest in Griffith's writing but gave him work as an extra. In 1908, a chance meeting on set with a cameraman led to Griffith's opportunity to direct shorts for Biograph.

D. W. Griffith's smooth career path was facilitated by a network of family and friends and marked by opportunities from which Black people were pointedly excluded. This makes Oscar Micheaux's ascent even more remarkable. Micheaux moved to Chicago at seventeen and worked a series of menial jobs, including as a shoeshine boy. He worked as a Pullman porter and in 1904, at the age of twenty, set out to South Dakota to become a homesteader, one of a handful of Black people who did so. Micheaux used his experiences in South Dakota as material for an autobiographical novel titled *The Homesteader* that he published in 1917. Six years later, Micheaux adapted his novel to make his first film, *The Homesteader*.

American society's rush to double down on white supremacy

after the end of Reconstruction foreshadowed the different reactions that the films of D. W. Griffith and Oscar Micheaux received. The extent to which their films were esteemed determined the extent to which the films were policed or protected by the law. Both filmmakers were making films during a period when Black Americans were victimized by the violent rule of Jim Crow in the South and the rigid, legalized segregation of redlining and employment discrimination in the North. In the early twentieth century, just prior to and during the First World War, the overwhelming majority of white Americans viewed Black people with fear and contempt.

In addition, as filmmaker and professor Bob Pondillo notes, citing *Mutual Film Corporation v. Industrial Commission of Ohio* in the First Amendment Encyclopedia database, there was an ongoing political battle to protect "white American culture" from the perceived threat posed by "Catholics, [Non-Protestants], immigrants and migrants." In the *Mutual Film Corporation* case, a film company brought a suit against the Ohio censorship board, alleging that its requirement that all films be submitted to the board before being distributed within Ohio was a violation of the film company's free speech rights. The Supreme Court opined that films were "business, pure and simple," that could be used for "evil," and held that films were not entitled to First Amendment protection.

State film censorship boards were one important mechanism of cultural control. The language of the court's decision in *Mutual Film Corporation* neatly summarizes the moral panic gripping white Protestant America over the nascent film industry. The court stated that motion pictures, thanks to "[t]heir power of amusement [were] . . . more insidious in corruption." Thus, film studios were at the mercy of the moral judgments of the men who comprised 208 different state and local censorship boards.

The divergent responses of these myriad censorship boards to *The Birth of a Nation* and *Within Our Gates* make clear that the predominant societal view was that audiences didn't need to be shielded from scenes of racial violence, but rather from images of the white perpetrators of that violence.

Although Black people's effort to condemn the overt racism of *The Birth of a Nation* was met with stiff resistance, they did manage to force Griffith to excise three of the most egregious scenes: one depicting the castration of Gus after his lynching; one depicting a white woman offended by the body odor of a Black child; and, most notoriously, a coda dubbed "Lincoln's Remedy," showing Black people on a ship being deported to Africa.

Griffith vehemently objected to even these concessions. He wrote a letter to *The New York Globe* casting Black opposition to his film as an attack on free speech, "the priceless heritage of our nation." As scholar David Rylance notes, through these justifications, "censorship became racialized," and arguments against it mirrored the film's central conceit—that white American culture had to be protected against uncivilized Black hordes. We can see echoes of the same tension today in the debate over "cancel culture," which typically involves the privileged and the powerful insisting on their right to deride the marginalized without consequence.

Black protests against *The Birth of a Nation* led to it being banned in eighteen states, but the controversy only contributed to its success. To get around censorship, Griffith toured the film in road shows across the country. *The Birth of a Nation* was not only a box office smash, but its smoothly effective demagoguery reinforced anti-Black violence for decades. In a case of life imitating art, the Klan only began wearing white hoods and burning crosses after seeing themselves depicted that way in *The Birth of a Nation*.

Black Illinois State Senator Robert R. Jackson responded by passing Illinois's first statewide censorship law in 1917. That statute prohibited "films which 'show[ed] the criminality, depravity, in chastity or lack of virtue'" of any "race, color, creed, or religion." Similar laws were passed soon thereafter in Denver, Colorado, and West Virginia, but the Illinois statute had the most specific language. Yet the Illinois statute was only sporadically deployed to counter racist media, because Jackson was unable to secure appropriations for enforcement. So it was left in the hands of the same white police force who were guilty of brutality against Black people during the outbreak of racial violence and the riots in Chicago during the Red Summer of 1919.

In 1920, when Micheaux released *Within Our Gates*, his unsparing depiction of white brutality repeatedly ran into stiff opposition from censors. Censorship boards in several states insisted that Micheaux cut powerful scenes showing the lynching of a Black man and woman. Even Chicago, home to Senator Jackson, sponsor of Illinois's antiracist censorship law, held up the release for two months. As a result, Micheaux had to edit multiple versions of *Within Our Gates* for the film to be seen at all. Trying to accommodate the varying demands of multiple state and local censorship boards had an adverse impact on a film's bottom line. The costly, time-consuming process of submitting a film to multiple boards was incompatible with the studio model of simultaneous film release. In addition, separate scandals, such as the rape and murder trial of silent film star Fatty Arbuckle, heightened scrutiny from bureaucrats charged with safeguarding public morality.

In response, the studios formed the Motion Picture Producers and Distributors Association (MPPDA) to devise a self-regulatory strategy. In 1922, the MPPDA appointed Will Hays, a Republican strategist who had orchestrated Warren G. Harding's successful presidential campaign, to develop standards for the studios to follow. According to historian Gregory D. Black, Hays was an anti-Semitic "puritan" who viewed it as "his mission to bring a Jewish-dominated industry the respectability of mainstream America." Hays developed "the Formula," a series of rules to screen out objectionable content. Unfortunately, the industry's efforts at self-policing did little to mollify the religious zealots who thought that Hollywood films were a corrupting influence. Beginning in 1930, the Catholic Church joined the fray. Staunch Catholic Martin Quigley launched a trade journal, the *Motion Picture Herald*, which asserted that films should take care to be "harmless entertainment" and took aim at studios' business model through various proposals.

In 1930, the MPPDA adopted a set of decency standards that had been drafted by Quigley, but enforcement was lax. By 1934, with its financial stability threatened by the twin impact of ongoing religious opposition and the Depression, the MPPDA was compelled to establish a production code administration tasked with enforcing the code. At the urging of the Catholic Church, Hays put a conservative Catholic layman named Joseph Breen in charge of enforcement. Breen went on to police motion picture content according to his ultraconservative standards until the mid-1950s.

The Hollywood Production Code contained only two mentions of race among its laundry list of prohibitions against the depictions of crime, sex, vulgarity, and obscenity. In its section on "sex," the code prohibited the depiction of "white slavery," the term coined by the Progressives to describe the sex trafficking of white women and girls, and "miscegenation," defined as "sex relationships between the [B]lack and white races." Though there was scant mention of race in the code, film studios steadfastly refused to produce films that grappled with the criminal violence of Jim Crow, preferring to depict Black people as subservient buffoons, deployed for comic relief.

The early experience of auteur Fritz Lang may point to one reason for filmmakers' reluctance to grapple with realistic depictions of racism. Lang, the brilliant Jewish director of the classic film *M*, fled Nazi Germany in 1933 for the United States. He wanted to make a powerful anti-lynching film, but Joseph Breen stopped him in his tracks. Lang's script did not violate the code's prohibitions against glorifying crime or suggest that sex was enjoyable, but Breen demanded significant edits to the script anyway. Breen decreed that the film could not show "racial prejudice, criticize Southern law enforcement or be a 'travesty of justice' story." In other words, Breen demanded a Disney cartoon, not a gripping tale of social realism.

Studios adhered to Joseph Breen's stultifying standards because the financial consequences of defiance were too great. Not only were the studios subject to stiff financial penalties for violating the Production Code, but failure to comply would also expose them to the vagaries of multiple local censorship boards. Over the next two decades, Breen passed judgment on twenty thousand films.

Although as an independent filmmaker Oscar Micheaux was not bound by the Production Code, the advent of talkies had a dramatic impact on his ability to produce and distribute films. During the silent film era, there were six hundred theaters nationwide catering to Black audiences, owned by Blacks and whites alike. Talkies crushed those outlets, which were ill-equipped to finance the upgrades required to exhibit films with sound.

Micheaux had a prolific output from 1918 to 1929, in which he produced twenty-three films, including Paul Robeson's debut, *Body and Soul* (1925). In the subsequent eighteen years, Micheaux was increasingly dependent on white financiers and produced nineteen films. Thus, just when the major studios were mass-producing demeaning and stereotypical images of Black people, the one filmmaker in a position to counter that narrative was less able to do so. The rigid segregation of American society kept the tools of filmmaking and the methods of distribution beyond the reach of Black people, so Micheaux's retreat meant that racist, one-sided, and damaging stereotypes circulated unchallenged.

There is no evidence that the Illinois censorship law was ever used to stop a film that maligned Black people or any other marginalized group. The one notable instance of prosecution under the law was detailed in the 1952 Supreme Court case of *Beauharnais v. Illinois*. Joseph Beauharnais, president of a white supremacist group, was prosecuted under the law for distributing handbills promoting residential segregation that implored the mayor and city council of Chicago to "halt the further encroachment, harassment, and invasion of white people, their property, neighborhoods and persons, by the Negro." He added that "if . . . the need to prevent the white race from being mongrelized by the Negro will not unite us, then the aggressions . . . of the Negro surely will." The Supreme Court found that Illinois's prosecution of Beauharnais for distribution of these truly noxious handbills did not violate his constitutional rights, a rare instance of the law actually policing racist speech.

Ironically, that same year, the Supreme Court finally decided that films constituted speech protected by the First Amendment, in the case of *Joseph Burstyn, Inc. v. Wilson*, also known as the *Miracle* case.

The Miracle was part of a film anthology directed by Italian neorealist Roberto Rossellini and cowritten by Rossellini and Federico Fellini. In the film, an unscrupulous character named Saint Joseph impregnates a delusional peasant woman who believes that she is the Virgin Mary. Although the picture was deemed Best Foreign Language Film by the New York Film Critics Circle, it was attacked as blasphemous. The New York State Board of Regents reviewed the film and revoked its distribution license on the grounds that it was "sacrilegious." The Supreme Court held that the New York law constituted an impermissible prior restraint on speech. The *Burstyn* decision, the rise of television, and the effect of the 1948 Paramount consent decree that broke the studios' vertically integrated control of the motion picture business combined to weaken the grip of what had come to be known as the Hays Code by the mid-1950s, until it was supplanted by the Motion Picture Association of America (MPAA) rating system in 1968.

The disparate treatment that *The Birth of a Nation* and *Within Our Gates* received from censors at the time of their releases can be read as an indictment of the widespread racism in America in the early twentieth century. Their fates in the one hundred years *after* initial release is damning evidence of the persistence of that racism and the ways in which intellectual property laws can reify the racialized hierarchy of whose art is valued.

Copyright law's purpose is to grant the author, or those to whom they sell or assign the copyright, a monopoly in the market for their work. Under the Copyright Act of 1909, in effect when both films were made, copyright owners had the exclusive rights of publication, reproduction, distribution, and sale for an initial period of twenty-eight years, with the right to renew copyright protection for an additional twenty-eight-year period, for a total of fifty-six years. After that, works fell into the public domain, where they could be freely exhibited or adapted by anyone, draining them of monetary value.

Under the United States copyright scheme, art that is not valued enough for its authorship to be registered is not protected by the law, and art that is not protected cannot be monetized. The 1909 law contained procedural hurdles that created myriad traps for those without the resources to retain skilled lawyers to protect their rights.

The Birth of a Nation was protected by copyright from its release in 1915 for the initial and renewal term, even though Epoch Producing Co., the copyright claimant for the renewal term, falsely claimed that it was the author of the film in the renewal application. This misstatement only came to light because Epoch sued Killiam Shows, Inc., which was distributing *The Birth of a Nation* pursuant to rights it obtained from the estate of D. W. Griffith. From 1942 until the 2nd Circuit's decision in 1975, two different companies were able to mine a film for profits that should have been in the public domain. We can only speculate about whether the film would have continued to maintain its hold on cinephiles if the ability to exhibit and license the film for a profit had ended in 1942.

Conversely, there is no record of a copyright registration for *Within Our Gates*. In fact, only five of Oscar Micheaux's films appear in the US Copyright Office database. Consistent with the truism that art that is not valued is not protected, several of Micheaux's films disappeared—not only from exhibition, but from distributors' catalogs as well. Although Paul Robeson's debut film, *Body and Soul,* was restored by the George Eastman Museum in 2009, *Within Our Gates* was lost for decades. The version available in the Criterion Collection is based on a copy of the film that was discovered in Spain in 1992, complete with translated title cards.

Despite the formidable obstacles that Oscar Micheaux faced—a racist film industry closed to Black filmmakers, censorship boards hostile to realistic depictions of Black people, and limited capital available to filmmakers outside of the studio system—he wrote and produced an astonishing forty-two films between 1918 and 1948. His final film, *The Betrayal*, was the first film by a Black filmmaker to be exhibited in a Broadway theater.

When Micheaux died in 1951, the absence of copyright protection for his films meant that his legacy nearly died with him. Without copyright protection, his heirs had no ability to license exhibition of his films to newly receptive movie theaters or to nascent television networks. The ability to view Oscar Micheaux's films was dependent on accessing physical prints. Given the fragile nature of film negatives, several of his films, such as his debut film, *The Homesteader*, have simply been lost.

Decades after his death, Oscar Micheaux was acknowledged as the pioneer that he was. He received a star on the Hollywood Walk of Fame in 1987 and a Directors Guild of America (DGA) Golden Jubilee Special Award in 1989. The town of Gregory, South Dakota, where Micheaux was a homesteader more than a century ago, holds an annual film festival in his honor. The US Postal Service honored him with a stamp in 2010, and the newly opened Academy Museum of Motion Pictures in Los Angeles has an exhibit dedicated to his work. The belated recognition is welcome, but the erasure of Micheaux's work for decades is the clearest example of how the American legal response to the cultural phenomenon of motion pictures operated ruthlessly to reinforce his country's stratified racial hierarchy.

FOUR

JAZZ AND THE FIRST
WAR ON DRUGS

In May 1947, Billie Holiday had a one-week engagement at Philadelphia's Earle Theatre, one of the biggest venues in the city for Black entertainers. The Earle Theatre was built as a vaudeville palace in 1924 on the ground floor of a seven-story office building. It had 2,768 seats and welcomed musical stars like Duke Ellington, Count Basie, and Benny Goodman.

Billie Holiday was at the height of her fame. In the fourteen years since John Hammond discovered her singing at Monette's Supper Club in Harlem, Billie Holiday had toured with Count Basie's band, been one of the first Black performers to integrate an all-white band when she joined Artie Shaw's orchestra, and, at the age of twenty-four in 1939, opened at Barney Josephson's groundbreaking integrated jazz club Café Society. It was at her inaugural gig at Café

Society that Billie Holiday introduced her signature song, the haunting anti-lynching ballad "Strange Fruit."

"Strange Fruit" catapulted Billie Holiday to stardom, but John Hammond, the white executive who had signed her to Columbia Records, had not wanted her to record it. Holiday signed a one-year deal with Milt Gabler's label to record the song. Although it is easy to criticize Hammond for his cowardice, he may have been prescient. The release of "Strange Fruit" put Billie Holiday in the crosshairs of racist federal and state law enforcement, who hounded her for the rest of her life. Beginning in 1940, the Federal Bureau of Narcotics (the predecessor to the DEA) began its obsessive surveillance of "Lady Day," hoping to use her drug addiction to silence her. Billie Holiday had often said that she modeled her singing voice after Louis Armstrong and Bessie Smith. By May 1947, she was sharing the bill with Louis Armstrong at the Earle, as an artist of equal stature.

None of this mattered to the federal agents gunning for her arrest. As Holiday herself described it in her memoir, *Lady Sings the Blues*, on the last night of her engagement at the Earle, she had a hunch that the feds would be waiting at her hotel to ambush her. She begged her bandmate Bobby Tucker and her road manager (and dealer) Jimmy Asundio not to go back to her hotel. They laughed off her concern, but when she pulled up to the hotel a short while later, the lobby was teeming with cops. When a federal agent walked up to her car, Billie claims she grabbed the wheel from her chauffeur and sped off in a hail of bullets.

Although much of her memoir has been criticized as a mix of exaggeration and self-conscious mythologizing, there is no dispute that Billie Holiday *was* ultimately charged with illegal narcotics possession based on that sweep of her Philadelphia hotel room. Her

manager, Joe Glaser, gave her the baffling advice to decline repre-
sentation and plead guilty. Holiday acquiesced, hoping to be sent to
a rehabilitation facility. Instead, in 1947, she was sentenced to serve
a year and a day in federal prison in Anderson, West Virginia. By all
accounts, Billie Holiday was a model prisoner, but during her entire
sentence, she didn't sing a note. Because of the criminalization of her
addiction, Lady Day would be silenced for far longer.

After her guilty plea, the New York Police Department revoked
Billie Holiday's cabaret card, banning her from the most lucrative
and consistent gigs in New York jazz clubs. Lacking the supportive
family, dedicated patrons, or honest managers that surrounded a jazz
great like Thelonious Monk, Holiday never regained her cabaret card
for the rest of her life. Although she performed in Europe and in
large concert halls, the inability to book jazz clubs severely limited
her earning potential.

Unlike Monk, the intellectual property that Billie Holiday created primarily drove revenue for others. She made her first recording in 1933 and recorded steadily over the next quarter century, but
like Bessie Smith before her, she did not receive any royalties for her
Columbia recordings. It was not until she signed with Milt Gabler's
Commodore Records in 1941 that Billie's contract included royalties.
Even then, the typical royalty rate for artists was between 1 and 4 percent, leaving the label with the lion's share of income for her recordings. As a result, when Billie Holiday died in a New York hospital in
1959, handcuffed to her bed by the sadistic NYPD, her only money
was the wad of $50 bills strapped to her leg.

In June 1948, the brilliant jazz composer and pianist Thelonious
Monk was leaving a gig at the Royal Roost, a New York City club,
when police approached and searched him. They found a small bag of

marijuana and arrested him. Although this was a misdemeanor even in 1948, after a trial on August 31, Monk was sentenced to thirty days in jail on Rikers Island. Sadly, Monk's real punishment for that nickel bag extended far beyond those thirty days.

Due to their convictions and incarcerations, the NYPD revoked the cabaret cards of both Billie Holiday and Thelonious Monk. Without cabaret cards, neither artist could work in any New York City establishment that sold alcohol, which eliminated every venue in the epicenter of jazz. Monk and Lady Day were barred from lucrative gigs on Fifty-Second Street—which boasted so many jazz clubs that it was nicknamed "Swing Street"—and from Harlem clubs like Minton's Playhouse, where Monk got his start as the house pianist in 1941.

Although the NYPD did not start requiring musicians to have cabaret cards until 1940, the law had its origins in Prohibition-era New York City. During the 1920s, Harlem became a mecca for Black artists, writers, and musicians. Harlem clubs attracted high-society white people who came to mix with artists like Langston Hughes and Zora Neale Hurston and to indulge in the illicit thrill of mingling across the rigid color line. As detailed in the legislative history of the cabaret card law, New York politicians panicked at the thought that tourists or naive (white) New Yorkers would "run wild" in New York clubs and dance halls after rubbing elbows with people of "poor moral character," and in 1926 legislation was passed requiring that the character of every staff person who worked in entertainment venues such as clubs and dance halls pass muster with the NYPD. The original legislation addressed permanent workers such as maître d's, waiters, and kitchen staff. In 1940, at the urging of Mayor Fiorello La Guardia, the law's scope was expanded to monitor musicians who appeared at any venue that served alcohol, regardless of whether their employment was a one-week engagement or as part of the house band.

In 1941, the union covering bartenders and hotel and restaurant workers sued the NYPD to invalidate the cabaret card law. In *Friedman v. Valentine*, the union challenged the entire cabaret card scheme as exceeding the scope of the police department's authority. The union also argued that the requirement that all applicants seeking work in restaurants, dance halls, cabarets, and nightclubs pay the police department a $2 application fee and be fingerprinted violated their due process rights by imposing an undue burden on their ability to find employment.

The court blithely dismissed both arguments. Justice Ferdinand Pecora of the New York State Supreme Court endorsed the New York City Council's view that workers in dance halls and cabarets were uniquely positioned to take advantage of patrons. The court stated that the test of a law's constitutionality was "whether an evil exists and whether there is a logical relation between the eradication of the evil and the enactment of regulations intended to cure the condition."

Although the opinion was written ten years after the end of Prohibition, the Puritanical contempt oozes off the page. Judge Pecora rejected the contention that the fingerprinting requirement imposed an undue burden, citing the myriad professions that required fingerprinting as a prerequisite to obtaining a license. The judge ignored the fact that these other professions involved business operators, rather than low-level workers. It gave short shrift to the fact that the law gave the police department the discretion to prevent every type of worker in an entire segment of the hospitality and entertainment industry from earning a living. The law allowed the NYPD to withhold cabaret cards from those convicted of *misdemeanors* involving disorderly conduct or relating to "narcotic drugs." Once the regulations were amended in 1940 to define jazz clubs as cabarets and to require musicians with limited engagements of one or two weeks to obtain a cabaret card in order to perform, the NYPD had a powerful tool for controlling the lives and livelihoods of Black musicians.

The NYPD of the 1940s boasted very few Black officers. In 1943, Black New Yorkers were 6 percent of the city's population but less than 1 percent of the police force. Given that the cabaret card law originated in politicians' fear that jazz music and alcohol would lead to debauchery and interracial socializing, it is hardly surprising the NYPD would focus its attention on placing Black jazz artists in legal jeopardy to imperil their livelihood.

The criminalization of a range of recreational drugs from heroin to marijuana made it much easier for the police to achieve that goal. That criminalization was thanks to Harry Anslinger, the virulent racist in charge of the federal government's narcotics policy for thirty years. Anslinger got his start during Prohibition, chasing down bootleggers for the federal government. Once Prohibition was repealed, he feared he would be unemployed and looked for another illicit substance to police.

According to journalist Laura Smith, Anslinger initially "focused [his agency's enforcement efforts] on cocaine and heroin," but the small number of users threatened his agency's relevance, so he pivoted to marijuana and embarked on a campaign to demonize the drug in order to criminalize it. He began with the name. In the early twentieth century, cannabis was known by many nicknames, including *juju*, *tea*, and *reefer*. Anslinger popularized the term *marijuana* so that the public would associate the drug with Mexican immigrants. He asserted that there was a link between marijuana use and violence, although research showed that this assertion was completely false. Throughout the 1930s, Anslinger worked to conflate race, drugs, music, and crime in the minds of the public. Anslinger's efforts culminated in the passage of the Marihuana Tax Act of 1937, which made the drug illegal.

Anslinger's efforts were successful because the criminalization of recreational drugs was racialized from the start. The first widespread use of opiates was among wounded Civil War veterans, who used the drugs to ease the pain of injuries sustained during what still holds the record as the deadliest war in American history. After the Civil War, male doctors commonly prescribed morphine to female patients to help with menstrual cramps, "diseases of a nervous character," and even morning sickness. From the late nineteenth century into the twentieth century, most opiate addicts were middle- and upper-middle-class (white) women. San Francisco passed the first law criminalizing the drug when it outlawed the operation of Chinese opium dens in 1875. It is telling that private sale and use were not outlawed, insulating white dealers and users from arrest and prosecution.

Once drug use crossed class and racial lines, the Harrison Narcotics Tax Act was passed in 1914, a federal law criminalizing the sale and use of opiates. Laws criminalizing the entire range of recreational drugs were a powerful weapon with which hostile law enforcement could target Black people in general and Black jazz musicians in particular.

At its birth in the early twentieth century, jazz was viewed with contempt and suspicion by the larger white society. The reasons aren't complicated. Black people in America were widely hated and viewed as inferior. Jazz, as an unequivocally Black creation, was condemned and feared by white music critics and listeners. Initial critical reactions to jazz presage the reception that bebop, rock and roll, and Hip Hop later received, often using the same adjectives.

In mainstream periodicals of the day such as *Current Opinion* and *The Literary Digest,* critics derided both jazz music and the Black musicians who played it. In an article titled "The Appeal of Primitive Jazz," the author described Black jazz musicians who "shake and jump and writhe in ways to suggest" Saint Vitus's dance, a medieval term for an illness characterized by involuntary movement. It dismissed the music as the "delirium tremens of syncopation . . . strict rhythm without melody."

This article appears to have been the first of many racist attacks on jazz under the guise of artistic "criticism." At least one Black musician, James Reese Europe, attempted to rebut the scurrilous attacks in an article titled "A Negro Explains Jazz." Europe was a famous musician and World War I veteran who served as a lieutenant in the famous Harlem Hellfighters regiment. As such, he had the gravitas and the authority to defend jazz from ignorant condemnation.

Europe described how the colonel of his regiment had recruited him to find a band to serve and play with him at the front lines. Although Europe and his band members spent time in the trenches seeing active combat, the purpose of his article was to defend jazz music. Europe details the "wild" reception French audiences gave his band in Paris that turned a one-night concert into an eight-week engagement. Europe returned from the war even more convinced of the artistic merit of Black jazz music. He argued that even Black classical composers like Harry Burleigh and Will Marion Cook did their best work when drawing on the cultural heritage of "their race."

Unfortunately, Europe's passionate defense did nothing to stem the steady flood of mainstream condemnations of jazz, rooted in racism. Outlets as disparate as *Ladies' Home Journal* and *The New Republic* ran articles characterizing jazz as a "known danger" and expressing fear that the mere act of *listening* to jazz could turn white people into the "savages" they believed Black people to be.

Commencing with the emergence of jazz as a popular art form around World War I, white critics relentlessly condemned it as nothing more than cacophonous "jungle music" and its Black practitioners as untutored savages. By the end of Prohibition, a wide swath of mainstream white America viewed jazz musicians as immoral, corrupting influences per se. Even the white critics who loved jazz often viewed its Black innovators with condescension born of racism. These attitudes made Black musicians ripe targets for persecution by zealous law enforcement, at great cost to their mental health, livelihoods, and their very lives.

Billie Holiday and Thelonious Monk are unquestionably two of the greatest jazz musicians that America has ever produced. Both left an indelible mark on the music, innovating and inspiring an untold number of their contemporaries, as well as generations of musicians who came after them. Despite—or perhaps because of—their genius, law enforcement persecuted them continually. Harry Anslinger, the viciously racist head of the Federal Bureau of Narcotics, specifically targeted both Billie Holiday and Thelonious Monk. Anslinger hired a Black undercover agent to infiltrate Billie Holiday's circle and colluded with her abusive husband to set her up for arrest. Billie was vulnerable thanks to a heroin addiction aided and abetted by enablers in her inner circle. Monk was harassed for "offenses" as disparate as possession of marijuana or refusing to snitch on pianist Bud Powell when heroin was found in their car.

Both Holiday and Monk lost their cabaret cards, and thus their ability to work in New York City clubs, because of these arrests. Despite his battle with racist law enforcement and mental health challenges, Monk left behind a jaw-droppingly large and brilliant body of work comprised not only of recordings but compositions for which he retained copyright ownership. Monk's catalog includes such classics as "'Round Midnight," "Crepuscule with Nellie," "Epistrophy," and "Ruby, My Dear."

Conversely, when Billie Holiday died handcuffed to a hospital bed, despite her extensive and brilliant body of work, she was nearly destitute. Her lawyer claimed that he was entitled to 10 percent of her record royalties, which were only disgorged after her husband, Louis McKay, successfully sued on behalf of her estate.

There are multiple reasons for the wildly disparate fates of Monk and Lady Day, from their gender to their family backgrounds, to formal training or its absence, to being surrounded by supportive managers or exploitative ones. A key difference between Thelonious Monk and Billie Holiday, though, was in whether their particular form of creative expression could be protected under intellectual property laws, and therefore monetized by them.

A TALE OF TWO COPYRIGHTS

We can best examine the role intellectual property played in Monk's ability to build intergenerational wealth despite pervasive racism and struggles with mental illness, and Billie Holiday's inability to overcome the triple threat of racism, misogyny, and addiction that she battled in her life, by exploring the journey of their best-known songs: "Strange Fruit" and "'Round Midnight."

Billie Holiday first performed "Strange Fruit" at Barney Josephson's pioneering New York City club Café Society in 1939. Josephson envisioned his club as a venue where integrated audiences could enjoy top-notch entertainment from a wide array of artists, becoming New York's first integrated nightclub. Café Society booked artists as disparate as Sarah Vaughan and Sister Rosetta Tharpe on the one hand, and Zero Mostel and Danny Kaye on the other. It was the ideal setting for Billie Holiday to debut this haunting protest song.

Certain facts about the authorship of "Strange Fruit" are not in dispute. It was originally a poem titled "Bitter Fruit," written by Abel Meeropol under the pen name Lewis Allan. Meeropol and his wife, Anne, set the poem to music, and it was performed publicly on several occasions. Café Society's floor-show manager Robert Gordon "heard the song at a union meeting, and brought it to Barney Josephson and Billie Holiday."

According to Josephson, Billie Holiday was "initially unenthusiastic" about performing the song and didn't really understand what it was about. The idea that a Black woman born on the Mason-Dixon Line who had just endured horrible racism in the Jim Crow South while traveling as the lone Black member of Artie Shaw's band would need white men to explain lyrics about lynching to her beggars belief.

Holiday's account in her memoir is the polar opposite. According to Holiday, when she heard the song, she "dug it right off." She recounts that Meeropol suggested that she and her pianist Sonny White "turn it into music [and that] the three of them got together and did the job in about three weeks."

Once "Strange Fruit" was added to Billie's set list, Josephson made sure that nothing would blunt the song's emotional impact. According to music historian John Szwed, "Strange Fruit" was programmed to be the last song for each of her three nightly sets, and

Josephson instructed "club staff to cease all activities while Billie sang. [He] turned out all the house lights [except for] a small spotlight on her face."

Despite the fact that Billie made it her signature song, despite her collaboration on its authorship, "Strange Fruit" was copyrighted in Meeropol's name alone when it was first published by the Edward B. Marks Music Company in 1939. Meeropol alone received public performance royalties from Billie Holiday's countless live performances. Meeropol alone received mechanical royalties from Holiday's recording of the song in 1940 for Gabler's Commodore Records.

Meeropol, not content with earning 100 percent of the copyright royalties for "Strange Fruit," also jealously policed any suggestion that Billie Holiday had contributed to the creation of the song. When Holiday gave an interview to *PM* newspaper repeating her version of how the song was created, Meeropol wrote a letter to the editor contesting her account. A decade later, when Billie Holiday published *Lady Sings the Blues,* she included her account of how "Strange Fruit" became her "personal protest" song. Meeropol immediately wrote to her publisher, Doubleday, and threatened to sue if they did not issue a retraction. Meeropol's position was supported by Barney Josephson, who repeated his assertion that Billie Holiday had not understood the song when she initially heard it. Holiday never said that she contributed to the lyrics, but to the *music,* so it's decidedly beside the point. William Dufty, the cowriter of Holiday's memoir, immediately rose to her defense. Dufty saw the misogyny and racism embedded in Meeropol's insistence that *he alone* was responsible for the haunting power of "Strange Fruit." In a letter to Doubleday, Dufty wrote that Billie Holiday's creative process involved "doing her own variations." Dufty asserted that if Meeropol's sheet music and Billie Holiday's record were compared, "if the melody was the same, I'd eat the record."

The view that Billie Holiday had made no creative contributions to what became her signature song, the song that made her a target of the FBI and the Federal Bureau of Narcotics, depends on a belief that she was nothing more than an unlettered vessel for the creativity of white men. The fact that biographers and critics did not question the racism and sexism inherent in the assumption that white men had to school a Black woman about lynching is all the more ironic given that Holiday's insistence on performing the song brought the full weight of federal law enforcement down on her.

The failure to credit Billie Holiday with any authorship of such a pivotal song in her career is a consequence of the persistent foregrounding of her personal tragedies over her artistry. We hear again and again about Lady Day's drug addiction and her victimization at the hands of both law enforcement and a string of truly horrible men, both Black and white. We don't stop to think that her heart-stopping musical brilliance is the only reason we care about these salacious details. As Frank Sinatra said in a 1958 interview, "Billie Holiday was and still remains the greatest single musical influence on me. . . . With a few exceptions, every major singer in the US during her generation has been touched in some way by her genius." In this century, Holiday has influenced singers like Erykah Badu and Andra Day.

"'ROUND MIDNIGHT," OR THE EDUCATION OF THELONIOUS MONK

Thelonious Monk, born in Rocky Mount, North Carolina, in 1917, is widely known as a groundbreaking musical genius. Along with Charlie

Parker and Dizzy Gillespie, Monk was one of the progenitors of the bebop style of modern jazz. He composed several songs that became jazz standards, but none was as famous as "'Round Midnight." According to Tom Lord's The Jazz Discography archive, as of 2021, 1,780 different recordings of "'Round Midnight" have been released, making it among the most frequently recorded jazz compositions in history.

Monk grew up in the San Juan Hill neighborhood on Manhattan's West Side, a neighborhood teeming with a mix of Southern Black people who fled Jim Crow during the Great Migration, West Indian and Cuban immigrants, Irish Americans, and transplanted Puerto Ricans. He grew up hearing a polyglot mix of music, along with Tin Pan Alley standards. Monk began studying piano as a child, initially looking over the shoulder of his older sister Barbara during her lessons before formally starting lessons himself at age eleven. Monk's first teacher, Simon Wolf, gave him a strong classical foundation, teaching him pieces by Chopin, Beethoven, Bach, and Mozart.

Monk's musical education was profoundly impacted by hearing the many jazz musicians who lived in his neighborhood, as well as by the lessons he took with Alberta Simmons, a jazz musician and educator. Monk learned various stride piano techniques from Simmons.

When he was seventeen, Monk left high school to tour the Southwest for two years with a Black woman evangelist. Jazz historians have been unable to uncover much about that period in Monk's musical evolution. Even the name of the evangelist Monk toured with has not been confirmed.

When Monk returned to New York in 1937, New York City, like the rest of the country, was in the grips of the Great Depression. Although all musicians found it challenging to make a living, Black musicians had it tougher. Local 802 of the musicians' union established an emergency relief fund for its members, but according to Monk's biographer, Robin D. G. Kelley, "few Black musicians benefited." Monk began playing in small clubs in Harlem, but thanks to the fact that Local 802 set a lower union minimum for Harlem venues, he was barely able to eke out a living.

Even though Black musicians were the creators and innovators in jazz, structural racism made it exceedingly difficult for them to monetize their talent. Popular musical radio shows featuring big band music were broadcast from Midtown hotels, whose strict segregation policies made it impossible for Black bandleaders to perform there and be featured on the radio. Since radio play led to increased recognition and record sales, an artificial ceiling was placed on the income potential of Black jazz musicians.

Against this backdrop, Monk made only a meager amount by playing in small Harlem clubs. But a steady job he secured in 1941 as the house pianist in a Harlem club called Minton's Playhouse helped change the course of jazz history. Minton's Monday-night jam sessions attracted a broad range of musicians and were fertile ground for the experimentation that led to the birth of bebop. It was during his stint at Minton's that Monk registered his first copyrights—for the compositions "Epistrophy" (a future classic cowritten with Minton's house drummer, Kenny Clarke) and "Harlem Is Awful Messy" (cowritten with "Hot Lips" Page and Joe Guy but never recorded).

At the end of 1941, Monk was let go from Minton's and was back to scrambling for gigs. He realized that he needed to supplement his income. Monk wanted to get his compositions published so they could be played and recorded by other musicians and generate public performance income, as monitored and collected by ASCAP, and mechanical royalty income from the sale of records.

Lacking any publishing connections of his own, Monk turned to Teddy McRae, an arranger for bandleader Artie Shaw (Shaw had toured the segregated South with Billie Holiday as his featured vocalist a few years prior). McRae submitted "The Pump" and "You Need 'Na" to Regent Music Corporation to be registered and published in early 1944. As "payment," McRae claimed 50 percent authorship and copyright in both tunes, although he had not written a single note!

Furious at McRae's deception, Monk cut ties with him. He later revised and reregistered the songs under the titles "Little Rootie Tootie" and "Well, You Needn't," listing himself correctly as the sole composer.

Over the summer of 1943, Monk finalized a song that he had been working on for a year. He asked his friend Thelma Elizabeth Murray to write lyrics and registered the song in both of their names with the copyright office in September 1944, under the title "I Need You So."

The composition languished in absence of a publisher until early 1944, when bandleader Cootie Williams began playing it as part of his set. It is not clear whether Williams learned of the tune through pianist Bud Powell, his band member and Monk's good friend, or directly from Monk himself. Williams revised "I Need You So" by adding an eight-bar interlude and soliciting Broadway tunesmith Bernie Hanighen to write lyrics. Williams filed for copyright in this revised version, now titled "'Round Midnight," in November 1944 through publisher Advanced Music Corporation, listing himself, Hanighen, and Monk as cowriters with one-third credit each. Although Williams's revision has only been recorded once and Hanighen's lyrics are infrequently performed, two-thirds of the revenue from Monk's most popular composition is paid to their estates to this day.

Monk was already wary of the unscrupulous club owners and promoters who took advantage of jazz musicians with punishing schedules and subpar pay. He often refused to work in conditions that he deemed exploitative, and Robin D. G. Kelley speculates that Monk's early reputation as "difficult" was stoked by music business figures who resented Monk's clear-eyed view of the power imbalance between talented musicians and those who merely profited from their art.

Stung by these early experiences being hoodwinked out of his proper share of copyright, for the rest of his life Monk policed his copyright ownership of the many tunes he composed. In 1955, Monk signed with Melotone Music, the publishing company established by Gigi Gryce, a conservatory-educated Black jazz saxophonist, composer, and arranger. Gryce was a passionate advocate for jazz musicians and composers who sought to protect them from the rampant exploitation in the music business.

Through Thelonious Monk's advocacy of his work, careful eye over copyright, and working with Melotone Music and Gryce, the fate of his music and estate after his death diverged from Billie Holiday's. While both were unjustly deprived of the ability to earn a steady living in New York City due to losing their cabaret cards, their legacies differed based on the intellectual property they created during their lives.

Musical compositions like those Monk created generated multiple streams of income: (1) mechanical royalties on each copy of sound recordings; (2) public performance royalties from ASCAP or Broadcast Music, Inc. (BMI) for radio airplay; and (3) royalties on sales of sheet music. Songwriters who entered publishing agreements where they retained 50 percent of their copyright ownership received

75 percent of the income generated by their compositions. Later in his career, Monk recorded songs for the soundtrack of Roger Vadim's *Les Liaisons dangereuses*, which generated synchronization license payments. This foundation of copyright ownership generated passive income for Monk's family after his death in 1982 and continues to this day.

Conversely, Billie Holiday, arguably denied proper credit on "Strange Fruit," relied primarily on record royalties and income from live performances. For Holiday, the loss of her cabaret card was a devastating blow; she relied on performing, given that she did not have music copyright income to fall back on. Although Billie Holiday was one of the most frequently photographed artists of her era, she earned nothing from the licensing or reproduction of her image, because copyright ownership in photographs was held by the photographer. Although New York State passed the first right of publicity statute in 1903, prohibiting the use of a person's image for advertising or trade, it did not recognize a postmortem right of publicity until November 30, 2020 (trailing states like California and Tennessee by decades).

For years after her premature death in 1959, copyright holders of the numerous images of Billie Holiday were free to commercialize and profit from her image without paying her estate a penny. Noted scholar Farah Jasmine Griffin detailed the extent to which Billie Holiday's image and persona was commodified by a range of advertisers and retailers who "decontextualized the image from the lived life, marr[ied] the Holiday image to particular products and services," without any requirement to compensate her estate for the use.

Monk and Holiday may have had different levels of success in resisting the music industry's efforts to separate them from the wealth their music created, but their artistic legacies remain undimmed decades after their deaths. As American popular taste shifted away from jazz in the 1950s, the power brokers in the entertainment industry discovered how to not only extract the majority of the wealth created by Black artists but to erase the very fact of their roles as innovators of rock and roll, to the point where decades later, Black people were not even associated with the genre they had created.

FIVE

HAIL, HAIL, ROCK AND ROLL

The Rock & Roll Hall of Fame is a physical oxymoron—a gleaming I. M. Pei–designed monument to the music that exemplifies youthful rebellion. Inductees are chosen annually by a panel of "experts," predominantly composed of those who write about or profit from rock and roll, rather than those who actually play it. The Rock Hall nominating committee skews overwhelmingly white and male, which may explain why, as of 2024, only 15 percent of the inductees have been women (and only 8.8 percent if you don't count every individual member of a musical group inductee).

The Rock Hall was also founded by a team dominated by record business executives and lawyers, none of whom were Black. In 1983, Atlantic Records founder Ahmet Ertegun recruited Jann Wenner, the editor and publisher of *Rolling Stone*; attorneys Allen Grubman and Suzan Evans; and fellow record executives Seymour Stein,

Bob Krasnow, and Noreen Woods to form the Rock & Roll Hall of Fame.

Equally as pernicious, while less obvious, is the narrative that the Rock Hall tells about the genesis and development of rock and roll, about who is merely "foundational" or an "early influence" and who "perfected" it. Rock music has the distinction, among all uniquely American musical art forms created by Black people, of being so thoroughly co-opted by mainstream white America that Black musicians have been almost completely erased. By 1985, musician and writer Greg Tate and guitarist Vernon Reid felt compelled to form the Black Rock Coalition to reclaim the very right of Black rock musicians to exist.

The inaugural class of the Rock & Roll Hall of Fame included such undeniable Black musicians as Chuck Berry and Little Richard. But Sister Rosetta Tharpe—the Black woman credited with releasing the first rock-and-roll record in 1945, the Black woman cited as an influence by everyone from Chuck Berry to Johnny Cash, the Black woman revered by British rock royalty like Mick Jagger and Eric Clapton, the Black woman who brought a fourteen-year-old Richard Penniman onstage in Macon, Georgia, before he was known as Little Richard—was not inducted into the Rock Hall until 2017!

Sister Rosetta Tharpe had a fascinating career that spanned from the 1940s to the 1960s, crossed genres from the sacred to the secular, appealed to Black and white audiences alike, and sold out stadiums from DC to Atlanta. Yet, by the time of her death from complications of diabetes in 1973, she had been eclipsed by younger white artists, who so thoroughly appropriated her guitar-playing techniques that her propulsive style became synonymous with white male "rock gods" like Keith Richards and Eric Clapton.

Conversely, everyone knows that rhythm and blues is Black music.

Legendary Atlantic Records co-head Jerry Wexler, then a *Billboard* reporter, coined the term in 1949 to replace the *Billboard* chart title of "Race Records" to denote what Wexler later defined as "Black music by Black musicians for Black adult buyers."

The sound of Black R & B music is ineffable. Critic Wesley Morris has described Black music as "uncatchable"—often imitated, but never duplicated. As Danyel Smith said, "To listen to Aretha Franklin or Whitney Houston or Mary J. Blige is to feel seen—as if each woman knew your deepest sadness or your greatest joy, plucked them out and delivered them back to you in a powerful, beautiful, shimmering package, with each note evoking a sympathetic physical vibration, where you become another instrument in their backing band."

We often explain this ability by pointing out that great Black singers got their start "in the church," but that shorthand does not tell the whole story. It is true that the rigors of Black church choirs train singers to be disciplined in their musicianship, providing them through practice and performance with more than the requisite ten thousand hours supposedly needed for mastery. Yet it is more than that. The call-and-response interplay among preacher, choir, and congregation is a direct descendant of the African spiritual practice of "hush harbors," where enslaved Black people convened to express their Christian faith. The ability to imbue every note with emotion that elicits a strong response from the listener is an outgrowth of the blues, itself a secular descendant of those same hush harbors.

The story of how the anguished cries of enslaved Black people in the hush harbors became Negro spirituals, diverged into the secular through the blues, and converged in the gospel blues, which gave birth to both rock and roll *and* rhythm and blues, can be told through the careers of Sister Rosetta Tharpe and musician and composer Thomas

Dorsey. Both created original, earth-shattering musical genres, but only one, by harnessing copyright law, ensured that Black people's role in that creation could not be erased.

Thomas A. Dorsey is the man responsible for bringing both the rigor and the emotion to the music of the Black church in the twentieth century. Although Dorsey may not be widely known outside of the Black community, it can be argued that Dorsey's understanding of the importance of intellectual property and institutional infrastructure is responsible for the fact that both Black gospel music and the music it gave birth to, rhythm and blues, continue to be recognized as Black cultural creations that cannot be appropriated by mainstream white culture.

Cotton Plant, Arkansas, where Sister Rosetta Tharpe was born, was founded as the town of Richmond in 1820, when white settlers, attracted by plentiful timber, moved to the area after Indigenous Cherokee people were forcibly removed in 1817. In 1846, a Mississippi transplant named William Lynch moved to Richmond, opened a general store, and planted cotton seeds in the field next to it. Lynch's cotton proved to be such a novelty that it gave the town its official name, Cotton Plant, when it was incorporated in 1852. The arrival of the Batesville and Brinkley Railroad in 1881 aided Cotton Plant's development, but the completion of a rail line connecting Helena to Cotton Plant in 1908, together with the growth of the timber industry, led to Cotton Plant's significant growth. Cotton Plant became a thriving cultural center as well as an industrial one, boasting an opera house and several music and literary societies. Early-twentieth-century Cotton Plant was also home to a thriving Black middle class who could send their children to the private Cotton Plant Academy, which had been established in 1878 to educate Black children.

Rosetta, known as Rosa in her youth, the only child of Willis Atkins and Katie Harper, was born in Cotton Plant in 1915. Willis was a farmworker, like most Black men in the rural South at that time. Both Willis and Katie played instruments and encouraged Rosa's precocious musical ability. Willis and Katie were also devout members of the Church of God in Christ (COGIC). An understanding of COGIC is key to understanding Sister Rosetta Tharpe's development as a musician. As Gayle F. Wald details in her biography of Sister Rosetta Tharpe, COGIC was a Black Christian denomination founded in the early twentieth century by Charles Harrison Mason. Mason was a Baptist minister who "split with the mainstream Baptist ministers because of his holiness beliefs." The denomination's popularity was "sparked by a 1906–07 Holiness revival initiated by five Black women [evangelists] in Los Angeles who began speaking in tongues."

COGIC was the first Black Baptist denomination in the US that was unabashedly African in its roots. Its emphasis on speaking in tongues and catching the Holy Spirit directly evoked the religious practices of enslaved people, which fused African spiritual practices with Christianity. COGIC embodied a paradox. While it held its members to a strict moral code, forbidding women from wearing makeup or jewelry, according to Wald, COGIC had an expansive definition of religious music, using instruments like "trumpets and guitars" and interpolating elements normally found in blues and ragtime in their gospel hymns.

This was the church that encouraged Tharpe's precocious musical gifts. In 1920, after divorcing Willis Atkins, Rosetta's mother, Katie, decided to move the two of them from Arkansas to Chicago to pursue her evangelical ambitions. While Katie Harper may have been motivated by the greater opportunities available in Chicago to spread the gospel, she may have been equally motivated by a desire to escape the capricious and deadly violence of white Southerners.

In the aftermath of the Civil War, most Black Americans remained in the South, pursuing a livelihood in agriculture. The political and economic gains Black people achieved during Reconstruction made wealthy white Southerners terrified of Black power, and they considered the growing alliance between poor whites and Blacks to be an existential threat. In response, in the twenty years between 1890 and 1910, every state south of the Mason-Dixon Line established Jim Crow laws that imposed rigid segregation in every facet of public life, from separate schools and hospitals to separate entrances and water fountains. Jim Crow was an apartheid regime that enforced its hierarchy through terroristic violence, with fatal consequences for any Black person found to have committed the slightest transgression. Black communities that were too prosperous, like the one in Tulsa, Oklahoma, were targeted for wholesale destruction by resentful white mobs.

Despite this, Black people did not move north in large numbers until the advent of World War I in 1916. The combination of the draft, the interruption of European immigration, and the ramp-up of wartime production created a labor shortage that Black people were eager to fill. According to historian James Grossman, factories sent recruiters south, and Black newspapers like the *Chicago Defender* urged Black Southerners to come north for opportunities. Southern whites used violence and intimidation to try to stem the exodus, "detaining" Black people at train stations until northbound trains had departed and refusing to "accept prepaid tickets." Despite these tactics, between 500,000 and 750,000 Black Southerners migrated to the North after the start of WWI, with 50,000 to 75,000 moving to Chicago alone.

Once the war ended, Black veterans fresh from "making the world safe for democracy" returned home to a country that still did not respect them as citizens or as human beings, while white veterans returned to Northern cities where they suddenly had to compete with Black people for housing and jobs. This combustible mix led to an eruption in racist violence against Black people in 1919. Around the country—from New York City to Monticello, Mississippi; from New London, Connecticut, to Omaha, Nebraska—white people waged a campaign of terroristic violence against Black citizens. There were a total of thirty-eight separate race riots waged by white people during the Red Summer of 1919, as cataloged by Labor Department Assistant Secretary and National Urban League cofounder George Edmund Haynes.

Katie and Rosetta's future home of Chicago was hardly immune to the racist violence sweeping the country. On July 27, 1919, a riot broke out when a Black teenager drowned after being stoned for drifting into the water on the "white" side of the beach at Lake Michigan. Violence consumed the south and west sides of the city for days. Twenty-three Black people were killed, 537 were injured, and one thousand were left homeless thanks to the arson and destruction of white mobs, before the state militia was called in to quell the rampage.

By far, the single deadliest event of the Red Summer occurred a mere sixty-six miles from Rosetta and Katie's hometown of Cotton Plant. In Elaine, Arkansas, as in other Southern agricultural towns, white landowners and shopkeepers colluded to cheat Black farmers out of the full value of their crops to keep them in economic peonage.

Beginning in 1919, Black farmers in Elaine began organizing a union to combat this economic exploitation.

When the white landowners learned of the Black farmers' plans, they sent two spies to infiltrate the organizing meetings. The Black farmers discovered the spies and shot them both, killing one. In retaliation, a white mob went on a rampage in Elaine, indiscriminately murdering hundreds of Black men, women, and children. The governor had to enlist soldiers to stop the violence, and in the end, hundreds of Black people were killed, but only five white people. No white people were ever prosecuted for their violent acts.

The Red Summer of 1919 was characterized both by the ubiquity of white violence and the emergence of Black resistance to that violence. Rather than simply plead for an end to the mob violence, whether emboldened by their recent military service or heeding the exhortation of Black leaders like W. E. B. Du Bois, Black people fought back.

Out of the ashes of this widespread destruction, new Black urban communities were born, united in their demands for dignity and opportunity. In cities like New York and Chicago, these Black communities gave birth to new artistic movements—the Harlem Renaissance in New York, and the gospel blues in Chicago.

The Black population of Chicago grew by 50 percent between 1916 and 1919, and doubled between 1919 and 1930, due to the influx of Southern migrants. Efforts to integrate these new arrivals into one cohesive Black community centered around the Black church. Even before the Great Migration, Chicago was home to several large, influential Black churches, such as Olivet Baptist Church, Metropolitan Community Church, Ebenezer Baptist Church, and Pilgrim Baptist Church. These churches were dedicated to the uplift of Black people, and their pastors believed that it could be achieved by securing stable education, employment, and housing, as evidenced by the robust church-sponsored social programs. As an example, by 1920, there were sixteen people on the social-program staff of Olivet, which included an employment office, childcare, a kindergarten, and a welfare department.

Chicago in the 1920s was fertile ground for nurturing young Tharpe's musicianship. The influx of Southern Black people during the Great Migration made Chicago an epicenter in the development of jazz and blues. Upon their arrival in Chicago, Katie joined the Roberts Temple Church of God, locally known as the Fortieth Street Baptist Church, pastored by Elder W. M. Roberts, one of Mason's early disciples in COGIC. It was a point of pride for the Fortieth Street congregation that they had built their church home from the ground up, rather than simply repurpose a preexisting building.

Although COGIC's strict moral code prohibited its adherents from engaging in secular entertainment, blues and jazz sounds found their way into sacred music through the person of Thomas Andrew Dorsey, known as the "Father of Gospel Music." At the same time that pint-sized Tharpe was drawing crowds to Fortieth Street Church with her precocious singing and guitar playing, Thomas Dorsey was zigzagging between the sacred and the secular, between Atlanta and Chicago, trying to make a name for himself in music.

Thomas A. Dorsey was born in 1899 Villa Rica, Georgia, to Thomas M. Dorsey, an itinerant preacher, and Etta Plant Spencer Dorsey, a homemaker. Although the elder Dorsey graduated from Atlanta Baptist College—later known as Morehouse College, whose most famous alumni is Dr. Martin Luther King Jr.—he never found a single church base or a stable living through preaching. Instead, like most other Black people in the rural South at the turn of the twenti-eth century, the elder Dorsey made his living as a tenant farmer. Despite their education, the Dorseys were unable to sustain their family from sharecropping and moved to Atlanta in 1908, when Thomas was nine years old. The elder Dorsey found work as a gardener, and Etta took in washing. In Atlanta, classmates steeped in colorism and the respectability politics of the early twentieth century mocked Thomas for his poverty and his dark-skinned complexion.

By the age of eleven, Thomas was disenchanted with school and church and found a job selling soft drinks at vaudeville venue 81 Theatre. The famed 81 Theatre was a launching pad for Black stars like Bessie Smith and decades later for Little Richard. Dorsey decided that music would be his ticket out of poverty and began to learn the rudiments of piano playing from Ed Butler, 81 Theatre's house pianist. Dorsey supplemented his on-the-job training with formal lessons from Mrs. Graves, a local piano teacher from Morehouse who taught Dorsey the rudiments of music theory. Armed with this knowledge, Dorsey was able to eke out a living playing at rent parties and brothels. He quickly realized that, given his low position in the pecking order of professional musicians in Atlanta, he would need to travel north for greater opportunity.

In the summer of 1916, Dorsey first went to Chicago, earning a living through a combination of odd jobs and the same rent-party piano gigs he had secured down South. Dorsey returned to Atlanta later that year to avoid the famously brutal Chicago winter, a pattern he repeated over the next two years. Dorsey planned to settle permanently in Chicago when he returned in the fall of 1919, just after the Red Summer.

Dorsey's return to Chicago coincided with the explosion of the blues in popularity. Secular Black music derived from Negro spirituals, the blues first emerged in the late nineteenth century in the aftermath of the Civil War. Blues music featured a call-and-response that echoed the hush harbors of enslaved Black people but was lyrically focused on worldly concerns, such as the continuing injustice suffered by newly emancipated Black people, or the intimate concerns of romantic and sexual relationships. As Lucy Chaudhuri explained in her blog post for the BBC's music website, the blues scale "is a six-note scale consist[ing] of the minor pentatonic scale plus an extra flattened fifth note. . . . The most common form is the twelve-bar blues."

Blues was the music of Black working people, rather than of the educated, upper-class Black people that W. E. B. Du Bois dubbed the "Talented Tenth." It was the music of roadhouses and rent parties. As noted in Chapter Two, in February 1920, New York blues musician Perry Bradford convinced Okeh Records to record Mamie Smith's rendition of "Crazy Blues." The song became a runaway success, igniting a feeding frenzy among labels that each wanted their own blues hit.

Chicago was second only to New York as an epicenter of blues talent, and Dorsey desperately wanted to become successful in this important market. Recognizing that Black musicians who could read music were in short supply, Dorsey enrolled in a local music school to study composition and arranging. By October 1920, Dorsey had registered his first composition, "If You Don't Believe I'm Leaving, You Can Count the Days I'm Gone."

Unfortunately, Dorsey suffered a mental health crisis later that fall that prevented him from capitalizing on the newfound commercial success of the blues. Dorsey returned to Atlanta to recover and didn't get back to Chicago for another year. When he returned to Chicago a year later, Dorsey attended the National Baptist Convention at his uncle's urging. While there, Dorsey heard a "Professor" W. M. Nix promoting the convention's first songbook, *Gospel Pearls*, by performing spiritual songs with the same rhythmic and melodic embellishments common in the blues. Dorsey had an epiphany, realizing the power of the combination of spiritual lyrical content and blues musical style. He credits Nix's performance with prompting his first religious conversion. Dorsey abandoned secular music and began working with New Hope Baptist Church on the South Side of Chicago. In September 1922, Dorsey registered his first gospel song, "If I Don't Get There." Yet the prospect of worldly fame was too tempting, and Dorsey left New Hope to join a jazz band called the Whispering Syncopators.

While Dorsey was making another run at secular stardom with the Syncopators, little Rosetta was becoming a local celebrity on the Black church circuit. Rosetta's mother Katie's choice of Fortieth Street Church of God in Christ as their church home was propitious. Elder W. M. Roberts, the pastor of Fortieth Street, strongly believed in the power of musical ministry. Fortieth Street had a saying: "Rock, church, rock!" Wald described Fortieth Street's services as marked by "loud, lively, swinging music."

Since Rosetta was raised in a home equally steeped in music and spirituality, her musical gift was recognized and developed at an early age. She found the perfect stage at Fortieth Street, where the pastor would perch the pint-sized musician and her full-sized guitar on top of the piano so that the congregation could see and hear her. Fellow gospel singer Geraldine Gay Hambric described Tharpe's guitar playing style as "fly," and it soon became the norm for the congregation to take up a special collection just for Tharpe, which they would give to her mother, Katie. As word of Tharpe's musical gifts spread outside of the congregation, crowds began frequenting the Fortieth Street Sunday evening service just to hear Rosetta sing and play.

Rosetta's formal education ended when her mother decided to capitalize on her daughter's growing fame and travel the gospel circuit. In its stead, Rosetta developed an exquisite sense of timing and a keen ability to gauge audience response. Katie's decision to take Rosetta on the road at such a young age had far-reaching implications. Not only did it mean the end of her formal academic education, but it also meant that Rosetta had no further formal musical education in composing and arranging. This meant that Tharpe—like Bessie Smith before her, and like her secular contemporary, Billie Holiday—would have to rely on live performances for the bulk of her income, reifying a pattern of Black people being paid for their physical labor rather than their intellectual production.

While Tharpe was soaking up musical technique from artists like Juanita "Arizona" Dranes, a blind gospel artist who was the pioneer of the sanctified piano-playing style, Thomas Dorsey was getting an object lesson in the importance of copyright ownership. The blues explosion that began with the release of Mamie Smith's "Crazy Blues" in 1920 created a market for the Southern improvisational blues style in which Dorsey performed, rather than the structured, formal style performed by Northern vaudevillians.

In the Northern blues style, musicians performed and recorded fully composed songs with lyrics, but the Southern blues style was amorphous and improvisational, only becoming fixed in recording. This allowed unscrupulous record companies to copyright versions of songs recorded by Southern-style artists, thereby avoiding paying mechanical royalties. The only way around this was to deliver artists to record companies with fully composed and arranged repertoires, which prevented the record companies from evading the obligation to pay mechanical royalties, a process perfected by J. Mayo "Ink" Williams, a Black Chicago-based blues talent scout for Paramount Records, credited with discovering Ma Rainey. Williams also owned the Chicago Music Publishing Company (CMPC) and outsmarted record companies by delivering fully packaged artists with arranged and copyrighted repertoires. Dorsey became a cog in this machine, composing and copyrighting seven blues tunes in 1923. For blues artists who were still cheated out of copyright ownership of songs that they composed, this merely substituted a Black face for a white one that separated artists from the profits their artistry produced.

Williams's CMPC hired Dorsey as an in-house arranger and vocal coach, thanks to his formal training and facility with both styles of blues. This role gave Dorsey critical insight on how to use copyright ownership to profit from a burgeoning musical trend. Dorsey's position led Ma Rainey to hire him as her accompanist, and he debuted with Rainey at Chicago's Grand Theater in April 1924.

In 1925, Dorsey married Nettie Harper, whom Ma Rainey promptly hired as her wardrobe mistress in order not to risk losing her accompanist. Dorsey toured with Ma Rainey for three years, from 1925 to 1928, interrupted by another bout of severe depression in 1926. In 1928, Dorsey cowrote and recorded the blues song "It's Tight Like That" with Hudson Whittaker, performing under the stage names Georgia Tom and Tampa Red. The record sold seven million copies.

As Michael W. Harris elucidates in his biography, Dorsey's experience in the 1920s hopscotching between the blues and gospel helped synthesize his musical philosophy that "different types of music [were] vehicles for your feelings," and that the key distinction between blues and gospel was that "the words are different." To

Dorsey, improvisation, spontaneity, and emotion were hallmarks of Black secular and spiritual music. When the death of his wife and infant son in childbirth in 1932 sent Dorsey into his deepest and most profound depression to date, he emerged committed to using his musical gifts exclusively in the service of the Lord.

Throughout this same period, young Rosetta had been crisscrossing the country with her mother, honing her musical gifts and saving souls in churches and revival tents in the Midwest and the South. Unlike Thomas Dorsey, whose formal training provided him with the means to make passive income through arranging and composing, Tharpe's only source of income was what she could make performing. Those years on the revival circuit taught her that the performances that attracted the most congregants and elicited the most fervor also resulted in the fattest collection plates.

At nineteen years old, Rosetta struck out from her mother by marrying itinerant COGIC preacher Thomas J. Tharpe in Chicago in November 1934. Rosetta and her husband began traveling the circuit as a duo, with Tharpe preaching and Rosetta singing and playing. The pair ultimately settled in Miami, making the Reverend Amaziah Cohen's Miami Temple their home base. Reverend Cohen featured Rosetta and Thomas on the Sunday-night radio program that was broadcast from WKAT, a white pop music station, and soon after, waves of white people crowded the Miami Temple for the live broadcast.

Although Sister Rosetta Tharpe's fame increased thanks to the weekly broadcasts, she was simultaneously enduring a personal and professional partnership with a physically abusive and unfaithful husband. As a Black woman gospel performer in the 1930s, Tharpe could not simply divorce her husband without alienating her audience, so she did the next best thing and snatched the opportunity to pivot to a secular career in New York, signing a two-week engagement with Harlem's storied Cotton Club in 1938.

The Cotton Club was infamous for simultaneously booking the biggest Black musical artists of the day, like Duke Ellington and Cab Calloway, and employing dazzlingly beautiful but uniformly light-skinned chorus girls like Lena Horne, while barring Black patrons. Gangster and bootlegger Owney Madden opened the Cotton Club in 1923, taking over the lease from Black heavyweight boxer Jack Johnson, who had opened a supper club, Club Deluxe, in the building in 1920. In his memoir, *The Big Sea*, Langston Hughes called the Cotton Club "a Jim Crow club for gangsters and monied whites."

When Sister Rosetta booked her engagement at the Cotton Club, it was located at Forty-Eighth Street and Broadway in the Theater District, where it moved after the Harlem riot of 1935. Tharpe debuted in the Cotton Club's 1938 fall revue alongside established stars like Cab Calloway. Her distinctive singing and playing style had an immediate impact on audiences and drew comparisons to Bessie Smith from critics, one of whom described Tharpe as a "hymn swinging evangelist."

Soon after her debut, Tharpe signed with manager Moe Gale, a well-known manager of Black artists and co-owner of Harlem's famous Savoy Ballroom. She then signed an exclusive music publishing deal with Mills Music for her compositions. The songs in Mills's *Eighteen Original Negro Spirituals* would form the core of Sister Rosetta's repertoire for years to come. While we don't have a copy of that publishing contract, even if it were an agreement where Tharpe sold her entire copyright interest to Mills, she would have been entitled to receive 50 percent of the income derived from her songs as her "writer's share," which was sacrosanct. Thus, Tharpe was protected from the fate suffered by so many Black artists of having their copyrights stolen by unscrupulous record company executives. She also signed with the "race records" division of Decca Records, headed by J. Mayo Williams, who a decade earlier had served as the crafty blues talent scout for Paramount Records. Tharpe's publishing deal prevented Decca from exploiting her by registering the copyright to her music in the label's name to deprive her of mechanical royalties. At the same time, signing the publishing deal with Mills—rather than establishing her own publishing company—cut the money Rosetta could earn from her compositions in half.

The success of Sister Rosetta's Decca recordings and the enthusiastic response to her Cotton Club engagement led to other high-profile opportunities. In 1938, she shared the bill with Count Basie at the Paramount Theatre and appeared in December on a star-studded bill for the Apollo Theater's annual Christmas fundraiser. Most notably, Sister Rosetta was one of many artists to perform for John Hammond's famous Carnegie Hall concerts, *From Spirituals to Swing*. Hammond, the Vanderbilt scion credited with discovering Billie Holiday, envisioned the concert as nothing less than a "populist challenge to racism." Hammond's Carnegie Hall concerts may not have eradicated racism, but they definitely expanded Tharpe's audience. According to musicians Count Basie and Harry "Sweets" Edison, the audience, which was largely unfamiliar with Black gospel music, was bowled over by Sister Rosetta's performance.

These engagements solidified Sister Rosetta's appeal to a secular audience and cemented the regard in which she was held by fellow musicians. The inclusion of Tharpe in a "jazz jam session" organized by *Life* magazine in 1939 for a story that never ran is evidence of the latter.

Cab Calloway, Billie Holiday, Duke Ellington, and Johnny Hodges were among the other attendees. A photo from the session shows Rosetta mid-performance—eyes closed, completely unselfconscious—as Calloway, Ellington, "Hot Lips" Page, and trombonist J. C. Higginbotham look on in admiration.

Sister Rosetta Tharpe's growing secular fame was not without a cost. There was a tension, after all, between the lyrics of heavenly salvation and love for the Lord set to a beat that you could dance to. None other than Thomas Dorsey inveighed against the practice in the pages of the *Chicago Defender*. Harlem Renaissance writer Arna Bontemps acknowledged the common roots of blues and gospel but ventured that Black religious folks were right to be upset that their sacred music was being repurposed for swinging secular entertainment in dance halls and smoky nightclubs.

While Tharpe was saddened by this criticism, there is no indication that she reconsidered her decision to pursue a secular career. Her talent and ambition were both too great to be contained on the revival circuit. After the Cotton Club closed in 1940, Sister Rosetta segued to an engagement at Barney Josephson's integrated Café Society. Here she performed in front of an audience of "Black elite and white intellectuals."

In February 1941, manager Moe Gale put two of his clients together: Tharpe signed to play with Lucky Millinder's big band. Millinder and Tharpe collaborated on big band arrangements of her repertoire (compounding her sin of swinging the spirituals) and began a regular engagement at Harlem's Savoy Ballroom, which Moe Gale owned with businessman Jay Faggen.

The Savoy was not just any venue. The Savoy Ballroom, located on Lenox Avenue between West 140th and 141st Streets, was a ten-thousand-square-foot, block-long palace of dance that could hold four thousand people. The Savoy featured two bandstands to allow for nonstop music and attracted scores of the most talented, acrobatic Lindy Hoppers, who spent evenings trying to outdo each other. In contrast to the Cotton Club, the Savoy was integrated from its inception in 1926. Although the Savoy was predominantly Black, on some nights the crowd had an equal number of Black and white patrons.

Once Tharpe began a regular engagement at the Savoy, aka "the home of happy feet," her crossover to a popular secular artist was complete. Although her repertoire consisted of a mix of contemporary gospel songs and public-domain spirituals, Tharpe performed them with Lucky Millinder's big band arrangements that swung hard. The Savoy's weekly broadcasts increased Sister Rosetta's reach and popularity, and in 1943, she traveled with the band on a chitlin circuit tour all over the country. Gayle F. Wald covers the exhausting schedule that Millinder's band had as it zigzagged the country, playing one-nighters in venues from "Jacksonville, Florida . . . to Tulsa, [Oklahoma, to] . . . Flint, Michigan . . . with stops at US Army camps" in between.

Tharpe's guitar-playing prowess came to the fore during her time with Millinder's band. By the time she appeared with the band at the Apollo Theater in August 1943, she was billed as "Sister Rosetta Tharpe and Her Guitar." During World War II, Tharpe was a favorite of the troops and one of the few Black gospel musicians to record V-Discs—government-issued recordings shipped to soldiers overseas. She also continued to record for Decca Records, but the bulk of her time and money came from live performances—lucrative in the moment, but incapable of generating an ongoing income stream like music publishing (or even record) royalties could.

Still, the fame was surely rewarding in its own right. At the height of their appeal in 1943, Lucky Millinder and Sister Rosetta Tharpe drew an integrated crowd of more than ten thousand people to Atlanta's Municipal Auditorium and attracted similar crowds in St. Louis and Philadelphia. Notwithstanding the success Sister Rosetta found with Lucky Millinder, or perhaps because of it, she abruptly left the band in September 1943 to resume her career as a solo artist. This also marked her effort to recommit to being a gospel artist, dubbing herself "America's greatest spiritual singer."

During this iteration of her career, Tharpe recorded "Strange Things Happening Every Day," her most influential song and the one that cemented her role as the progenitor of rock and roll. "Strange Things Happening Every Day" has been cited as a key influence by all of rock and roll's earliest acknowledged stars.

Tharpe wrote "Strange Things" and recorded it for Decca in September 1944. On the song, she sings and plays her resonator guitar—an acoustic guitar outfitted with "one or more metal discs within the body," amplifying the sound and producing a tone favored by blues and bluegrass musicians. She was backed by the Decca house band, featuring jazz musician Sammy Price on the piano.

"Strange Things" eerily presages the rock-and-roll sound that would explode in popularity ten years later. The song features a compelling, danceable 4/4 beat and catchy tune, but what grabs you immediately, beyond Tharpe's bright, clear vocals and Price's percussive piano, is the sound of Sister Rosetta's guitar. Her propulsive and intricate "pickin'" and "shredding" is later echoed in the records of Chuck Berry and Elvis Presley.

The record that was so clearly ahead of its time was a smash. It was the first gospel record to cross over onto *Billboard*'s then-named

Race Records chart, peaking at #2. Through "Strange Things," Sister Rosetta would become a model for male musicians, Black and white, in the US and the UK, who have since been widely credited as the creators and perfectors of rock and roll. In 1945, when Tharpe was about to play a gig at the Macon City Auditorium in Georgia, she heard a young man singing "Strange Things" as she unloaded her gear in the parking lot. Sister asked him if he wanted to perform, and later that night brought fourteen-year-old Richard Penniman onstage and paid him $35. A few years later, that young man would go by the name of Little Richard.

In 1946, shortly after the release of "Strange Things," Tharpe signed singer Marie Knight to perform with her as a duo. By all accounts, Knight was also Tharpe's lover, which was somewhat of an open secret within the industry but kept from the public.

The duo of Sister Rosetta and Marie Knight continued to enjoy success throughout the 1940s, playing sold-out venues of mixed audiences throughout the South. They scored another hit in 1947 with "Didn't It Rain," the same year that Tharpe began playing the electric guitar.

As intoxicating as this success must have been, it was ephemeral. Sister Rosetta Tharpe was well paid for her live performances, but since she was not a prolific composer and did not control her publishing, she had no stream of passive income from mechanical and public performance royalties. When white rockers meticulously copied her innovative guitar playing style, Sister Rosetta could not receive any financial compensation or even credit as the originator of making the guitar "talk."

A decade after its initial release, "Strange Things" had a resurgence in popularity and exposure thanks to pioneering Memphis DJ Dewey

Phillips. Phillips, the inspiration for the Broadway musical *Memphis*, had a nightly radio show in Memphis in the mid-1950s called *Red-Hot & Blue*. Like Cleveland's Alan Freed, Phillips rebelled against the segregated airwaves and played "good music for good people," with no regard to whether the artist was Black or white or if the song was a current release or a decade old. Phillips put "Strange Things" into rotation, where up-and-coming white musicians on the cusp of rock-and-roll stardom rediscovered it. Every member of the famous "Million-Dollar Quartet"—Elvis Presley, Jerry Lee Lewis, Johnny Cash, and Carl Perkins—name-checked "Strange Things" and Sister Rosetta Tharpe. Jerry Lee Lewis performed the song in his audition for Sam Phillips of Sun Records. Carl Perkins called it one of his favorite songs, and those close to both Elvis Presley and Johnny Cash said they loved Sister Rosetta Tharpe.

In the late 1950s, rock and roll exploded in popularity. Although Black artists like Little Richard and Chuck Berry were credited as originators and enjoyed tremendous success, they began to be eclipsed by white stars like Elvis Presley, who, as Tharpe biographer Wald pointed out, could take "the sound and style of Black music [and] reinterpret it for a mainstream [white] youth audience that he, but not his Black models, could access." In this climate, Sister Rosetta Tharpe's star began to fade. Although she had attracted twenty thousand fans to a "wedding concert" at Griffith Stadium in Washington, DC, when she married her manager, Russell Morrison, in 1951, by the late 1950s Sister Rosetta was no longer under contract to Decca Records and was playing before sparse crowds in small clubs. She was buffeted by changing musical tastes and suffered unfavorable comparisons to her friend and contemporary Mahalia Jackson. Jackson, an early protégé of Thomas Dorsey, refused to perform in secular venues, eschewed the glamorous costumes Tharpe favored, and, most important, never sang a secular love song like "Don't Leave Me to Cry," a 1953 record Tharpe released in an attempt to recapture R & B success.

In April 1957, the bank foreclosed on Sister Rosetta's suburban Barton, Virginia, house and she and her husband, Russell Morrison, moved to the Hotel Carlyle in Philadelphia. In November 1957, Tharpe's career received a much-needed boost when British musician Chris Barber invited her to perform with his traditional jazz band. At the time, Britain was in the throes of a postwar fascination with Black American blues music that had begun in 1949 with Leadbelly.

British fans associated early pre-bebop jazz, blues, and gospel music with "authenticity." Although Sister Rosetta received glowing reviews, they were embedded with stereotypes. Jazz critic Leonard Feather remarked on her "magnificent passion and folk quality unspoiled by her appearances before sophisticated audiences." Such reviews relegated Tharpe's artistry and musicianship to something innate and primitive, rather than the innovation and virtuosity that comes from intellectual production and diligent practice.

This view of Black music and musicians makes it easier for white artists to appropriate their styles without attribution. If Black music is merely the untutored expression of something "innate," nothing prevents white people from taking that music while failing to credit Black authorship. In addition, since the styles and techniques emerge in performance, which is by its nature ephemeral and not fixed, there is nothing copyrightable that can be monetized by those original creators.

The darkest manifestation of this view of Black music was exemplified by Britain's "teddy boys," a group of nattily dressed obsessive rock-and-roll fans who emerged in the mid-1950s. As music historian Jack Hamilton writes, teddy boys were simply "the earliest in a long line of white rock-and-roll fans who have mined the music for racialized fantasies of hypermasculinity while strategically ignoring any real connection to Black people." The virulent racism of the teddy boys culminated in the 1958 Notting Hill race riots, where they waged a campaign of indiscriminate violence against the Black Notting Hill residents who had immigrated from British colonies.

The more benign strain of white fascination with Black blues and gospel still had the effect of policing the borders of Blackness. The white folk and blues revivalists of the late 1950s and early 1960s appointed themselves the arbiters of what constituted real Black music. In their eyes, "modernity and 'authentic' Black music" could not be reconciled with each other. They believed they were "saviors" of Black culture and viewed Black commercial success or artistic innovation with suspicion. White fans and musicians alike conflated *unlettered* with *unstudied* and did not believe that Black blues and gospel musicians had the capacity to innovate within established genres, a privilege they reserved for white artists. This created the permission structure for white musicians to erase astonishing virtuosos like Sister Rosetta Tharpe and appropriate her techniques as their own. As her artistry was grounded in performance, Sister Rosetta Tharpe had no protection against her erasure. The same type of exploitative fandom would be a defining feature of the rise of Hip Hop in the United States five decades later.

Thomas Dorsey, on the other hand, understood the value of owning his copyrights thanks to his early experiences hawking his songs at the National Baptist Convention in 1923 and his work as an in-house arranger for J. Mayo Williams during the blues craze of the mid- to late 1920s. Dorsey established his own publishing company, Dorsey House of Music, in 1930, and is credited with writing four hundred jazz and blues tunes and writing and/or publishing one thousand gospel songs.

In contrast to Sister Rosetta Tharpe, once Thomas Dorsey dedicated himself exclusively to the church, he spent all his time and energy perfecting and institutionalizing the genre of gospel blues music within the Black church and its affiliated institutions. Dorsey remained president of the National Convention of Gospel Choirs and Choruses (NCGCC) from its inception in 1933 until his death in 1993. Through his stewardship of NCGCC and his prolific composition of gospel songs, Dorsey influenced the sound of Black gospel music throughout the country. Through his close working relationship with Mahalia Jackson and his tutelage of seminal gospel artists like Clara Ward, Dorsey's reach extended beyond the confines of the Black church. Through his ownership of his publishing company and control of his copyrights, Dorsey was able to personally profit from what he created.

When Dorsey died, he was widely acknowledged as the Father of Gospel Music and as someone who had built a robust institution that incubated gospel singers who went on to create and innovate the next iteration of secular Black music, like Bobby Womack and Sam Cooke. Dorsey left behind a large body of copyrights that could be reinterpreted and monetized by his estate for years after his death. When Sister Rosetta Tharpe died from a massive stroke in 1973, she had very little money. Despite her international acclaim, without a robust back catalog of recordings or compositions, Tharpe depended on live performances to earn a living. When she died, her husband, Russell Morrison, sold her white Gibson guitar, her white mink coat, and her Lincoln Continental, and buried her in an unmarked grave. After her death, white rock musicians were free to imitate and appropriate Sister Rosetta Tharpe's playing style of making her guitar "talk" and rechristen it as the exclusive province of white male rock musicians.

SIX

THE SOUND OF YOUNG AMERICA: THE RISE OF BLACK LABELS VEE-JAY RECORDS AND MOTOWN RECORDS

Thomas Dorsey and Sister Rosetta Tharpe laid creative and institutional foundations that made the postwar era fertile ground for Black people not only to perform and create new artistic genres, but to become entrepreneurs who profited from the production and distribution of Black artists' creative output. In the late 1940s and 1950s, the Midwestern industrial cities of Detroit, Michigan, and Gary, Indiana, gave birth to Black-owned companies that made an unforgettable mark on American popular music.

A generation after the Great Migration, several major Midwestern cities had given birth to significant Black communities. Even though the Black workers in Gary's steel mills and Detroit's auto plants were relegated to the most dangerous work, these union jobs still provided a solid income that helped to build a stable Black working class. Those communities in turn gave rise to a new Black entrepreneurial class poised to serve this new market.

When the U.S. Steel Corporation decided to establish a city to surround its Indiana mill in 1906, the company dubbed the town Gary, after its then-CEO Elbert Gary. The jobs at the Gary mill were arduous and dangerous, but the company believed they did not require the same skill level as those in the company's East Coast mills. As a result, U.S. Steel filled the Gary workforce with first-generation immigrants.

When Gary was founded, the Black population numbered only four hundred. During World War I, Black people from the South moved to Gary for job opportunities that had opened up during the war, as Black families did throughout the country. By 1919, there were 2,699 Black workers in the Gary mill. The Black population of Gary grew further when the American Federation of Labor (AFL) called a national strike in September 1919 against U.S. Steel, seeking an eight-hour workday and safer working conditions. The walkout of three hundred and fifty thousand ironworkers and steelworkers across the country was "the largest national strike recorded up to that time." Instead of engaging in negotiations, rabidly anti-union U.S. Steel CEO Elbert Gary brought thirty thousand Black workers from the South to cross picket lines and work as scabs in their mills around the country. By 1920, the Black population of Gary had grown to five thousand.

Unlike virtually every other American city in 1919, Gary was remarkably free of the racist mob violence that plagued other Northern industrial cities, thanks to its largely first-generation immigrant populations *and* the work done by Black labor organizers Louis Caldwell and C. D. Elston. Despite this auspicious beginning, by the 1930s, Gary's elite had succeeded in thoroughly segregating Gary, cementing its Black residents to second-class status, colluding to exclude Black people in Gary not only from housing, but from employment, education, hospitals, and public spaces like parks and beaches. Realtors, for example, conspired with property owners to limit Black residents to overcrowded, substandard housing in the city's Midtown district, but charged them 20 percent more than white residents who paid for better accommodations.

Yet like Black people throughout the US, Gary's Black community made a way out of no way, and by 1950, the Midtown district of Gary boasted several Black-owned businesses, including a large beverage distributor and many restaurants. One prominent Black business in Midtown was Vivian's Record Shop. Vivian Carter, a popular late-night DJ on "Gary's premiere radio station, WWCA," opened the shop in 1950 with her business partner (and later husband) Jimmy Bracken.

Vivian Carter was born in Tunica, Mississippi in 1921 and moved to Gary as a child when her family migrated in search of economic opportunity. Following her graduation in 1939 from Gary's segregated Roosevelt High School, Carter took business courses and then joined the Quartermaster Corps, the branch of the army responsible for maintaining and distributing supplies. She got her break by entering a 1948 contest sponsored by Black Chicago DJ Al Benson to identify a male and a female host to have their own fifteen-minute radio show. Carter beat out hundreds of competitors to win the female slot.

The path from a fifteen-minute show to helming a five-hour late-night show on Gary's top station involved detours at a small market station in Hammond, Indiana, and a stint working retail at a hat shop, but Vivian Carter was soon holding listeners spellbound six nights a week on WWCA. Carter called herself "the hostess with the mostest" and would play songs that she liked four or five times in a row.

When she and Jimmy Bracken opened Vivian's Record Shop in 1950, teenagers would gather at the store at 1640 Broadway to watch Vivian DJ through the window while music blasted from loudspeakers facing the street. A record company was the logical extension of Vivian's two other jobs as a DJ and record retailer. As a DJ, Carter could make or break a record by giving it airplay. As a retailer, she stood to profit from the popularity of the records she played. The only missing link in the chain was to make the records herself.

In 1953, Carter and Bracken borrowed $500 from a pawnbroker and started Vee-Jay Records, taking the name from the first initial of each of their names. Vivian was following a trail blazed by people like Billy Crystal's uncle Milt Gabler, who launched jazz label Commodore Records in 1937, out of Commodore Music Shop, a former radio and speaker supply store that Gabler had transformed into a retail epicenter for jazz lovers in New York City.

Once Vivian and Jimmy started Vee-Jay, the crowd of teenagers flocking to 1640 Broadway included high schoolers in search of a record deal. Vee-Jay's first signing was a group of Black kids who had just won a talent contest at Roosevelt High School. Lead singer James "Pookie" Hudson and Gerald Gregory, Ernest Warren, Willie C. Jackson, and Opal Courtney Jr. called themselves the Spaniels. Their first recording that Vee-Jay released was "Baby, It's You," and it was a bona fide hit, reaching #10 on the *Billboard* R & B chart.

Vee-Jay's third Spaniels record, "Goodnite, Sweetheart, Goodnite," was released in March 1954. Although the Spaniels' version was definitely a hit, reaching #5 on *Billboard*'s R & B chart, it was the explosive success of the insipid cover version by white pop group the McGuire Sisters that put the label on the map. The McGuire Sisters' cover, recorded in March 1954 and released later that year, hit #8 on *Billboard*'s pop charts and sold one million copies.

The trajectory of "Goodnite, Sweetheart, Goodnite" was depressingly common. In the mid-1950s, the music marketed to America's teens was so segregated that Black R & B hits were routinely covered by white artists, eclipsing them in sales. For example, in 1956, bland pop singer Pat Boone released a denuded version of Little Richard's raw, rocking hit "Tutti Frutti." Boone's version briefly bested Little Richard's on the Billboard Hot 100 chart, reaching #8 to Little Richard's #12.

The fate of the song "Hound Dog" was the most egregious example of a white artist's ability to completely erase the memory of the Black artist's version that preceded it. "Hound Dog" was written by prolific and legendary rock-and-roll composers Jerry Leiber and Mike Stoller for Willie Mae "Big Mama" Thornton. As Haben Kelati related in *The Washington Post*, Thornton "was an imposing, powerful singer who stood six feet tall" and "often performed in a suit jacket and tie wearing cowboy boots." Leiber and Stoller wrote the song for Thornton in 1952, and she released her recording in 1953. Thornton's version was a hit, reaching #1 on the *Billboard* R & B chart. Three years later, twenty-one-year-old Elvis Presley rerecorded "Hound Dog," and his version rocketed to #1 on the *Billboard* pop chart, staying there for eleven weeks. Elvis's version became so dominant that it nearly obliterated the memory of the Black woman the song was written for. What distinguished Elvis's cover of a Black R & B hit from the uninspired covers of other white artists was his embrace of the rawness of the original, which he infused with elements of country music style.

The fact that the Spaniels wrote "Goodnite, Sweetheart, Goodnite" should have lessened the sting of being outsold by the McGuire Sisters. In 1954, songwriting and publishing royalties on a million-seller could have equaled $20,000, the equivalent of $240,874 in 2025 dollars. The Spaniels never received a dime of that, though, because, as lead singer Pookie Hudson explained, Vivian Carter "had the power of attorney over all our money and all our rights . . . as far as receiving royalties or anything like that, uh-uh. They always had some excuse."

Vee-Jay was not uniquely villainous. It was merely signing artists to the same one-sided contracts that white-owned record companies did. Take Little Richard's smash hit "Tutti Frutti": When he released the song, Little Richard was signed to Art Rupe's Specialty Records. Specialty paid Little Richard a royalty of 5 percent on 90 percent of the retail price of each record sold. In the mid-1950s, a 45 rpm record sold for 89 cents, which translated into payment to Little Richard of a mere 4 cents per record sold.

His contract also granted Specialty Records ownership and control of all compositions he wrote while under contract, meaning that Specialty would receive all the "publisher's share" of income from his songs, and Little Richard would only receive his "songwriter's share." Specialty, as the publisher, controlled licensing of the composition and licensed "Tutti Frutti" to itself at a reduced rate of 50 percent of the then-applicable statutory rate. This resulted in Little Richard netting only one half of 1 cent per record in songwriter royalties and was a key factor in his decision to temporarily abandon his career in rock and roll.

Both "Goodnite, Sweetheart, Goodnite" and "Tutti Frutti" are powerful examples of the tremendous value of music copyrights and the systematic way that the music business operated to extract that value from the Black artists who created them.

Vee-Jay used the money and credibility gained from the Spaniels' hit to build on that success. They had a small, tight-knit team, consisting of Vivian, Jimmy, and Vivian's brother, Calvin Carter. Calvin was their A&R (artists and repertoire) man, responsible for scouting and signing talent and overseeing production of artists in the studio. After the Spaniels' hit, Calvin built out a tight house band to back their artists with a consistent sound.

By 1954, Vee-Jay had moved to Chicago's so-called Record Row on South Michigan Avenue to record in a Chicago studio. That's when they signed another doo-wop group, the El Dorados, whose song "At My Front Door" reached #1 on the *Billboard* R & B chart and #17 on its pop chart. Pat Boone's vanilla version of the song hit #7 on the pop chart.

Calvin Carter had an ear for a wide range of Black music, signing blues artists like Jimmy Reed and John Lee Hooker and gospel artists like the Staple Singers and the Highway Q.C.'s (the group that at different points featured Sam Cooke and Lou Rawls before their solo careers in secular music). He signed the Dells, who recorded their enduring hit "Oh What a Nite" in 1956, and the Impressions, which featured both Jerry Butler *and* Curtis Mayfield. The Impressions' first Vee-Jay record was "For Your Precious Love," a song written by Jerry Butler, Arthur Brooks, and Richard Brooks that they sang for Carter during their audition. Carter sensed a hit and rushed the song into production. Released in 1958, "For Your Precious Love" became a smash, selling five hundred thousand copies and later earning a spot on *Rolling Stone*'s 500 Greatest Songs of All Time.

Calvin helped build Vee-Jay into a reliable hit machine with his golden ear, and they generated significant earnings for a scrappy independent label. But Vivian and Jimmy still needed help with the business side of running a label, such as securing retail distribution and radio airplay beyond Vivian's late-night show.

Like many independent labels of the era, Vee-Jay had to license or "lease" its recordings to larger third-party record companies to get them into national retail channels. Vee-Jay leased its records to Chicago-based Chance Records, a company that both produced its own R & B and gospel recordings and handled pressing and distribution for several other independent labels. When Chance went out of business in 1954, Vee-Jay recruited Chance executive Ewart Abner to join Vee-Jay as general manager.

The combination of Calvin Carter's instinct for hits and Abner's record-business savvy fueled Vee-Jay's growth—such that, according to R & B historian Robert Pruter, by 1960, "it was the country's largest Black-owned record company." Vee-Jay's roster included pre-Motown Gladys Knight & the Pips and Gene Chandler, whose 1962 hit "Duke of Earl" was Vee-Jay's first million-seller.

In 1961, Vee-Jay signed its first white artist, a vocal group from New Jersey whose style was variously described as rock, pop, blue-eyed soul, and even R & B—the Four Seasons. Regardless of what their music was called, it proved to be unstoppable. The Four Seasons' first Vee-Jay release, "Sherry," hit #1 on *Billboard*'s pop chart in September 1962, where it stayed for five weeks, and hit #1 on the *Billboard* R & B chart. Featuring Frankie Valli's piercing falsetto,

"Sherry" was the first in a string of #1 hits that the Four Seasons scored for Vee-Jay. "Big Girls Don't Cry" and "Walk Like a Man" followed in quick succession, each reaching #1 on the *Billboard* charts in November 1962 and March 1963, respectively.

In 1962, Vee-Jay signed a group whose fame would eclipse even the Four Seasons. Vee-Jay was negotiating with EMI Records for US distribution rights to British singer Frank Ifield when EMI threw in a little-known Liverpool group called the Beatles.

Sadly, these two signing coups exposed the ingredients of Vee-Jay's implosion. Vee-Jay had long been accustomed to spending whatever it earned and not being accountable to its artists. The rapid succession of hits by the Four Seasons, together with the high royalty rate that their manager had negotiated, created cash-flow problems for a label that typically mollified its artists with cars, rather than accurate royalty payments. Vivian Carter blamed Ewart Abner's "unorthodox" accounting methods and profligate spending. Abner was known to keep the amounts owed to artists "in his head," and while all labels spent lavishly on entertaining DJs to ensure airplay for their releases, Abner took it to extremes. According to the Indiana Historical Society's account, he was known to rent entire floors of Las Vegas hotels for DJs to party and was also a "compulsive gambler who allegedly" used Vee-Jay's money to pay debts to the mob. Yet Vivian was hardly blameless. For years, she spared no expense on herself, and according to contemporaries was often seen tooling "around Chicago and Gary in a gold Cadillac, wearing an expensive mink coat." Notably, Abner would go on to serve as a high-level executive at Motown, which did not experience Vee-Jay's financial difficulties.

By the time of the Beatles' signing, rumors were flying about Vee-Jay's imminent demise. The industry chatter was that Vee-Jay had run out of money and would be folding soon. The Beatles got off to a slow start in the US. Their first Vee-Jay single, "Please Please Me," released in 1963, barely made a dent on US radio. The Beatles' second US release, "From Me to You" in April 1963, was overshadowed by Del Shannon's cover version and sank without a trace.

In August 1963, Vee-Jay fired Abner and brought in a new management team, but it didn't work. The same month, the Four Seasons sued Vee-Jay for unpaid royalties. When Vee-Jay discovered that the group was withholding its next single, "Dawn (Go Away)," the label countersued.

The turmoil surrounding Vee-Jay shook EMI's confidence in the label's ability to effectively distribute their artists, and they asked Vee-Jay to relinquish its rights to Frank Ifield. In the confusion, Vee-Jay's new management was under the mistaken impression that it had also relinquished the label's rights to the Beatles and held up the album, *Introducing . . . The Beatles*, that had been scheduled for release in the summer of 1963. Although the Beatles weren't making headway in the US market, by 1963 they had begun to have success in the UK. Their debut single on Parlophone Records, "Love Me Do," released in October 1962, hit #17 on the UK charts.

By the end of 1963, EMI was preparing to expand the Beatles' success to the other side of the Atlantic. In December, EMI-owned US affiliate Capitol Records embarked on a publicity blitz to promote the Beatles' imminent arrival in the US. Capitol plastered billboards and flyers everywhere to proclaim that THE BEATLES ARE COMING!, in what was reputed to be the most expensive music publicity campaign up to that time. On December 26, Capitol released the single "I Want to Hold Your Hand," with "I Saw Her Standing There" as the US B-side. It shot to #1 on the Billboard Hot 100 chart by January 13, 1964.

Not to be outdone, Vee-Jay released the Beatles single "Please Please Me," backed by "From Me to You," on January 15, 1964. EMI promptly hit Vee-Jay with an injunction, barring it from manufacturing or distributing any Beatles records. It is unclear what grounds EMI relied on, since Vee-Jay had a valid five-year contract with the Beatles in the US, and their previous releases had not sold enough copies to generate royalties. Perhaps EMI wagered that Vee-Jay's financial instability would cause it to fold under pressure, but that did not happen immediately. Vee-Jay fought back in court, got the injunction lifted, and rushed to press more Beatles records. By Vee-Jay's account, they sold 2.6 million Beatles records in one month!

Undeterred, EMI returned to court to wrest the rights to the Beatles back from Vee-Jay. The pressure proved too much for Vee-Jay, which was in the midst of fighting "no fewer than 64 legal actions," according to the label's then-president, Randy Wood. Vee-Jay reached a settlement with EMI that permitted them to retain the rights to masters that they already had, but no future Beatles recordings.

Losing the Beatles and the Four Seasons—along with popular Black artists like Gene Chandler and Dee Clark, who followed Ewart Abner out the door—turned out to be a fatal blow to Vee-Jay. In 1964 the label added to its woes by signing hitless artists like Buddy De-Franco and Gary LeMel. Between Vee-Jay's lack of hits and the cost of maintaining both LA and Chicago offices, the label sank deeper into debt. While their financial mismanagement certainly played a role in their demise, if Vee-Jay had been able to access a bank line of credit or other legitimate financing available to white-owned major labels, it might have been able to pay the Four Seasons the royalties they had earned or fight off EMI's aggressive litigation.

Alternatively, Vee-Jay could have leveraged its music publishing catalog, since its standard artist agreement granted the label rights to the compositions written by the artists. Sadly, there is no indication that Vee-Jay grasped the value of the copyrights it controlled, and it limped along from 1964 to 1966, when insolvency finally forced them to shut down. The IRS then seized the Carters' record store for unpaid back taxes. Vivian Carter died in a nursing home in 1989 from complications of a series of strokes brought on by diabetes and hypertension.

As Vee-Jay was enjoying its perch as the biggest Black record label in the country, less than three hundred miles away, in Detroit, Michigan, a pugnacious boxer turned songwriter was trying to figure out how to survive in the music business. By the time that Vee-Jay's signing of the Four Seasons and the Beatles precipitated its implosion, that Detroit striver had started a record company that would grow into a multimillion-dollar behemoth and launch the careers of superstars like Diana Ross, Stevie Wonder, and Michael Jackson. The Detroit company's mark on American culture would be so profound that its name would become synonymous with a musical genre. Motown Records' indelible impact on popular music nearly erased the memory of Vee-Jay.

Similar to Gary, Indiana, and other industrial Midwestern cities, the 1910 Black population of Detroit was minuscule, numbering a mere 5,700 residents. After Black people rushed to Detroit to take advantage of opportunities at Henry Ford's auto plants, the Black population grew such that by 1920, it had mushroomed by 611 percent to forty thousand residents. By 1930, the Black population had tripled from 1920 levels to 120,000.

Black Detroiters also paid higher rents than white residents for worse housing. Black residents were primarily relegated to the east side of the city, where neighborhoods like Black Bottom and Paradise Valley developed robust Black-owned-business districts to cater to Black residents.

Like most Black Detroiters, Berry Gordy Sr. came north as part of the Great Migration. In Gordy Sr.'s case, though, he came to Detroit to escape the threat of lynching that was ever present for Black men of means. Berry Gordy Sr. was born in 1888 in Oconee County, Georgia, to the first Berry Gordy, the son of an enslaved woman and her trafficker, plantation owner Jim Gordy. Thanks no doubt to his status as the plantation owner's son, the eldest Gordy learned to read, write, and do math "as well as any white man." Gordy's education helped him avoid the debt peonage that entrapped most newly emancipated people. He used his earnings to buy 168 acres of farmland, which he diversified by growing crops like collard greens, corn, and peanuts in addition to cotton.

When a lightning strike killed the eldest Gordy in 1913, Berry Sr. took over ownership of the land, resisting white men's offers to administer it for him and his mother, which frequently led to the outright theft of land from Black farmers. In 1922, when Gordy Sr. sold a timber lot for $2,600 (the equivalent of $50,266 in 2025 dollars), he feared that possession of such a large sum—along with his continued insistence on managing his own property—would make him a target for lynching. He decided to follow his brother north to Detroit, sending for his family soon after his arrival.

After working his way up from union plasterer to owning his own plastering and carpentry company, Berry Gordy Sr. bought a building on Detroit's east side. He opened the Booker T. Washington Grocery Store on the ground floor and installed his family in an apartment above it.

Berry Gordy Jr., the seventh of Berry Gordy Sr. and Bertha Gordy's eight children, born in Detroit on November 28, 1929, remembers this move to the east side as pivotal in his upbringing. Gordy was mesmerized by the vibrant community where number runners and pimps lived alongside hardworking, God-fearing businesspeople like his father. An indifferent student, he dropped out of high school, hoping to parlay his rudimentary musical training and passion for music into a career as a songwriter. His path to songwriting was anything but straightforward. It included being drafted to serve in the Korean War; opening a jazz record store when he returned to Detroit that went out of business; getting married, and with help from his mother-in-law, getting a job on the Ford assembly line, where he composed music in his head; and quitting to focus on music, leading to the breakup of his first marriage. Gordy moved in with his sister Loucye, and spent his days composing and his nights hanging out at Detroit's famous Flame Show Bar, where his other sisters Gwen and Anna ran the photo concession.

The Flame Show Bar booked artists like Sarah Vaughan, Dinah Washington, and Billie Holiday, and Gordy spent as much time there as possible, hoping to make a connection that would boost his songwriting career. His sisters consistently introduced Berry as a songwriter and connected him to Al Green, the manager of both the Flame Show Bar and R & B singing sensation Jackie Wilson. Green invited Berry to come to the offices of his Pearl Music Company the next day. At Pearl, Gordy met Roquel "Billy" Davis, who would become his songwriting partner for the next several years.

Gordy's first big break as a songwriter came when Jackie Wilson recorded Gordy and Davis's composition, "Reet Petite," that hit the Billboard Top 100 in 1957. Wilson recorded four other songs written by Gordy and Davis, including "To Be Loved," which reached #7 on *Billboard*'s R & B chart. According to writer and filmmaker Nelson George, signs of what would become hallmarks of Motown's signature sound can be heard in those compositions, including the "gimmicky use of establishment culture" references in the lyrics, "the use of tambourines to bolster the drumbeat, and the blistering baritone sax."

Gordy's experiences as a songwriter for Jackie Wilson planted the seeds for Motown's business success as well. Despite composing five hits for Wilson, two of which—"To Be Loved" and "Lonely Teardrops"—were bona fide smashes, Berry and his writing partners, Billy Davis and his sister Gwen Gordy, were still broke. When "Lonely Teardrops" went to #1 on the R & B chart and #10 on the *Billboard* pop chart, Gordy had an epiphany. He realized that not only did publishers earn more than writers from the exploitation of compositions, but the composers of B-sides earned just as much as those of the A-sides, despite receiving no airplay and driving no sales. Such is the nature of mechanical royalties, which have been paid on all physical reproductions of a composition since the days of the player piano.

It was a pivotal object lesson in the importance of controlling music publishing as well as the passive income potential of music copyrights. Gordy and Davis approached Nat Tarnopol, who became Wilson's manager after Green's death, to ask if their compositions could be the B-sides of future Wilson releases so that their writers' share of publishing income could come closer to the value of the hits they were composing. Tarnopol refused their request, preferring to continue putting compositions written by his aunt on the B-side of Jackie Wilson's singles.

In part because Berry Gordy Jr. came from an entrepreneurial family that owned successful businesses and real estate, he walked away from writing for Jackie Wilson, confident that he could build a music company of his own. Berry's older sister Gwen was actually the first one to start a label. Gwen partnered with Billy Davis in 1957 to create Anna Records, securing distribution for the new label through Chicago-based Chess Records. They invited Berry to partner with them, but he preferred to start his own venture and to be the sole decision-maker. Gordy did agree to produce records for his sister's new label, working with his new partner and second wife, musical prodigy Raynoma Liles, to provide background singers for some of their artists.

Before his break with Jackie Wilson, Gordy had met the man who would be a key component of his future label's success and one of the pillars of the unmistakable "Motown sound." In August 1957, the Matadors, a group of five recent high school graduates—four guys and one girl—came to audition for Nat Tarnopol. The group consisted of Ronnie White, Pete Moore, Bobby Rogers, Claudette Rogers, and the lead singer and songwriter, a light-skinned, green-eyed young man with the counterintuitive name of "Smokey" Robinson. Although the Matadors failed to impress Tarnopol, Berry Gordy saw potential in the young group. After their failed audition, Berry Gordy ran down the hall after them and asked Smokey if he had any more original songs, according to both Gordy and Robinson. Smokey took out a school notebook filled with page after page of "lyrics he had written in pencil."

Gordy yanked Smokey and the Matadors into a rehearsal room with a piano and asked Smokey to sing some of the songs he had penned. In Gordy's view, the fledgling writer's lyrics meandered and lacked the tight story structure that he knew to be the foundation of a hit. Still, Gordy believed Smokey to be a tremendous talent, who simply needed the guidance that Gordy could provide. Gordy became the group's manager, convincing them to change their name to the Miracles and booking them in "little gigs around Detroit."

Berry's faith paid off in January 1958, when Smokey brought him a song that he was certain would be a hit. Smokey had written a tune called "Got a Job," an "answer" record to "Get a Job," the #1 pop and R & B hit by the Silhouettes. The song's lyrics poetically but accurately detail the indignity and precarity of low-wage work.

"Got a Job" wasn't the only successful record that Berry Gordy produced for Anna Records. Despite that, he was still broke. The music industry was structured to extract value from the Black people who actually *made* the music—the songwriters, producers, musicians, and singers—and put that wealth in the hands of those with the capital to get those records sold—distributors and music publishing companies. It was no coincidence that in 1959, those with capital were overwhelmingly white.

Berry Gordy's frustration with a publishing company's refusal to pay him royalties on hits he had written for Jackie Wilson spurred the formation of his music publishing company, Jobete Music (named using the first two letters of his three children's names), to ensure that he and the Black songwriters he signed would actually get paid. The first writer signed to Jobete after Gordy himself was Smokey Robinson.

Similarly, after receiving a producer's royalty check of only $3.19 for "Got a Job," Gordy decided that it was time to launch his own label too. Both Gordy and Robinson recounted that the decision to launch the label was reached on a snowy drive that they took from Detroit to Owosso, Michigan, to pick up copies of Marv Johnson's single "Come to Me." Gordy knew that he wanted that to be the first record on his new label but, given his scant resources, did not know how he was going to do it. Black would-be businesspeople had no access to commercial banking services in 1958, and even if there had not been a color bar, a twenty-nine-year-old songwriter with little income would not have been a good credit risk.

Gordy was, however, able to lean on the resources of his entrepreneurial family. The Gordys had set up a family financial cooperative, with each family member contributing $10 per month to create a fund that individuals could access for a "good reason." So in January 1959, Gordy appeared before the family cooperative and pitched his record business to some initial skepticism. The family ultimately agreed to loan Berry Gordy $800 to launch his label, secured by his songwriting royalties from his Jackie Wilson hits, evidence that his family understood the value of Berry's intellectual property.

With that, Berry Gordy launched Tamla Records. The loan from his family paid the recording and pressing costs for "Come to Me," yet it was a stretch to call Tamla a record label. Tamla still had to license the record to United Artists Records to get it into retail channels. As Gordy explained, each record cost Tamla only 10 cents to manufacture, and it sold for $1, but the retailer paid 60 cents on each record to the distributor, which retained 30 cents for itself. That left Tamla with 30 cents to cover marketing and promotion costs as well as artist and songwriter royalties.

Giant distributors often took advantage of the cash disparity between themselves and independent labels by buying out the contracts of the artists whose records they were distributing. United Artists took over Marv Johnson's contract, once again relegating Gordy to serving as a mere songwriter/producer. Gordy was less cooperative when a large white distributor tried to poach the Miracles. He convened all of Detroit's Black DJs for a meeting and shared what he was facing. At that meeting, the DJs called the company president and told him that if he made good on his threat to steal the Miracles, they would collectively boycott all his label's releases. The president backed down, and the Miracles stayed with Tamla.

Incidents like these made it clear to Berry Gordy that he could not have long-term financial success unless he controlled marketing and distribution of the music he was creating. In 1959, he began developing the infrastructure for that success. He decided to move operations out of his apartment and purchased a house, 2648 West Grand Boulevard, that could serve as the label's Detroit headquarters, with offices and studio on the lower floors and his living quarters above. He named the building Hitsville U.S.A.

Gordy set up several corporations through which to run operations. In addition to Jobete, he established Hitsville, Berry Gordy Jr. Enterprises, and the company that would house Tamla and other subsidiary labels, Motown Record Corporation (its name a contraction of Detroit's nickname, Motor Town).

Buying a building and forming corporations did not magically transform Motown into a full-fledged label with national marketing and distribution capacities. Gordy learned that lesson with the record that was one of the first to be recorded at Hitsville, an anthem for the very issue that bedeviled his young company.

As Gordy tells it, he was pacing the floor of his new headquarters working out a song in his head when receptionist Janie Bradford asked what he was working on. Gordy sang a few lines and then went to the piano to demonstrate. Singer Barrett Strong slid in from the next room and continued to jam with Berry as the song came together, featuring lines such as:

The best things in life are free,
but you can give them to the birds and bees.
I need MONEY!
That's what I want!

"Money (That's What I Want)" starts with a "funky piano riff," and features what became signature elements of the famous Motown sound: a prominent tambourine amplifying the "tom-tom beat" of Benny Benjamin on the drums and a scorching sax.

In August 1959, Gordy released "Money" in Detroit and regionally in Baltimore/DC and Cleveland, but he did not have the capital to release the song nationally. Gordy's sister Gwen suggested that he put it out through her Anna Records, since she had national distribution through Chess Records. "Money" hit #2 on the *Billboard* R & B chart and #23 on its pop chart, but because of the revenue share taken by Chess and Anna, Motown made more from the three areas where he distributed the record directly than he did from the entire rest of the country.

While Berry Gordy didn't make much from the initial release of "Money," the song proved to be one of his most profitable as a songwriter and publisher. The Beatles recorded a cover in 1963 that sold millions, and new-wave band the Flying Lizards had a hit with their version in 1979.

After seeing the dramatic effect that not controlling distribution had on the company's revenues, Gordy decided that going forward, Motown would handle all aspects of the record business directly—songwriting, production, distribution, and marketing. That decision proved prescient when Motown's 1961 release, "Shop Around" by the

Miracles, became the label's first gold record, shooting to #2 on *Bill-board*'s pop chart.

Berry Gordy instituted specific business practices at Motown to ensure that the company maintained tight control over its artists, product, and money. Motown recording contracts and Jobete publishing contracts were cross-collateralized, meaning that costs under one agreement could be deducted from payments owed under the other. Thus, artists who were also songwriters would have recording costs deducted from their publishing royalties. Motown paid its artists a weekly salary, and that too was deducted from royalties.

Gordy signed Motown artists to talent management contracts with its affiliate, International Talent Management, Inc. (ITMI), to capture revenue from artists' live appearances. These policies were overreaching but legal, and they gave Motown a revenue stream that helped it weather the time lag between having a hit record and the payment for it from distributors.

Of course, no amount of organizational efficiency and savvy cash management would have catapulted Motown to the global fame and impact it achieved without extraordinary music. Motown built this catalog of incredible music by assembling a stable of talented song-writers and making them ruthlessly compete with one another to have their records released. Gordy instituted a quality control department, modeled after the departments in Detroit's auto plants, that evaluated every demo recorded and decided if it was worthy of moving on to the weekly product evaluation meeting run by Gordy. Quality control at Motown was headed at various points by Billie Jean Brown, whom Gordy described as "strong, opinionated, honest, and [with] a good ear," and earlier by future Temptations hitmaker Norman Whitfield.

The final key to Motown's cultural and chart dominance during the 1960s was the Motortown Revue, launched by Gordy in the fall of 1962. Although rock-and-roll revue tours had been commonplace since the 1950s, Motown was the first record company to package and invest in a tour comprised entirely of artists from its own label. The first Motortown Revue toured "19 cities in 23 days," fifteen of which were in the Deep South. While it was grueling for young artists who had never been out of Michigan to confront the segregation and hostility of the Deep South during the height of the Civil Rights Movement, Gordy recognized that getting his artists in front of audiences around the country would boost sales and ultimately be a wise investment. It took several years for other labels to follow suit and institute the practice of investing in their artists' live tours, or what became known as tour support.

The first revue revealed that, for all their talent, Motown's artists lacked a polished and professional stage presence. This was hardly surprising given that most of them were barely out of their teens—and in the case of Stevie Wonder, signed to Motown at eleven, barely in them. Harvey Fuqua, former member of doo-wop group the Moonglows and husband of Berry's sister Gwen Gordy, was in charge of rectifying this. Fuqua recruited Maxine Powell, head of an eponymous finishing and modeling school, choreographer Cholly Atkins, and musical director Maurice King to staff the artist development department. Together they created a legendary program that transformed gawky teenagers into polished, elegant performers who could wow audiences, from Black folks at the Apollo Theater to the British royal family at the London Palladium.

Although "bigger than Motown" in 1963, Vee-Jay Records' reign was short-lived. Vee-Jay suffered from its overspending and inability to capitalize on the rights it controlled. Conversely, since Gordy got his start as a songwriter, he understood that publishing royalties could provide a crucial hedge against the cash-flow issues that typically plagued independent labels.

Unfettered by the undercapitalization that plagued earlier Black-owned labels, Motown was free to concentrate on making the best music with the widest possible appeal, and then hiring an integrated sales staff, headed by white major label vet Barney Ales, to get past white music industry gatekeepers. It was an unbeatable formula.

As Nelson George observed, beginning in 1963, Motown began a run of success that "changed Black music's position in the record industry and in the culture." From the blues craze of the 1920s until the advent of Motown, major labels relegated music by Black artists to smaller subsidiary labels that were consciously marketed to Black audiences only. Rock and roll was largely the province of independent labels like Atlantic, Chess, and Sun, which emphasized singles over albums for economic reasons.

Motown changed all that. In the ten years between Motown's first #1 pop hit in 1961, "Please Mr. Postman" by the Marvelettes, and 1971, they had 110 songs appear in the top ten of the Billboard Hot 100 pop chart. Berry Gordy and Motown created an instantly recognizable sound that erased the boundaries between Black and white music, made an indelible mark on American culture, and for a time was, as its motto proclaimed, "the sound of young America."

In the 1970s, when popular taste began to shift away from the Motown sound, the company used its relocation to Los Angeles to expand into film. Motown produced the Billie Holiday biopic *Lady Sings the Blues* as well as *Mahogany* and *The Wiz*, among other films

Yet the move to LA disrupted the close-knit Detroit hitmaking machine, and Motown's fortunes as a label suffered.

The difference in Vee-Jay's and Motown's fates can be chalked up to many factors—the Gordy family entrepreneurial history that provided Berry Gordy with access to capital that Vee-Jay lacked, or Berry Gordy's insistence on an efficient organizational structure and tight financial controls versus Vee-Jay's undisciplined spending, chasing hit records, and lining the pockets of its owners. Yet there is no question that Berry Gordy's sophisticated understanding of the value of musical copyrights, grounded in his roots as a songwriter, was a key reason for Motown's longevity as a multimillion-dollar, independent, Black-owned company. Despite the public's shifting musical tastes, Gordy was able to keep the label afloat for decades, until selling it to MCA Universal in 1988 for $61 million. Tellingly, he held on to the music publishing company for another sixteen years, not relinquishing full ownership of Jobete until 2004.

SEVEN

FROM *SIR* TO *SWEETBACK*: SIDNEY POITIER AND MELVIN VAN PEEBLES, PIONEERS IN MODERN BLACK FILM

In 1963, when Motown was integrating and remaking American popular music, Black Americans were amid a pitched battle to integrate and remake American society, demanding their full rights as citizens and humans. Although Black Americans had been waging this fight since federal troops withdrew from the South in 1877, the landmark victory won by brilliant NAACP lawyers in *Brown v. Board of Education* in 1954 ushered in what is recognized as the modern Civil Rights Movement.

Brown, argued by a top team of lawyers led by future Supreme Court Justice Thurgood Marshall, overturned the odious 1896 precedent of

Plessy v. Ferguson, which held that segregation (and by extension Jim Crow law) was constitutional, as long as the segregated facilities funded by the government were "equal" to those provided for white people. Of course, Southern segregationists had no intention of providing equal facilities for Black citizens and no public facility was too small to be segregated, from state universities to water fountains.

The gruesome murder of fourteen-year-old Emmett Till by white racists that occurred a year after *Brown* in Money, Mississippi, on August 28, 1955, was the spark that truly galvanized a mass movement. The young boy's "crime" was making flirtatious remarks to a white Southern woman, Carolyn Bryant, in the store that she owned with her husband, Roy Bryant. As punishment for allegedly breaking the unwritten racial codes of the South, Roy Bryant and J. W. Milam kidnapped Till from his bed, beat him beyond recognition, shot him in the head, and then threw his body into the Tallahatchie River weighed down with barbed wire and a cotton gin fan. Decades later, we learned that Bryant had fabricated the entire incident. Mamie Till-Mobley's brave decision to have an open casket at his well-attended funeral in Chicago and to publish photos of her son's mangled body in *Jet* magazine, forced the world to witness the depraved brutality of the Jim Crow regime, and spurred Black people to mobilize in large numbers.

A few months later, civil rights leaders in Montgomery, Alabama, tapped twenty-six-year-old Martin Luther King Jr. as the spokesperson for the Montgomery bus boycott, propelling the young minister to national prominence.

In the aftermath of World War II, the United States was locked into a battle for global hegemony with the Soviet Union and China—the Cold War. The US government soon realized that the country's rampant segregation, disenfranchisement, and discrimination against its Black citizens undercut the country's argument that it was a beacon of freedom and democracy. President Harry S. Truman himself took up the cause, arguing for the passage of federal civil rights legislation. The State Department viewed sports, art, and culture as a way to create the impression that Black people's status in the United States was improving.

Hollywood, in a reflection of these societal shifts, slowly began to expand its depiction of Black Americans beyond demeaning mammies, maids, and servants. The reasons were not only a desire for geopolitical advantage, but were also a function of the changing economic realities of the movie business.

After the war in 1948, the government won a landmark antitrust case against Paramount Pictures that radically disrupted the structure of the film business, challenging the major studios' bottom lines. Originally brought by the US Department of Justice against the studios in 1938, the case removed the stranglehold that the major film studios had over every aspect of the motion picture industry, from production to distribution and exhibition, by outlawing practices like block booking (which forced theaters to take studios' B pictures along with the hits), and compelling the studios to divest from their ownership of movie theaters. This court-ordered divestment eliminated a key revenue safety net for studios. In addition, the rising popularity of the new entertainment medium of television during the early 1950s challenged movies' monopoly on Americans' leisure time.

The combination of legal and competitive challenges made studios risk-averse. The studios' caution created an opening for adventurous independent producers more willing to tackle commercially risky films. These producers were able to incorporate socially relevant themes in their films in part because they were working with much smaller budgets than major studios.

Stanley Kramer was one such independent producer who became known for his socially conscious "message pictures." Kramer, born in New York City in 1913, graduated from DeWitt Clinton High School at fifteen and NYU at nineteen. Thanks to his student journalism and family members in the movie business, Kramer was offered a writing internship in Hollywood by 20th Century Fox upon his graduation. Kramer worked as a writing and editorial assistant in Hollywood until he was drafted in 1943 during World War II. He spent the war stateside making training films for the US Army Signal Corps, along with established filmmakers like Frank Capra. This experience positioned Kramer to start his production company in 1947, after the war.

The first message picture that put Kramer on the map was *Home of the Brave*, a 1949 film centered on the racism that a Black soldier suffers in the army. Although the film received strong reviews, James Edwards, the Black actor at the center of the film, had his career derailed by his refusal to testify against renowned Black actor, singer, and activist Paul Robeson in front of the House Un-American Activities Committee, the congressional committee that ignited the anticommunist Red Scare in Hollywood and cost three hundred people their careers.

Yet Kramer was not the only producer tackling social issues in film during the 1950s. Other producers were making films that for the first time in Hollywood's history featured Black characters in roles that were not demeaning. Several of these films featured a young, up-and-coming Black Bahamian actor named Sidney Poitier.

In 1950's *No Way Out*, produced by Joseph Mankiewicz, Poitier plays a young doctor who is accused of murder when a white robbery suspect shot by the police dies in his care. He followed that up in 1951 with the role of a priest in director Zoltán Korda's adaptation of *Cry, the Beloved Country*, novelist Alan Paton's searing critique of South African apartheid.

Poitier, by his own account, came to New York from the Bahamas in the 1940s impoverished and barely literate. After starting as a janitor and understudy at the American Negro Theater in Harlem, Poitier worked his way up to featured roles on Broadway in *Lysistrata* (1946) and *Anna Lucasta* (1947). Favorable notices on Broadway led directly to Poitier's first film roles.

Yet the Hollywood of the 1950s had hardly undergone a sea change. Black actors still could not make a living working in Hollywood. Throughout the decade, Poitier was a reliable player for those producers using their films to tackle issues, like Darryl Zanuck, Joe Mankiewicz, David Susskind, and the Mirisch brothers. In 1955's *Blackboard Jungle*, twenty-seven-year-old Poitier plays a rebellious teen opposite Glenn Ford, who plays the white teacher trying to reform the delinquents in his charge. In 1957's *Something of Value*, Poitier plays native Kenyan Kimani Wa Karanja, a young man trying to reconcile the conflict between his role in the uprising for Kenyan independence and his friendship with Rock Hudson's white colonizer.

After years of featured and supporting roles, Poitier had his breakout starring role for the producer most closely identified with the "social issues" picture, Stanley Kramer. In Kramer's 1958 drama *The Defiant Ones*, Poitier and Tony Curtis star as convicts, one Black and one white, who escape from a chain gang while still chained together and must overcome the mutual distrust precipitated by the racism of Curtis's character to evade capture.

Over the course of the film, the two men bond, leading to the film's famous ending. The final scene of *The Defiant Ones* features an indelible image of Sidney Poitier's character choosing to tumble off a moving freight train and risk capture, rather than escape and leave Tony Curtis's character, too weak to hoist himself onto the train, behind. At the time, some Black people criticized the scene, wondering why Poitier's character would jeopardize his freedom to save a white man who had only recently rejected his racist beliefs.

While that was, and remains, a valid critique, it is important to understand the social context of the United States in 1958. The Supreme Court decision in *Brown v. Board of Education* that declared that "separate but equal" public schools were unconstitutional was only four years old. The year before *The Defiant Ones* was released, President Dwight D. Eisenhower had to federalize the National Guard and send the US Army to protect nine Black high school students attempting to integrate Little Rock, Arkansas's, Central High School.

The key message of Kramer's film was that proximity to, and interdependence with, Black Americans could reform the most inveterate white racists, and most important, that Black people could forgive and even save those same people. That message surely resonated with white audiences, who may not have seen themselves in the faces of the angry mobs in Little Rock but also may not have wanted a Black family to move in next door.

After his Oscar-nominated turn in *The Defiant Ones*, Sidney Poitier returned to the stage in 1959, starring as Walter Lee Younger in Lorraine Hansberry's groundbreaking play *A Raisin in the Sun*. When Poitier starred in the film adaptation one year later, producer David Susskind gave him valuable advice, telling Poitier "to learn how things worked on the inside of the film business," and not to be content with simply being in front of the camera.

Just as Hollywood was slowly embracing Black characters as human beings with the ambition and agency to be more than servile comic foils, white America was grappling with Black people's demand to be recognized as equal American citizens. Despite massive protests and court orders, white America often violently resisted this demand.

On August 28, 1963, Dr. Martin Luther King Jr. gave his famous, "I Have a Dream" speech in front of 250,000 people at the March on Washington. Two weeks later, on September 15, 1963, racist terrorists bombed the 16th Street Baptist Church in Birmingham, Alabama, murdering fourteen-year-olds Addie Mae Collins, Cynthia Wesley, and Carole Robertson, and eleven-year-old Carol Denise McNair.

Almost two weeks after that horrific act of white supremacist violence, the Sidney Poitier film *Lilies of the Field* was released on September 26, 1963. In it, Poitier does something that no Black film actor had been able to do before—he plays a role in which his circumstances are not defined or circumscribed by his race. An itinerant laborer named Homer Smith stops at a Catholic convent in the Arizona desert to get water for his car's radiator and ends up being convinced to stay and build a chapel for the local Mexican American townspeople. The film centers on the gentle, lightly humorous battle of wills between Homer Smith (called Schmidt by the German nuns) and the Mother Superior over whether Smith would stay and build the chapel.

As a contemporaneous review in *The Hollywood Reporter* put it, this was a "funny, sentimental, charming, and uplifting" film in which Poitier plays a "role [that] is not that of any Negro stereotype, however well-intentioned." Against the backdrop of a country where the battle for the right of Black Americans to be treated as full humans was met with gut-wrenching violence, a film with a quietly heroic Black protagonist with agency over his own life was groundbreaking.

Hollywood took notice, and in March 1964, Sidney Poitier became the first Black man to win an Academy Award for Best Actor for his role in *Lilies in the Field,* and only the second Black person to win an Oscar (after Hattie McDaniel's 1940 Best Supporting Actress award for playing Mammy in *Gone with the Wind*).

Poitier noted that his win was a milestone, but that "Hollywood had not kept it secret that it wasn't interested in supplying [B]lacks with a variety of positive images." Hollywood expected Black audiences to be content with repetitive depictions of what was ostensibly the same character—upright and completely lacking interiority. Although Hollywood was insufferably self-congratulatory about Poitier's Best Actor Oscar, it had little impact on Poitier's career or the progress of Black people in Hollywood. The NAACP's sustained public campaign to push Hollywood to integrate its workforce was largely responsible for what little progress took place. As film historian and journalist Mark Harris noted, for Poitier, his Oscar win was followed by several roles in mediocre pictures and the knowledge that his "Oscar would be less useful to him than to the organization that handed it out."

In 1965's *A Patch of Blue,* Poitier plays Gordon Ralfe, a selfless Black man who rescues a blind white woman from her abusive family. He also played Simon of Cyrene in the biblical epic *The Greatest Story Ever Told* and a reporter in the taut Cold War thriller *The Bedford Incident,* starring Richard Widmark. In each of these films, Poitier's characters are dignified and above reproach but lack any significant backstory or character development.

As Poitier's star was rising, Black people continued to risk brutality, imprisonment, and death in their push for equality under the law. In February 1965, Malcolm X was assassinated in New York's Audubon Ballroom. On March 7, 1965, civil rights marchers trying to cross the Edmund Pettus Bridge, en route from Selma to Montgomery, Alabama, were attacked by police, state troopers, and white vigilantes, landing seventeen marchers in the hospital. Reverend James Reeb, a white Unitarian minister, was killed during the follow-up march a few days later. The resulting media spotlight put pressure on Congress and Lyndon B. Johnson's administration, and President Johnson signed the Voting Rights Act into law in August 1965.

Poitier was far from a passive observer of Black people's freedom struggles in the United States. Along with his close friend, artist and activist Harry Belafonte, Poitier actively supported the Civil Rights Movement. Poitier and Belafonte not only attended the 1963 March on Washington but traveled to Greenwood, Mississippi, during Freedom Summer in 1964 to personally deliver $70,000 in cash to help fund voter registration efforts. As journalist Joan Walsh recounted, the pair were "chased by armed Klansmen" and "almost didn't make it out of the South alive."

Poitier's fame and cultural impact reached its apex in 1967, when he had not one but three of the top-ten grossing films in the United States for that year. In each of the three films, Poitier created indelible characters that remain seared in the imagination of baby boomers.

In *To Sir, with Love*, released on June 14, 1967, in a role reversal from his character in 1955's *Blackboard Jungle*, Poitier's character is a teacher tasked with taming a class of unruly, white British working-class teenagers. Poitier plays Mark Thackeray, a West Indian immigrant to London who turns to teaching after being unable to secure an engineering job. Thackeray is assigned to a last-chance school for troubled teens in London's East End. His students are initially dismissive and disruptive, but Thackeray's unfailing dignity and the respect that he affords them gradually win his students over. Though the film was derided by critics as unrealistic and criticized as an early example of the "Magical Negro" trope, it was a bona fide hit, grossing $42 million on a budget of $640,000. In an early example of taking David Susskind's advice to heart, Poitier's deal on the film paid him a percentage of the film's gross in exchange for accepting a fixed fee of $200,000, half of his usual quote. Given that the picture eventually grossed $27 million, that was a savvy business decision.

Two months after the release of *To Sir, with Love*, Poitier starred as Detective Virgil Tibbs in the Southern murder mystery *In the Heat of the Night*. The white filmmaking team—director Norman Jewison and screenwriter Stirling Silliphant—were determined to make a film that was responsive to the righteous Black anger being expressed on the streets of Los Angeles during the 1965 Watts Rebellion and on the pages of posthumously published *The Autobiography of Malcolm X*.

In the Heat of the Night spawned a classic line *and* a classic scene that resurfaced as a meme in 2024. In the beginning of the film, Poitier's Virgil challenges the white sheriff (played by Rod Steiger in an Oscar-winning performance), contradicting his theory about who committed the murder. Police chief Bill Gillespie responds angrily, snarling, "Virgil's a funny name for a n——ger boy that comes from Philadelphia. What do they call you up there?" Through gritted teeth, Tibbs looks him in the eye and responds icily, "They call me *Mr. Tibbs!*" The line was a pointed vindication for Black audiences who had endured a century of disrespect from white Southerners who called Black men and women *boy* and *gal*, never *Mr.*, *Miss*, or *Mrs.*, no matter their age.

The second, even more impactful scene occurs later in the film, after Tibbs and Gillespie have formed a grudging partnership to solve the crime. They arrive at the home of cotton plantation owner Endicott to question him about his activities the night of the murder. Endicott becomes enraged by Tibbs's line of questioning and slaps him. Without missing a beat, Tibbs slaps him back. According to Steve Ryfle's essay in *Cineaste,* the scene marked "the first known act of physical defiance in a studio film by an African American character that did not result in punishment or death."

If Virgil Tibbs represented a departure from Poitier's other film roles by being a man who refused to be "accommodating," his last big film of 1967 represented a reversion to type. In Stanley Kramer's *Guess Who's Coming to Dinner,* Poitier stars alongside lions of the screen Katharine Hepburn and Spencer Tracy, who play the parents of his character's white fiancée. Poitier plays Dr. John Wade Prentice, a preternaturally perfect human being: a brilliant physician dedicated to eradicating disease in Africa, a gentleman who refuses to have premarital sex with his fiancée, one so honest that he leaves change on the table of his hosts to pay for a long-distance phone call.

Guess Who's Coming to Dinner was an anodyne drawing-room comedy whose message was that prejudice was no match for the power of true love. Even in 1967, reviewers noted that the film, though excellent, was "old-fashioned," though the year of its release coincided with the Supreme Court decision, *Loving v. Virginia,* that legalized interracial marriage. Stellar performances by Tracy, Hepburn, and Poitier and a deftly written script by William Rose led the film to earn nearly $57 million at the box office and win two Oscars, for Best Screenplay and Best Actress for Katharine Hepburn.

Within six months of the release of *Guess Who's Coming to Dinner*, the winds shifted dramatically in the country, with profound implications for Sidney Poitier's career. In the aftermath of the assassination of Dr. Martin Luther King on April 4, 1968, Black communities around the nation erupted in anger, sparking uprisings in cities from Washington, DC, and Baltimore to Chicago. The spontaneous rebellions were an expression of Black people's collective shock that an apostle of nonviolence, a crusader who was pleading with America to grant Black people the rights that they were *entitled to* as human beings and citizens, had been violently murdered by a white racist.

Two months later, on June 5, 1968, Democratic presidential front-runner Robert F. Kennedy was assassinated during a campaign event at the Ambassador Hotel in Los Angeles. It is hard to overstate the devastating impact of the tragic back-to-back murders of Dr. King and Bobby Kennedy on a country already reeling from protests against the widely unpopular Vietnam War and rebellions in major cities waged by Black people whose patience had run out.

The turmoil culminated with the violence that rocked the Democratic National Convention, held in Chicago in August 1968. Thanks to LBJ's escalation of the Vietnam War, five hundred thousand American soldiers were serving overseas in 1968. Despite the massive troop presence and constant bombing by American forces, North Vietnam showed no signs of backing down. Opposition to the war was so widespread that President Johnson decided not to seek reelection.

Anti-war protesters were determined to make their voices heard by the party of the president responsible for this conflict. On the third night of the convention, protestors broke out of their designated area to march toward convention headquarters on Michigan Avenue. Their move enraged "dictatorial" Mayor Richard Daley, who unleashed Chicago cops and the National Guard on them in what was later described in an Illinois State investigative commission report as a "police riot."

Eight of the protest leaders were indicted and tried for inciting a riot: The "Chicago 8" included Young Independent Party ("Yippie") leaders Abbie Hoffman and Jerry Rubin and the only Black defendant, Black Panther Party leader Bobby Seale. Judge Julius Hoffman's unabashed racism was on full display when he denied Seale his choice of counsel and ordered him to be bound, gagged, and *chained* in the courtroom during the trial.

Republican presidential candidate Richard Nixon defeated Vice President Hubert Humphrey in November 1968 by cynically exploiting the fault lines that exploded in American society, claiming to speak for a "silent majority" and promising to restore "law and order."

War, assassinations, and political turmoil darkened the nation's mood. Between white backlash to Black people's push for equality and Black people's rage and despair at continued violent resistance to their demands for civil rights, there was little appetite for the kinds of films that made Sidney Poitier a star—films with an unimpeachable, brilliant, and dignified Black protagonist who could defeat racism through the sheer force of his respectable perfection. The bullet that murdered the Rev. Dr. Martin Luther King Jr. while he was wearing a suit and tie shattered that illusion.

As a consequence, Black audiences began to abandon Poitier, with some critics calling him an "Uncle Tom" or a "house n—ger." Sidney Poitier was acutely aware that his roles represented "one-dimensional, middle-class imagery." Poitier's response was not to get defensive, but to use his power to expand the type of Black people depicted on-screen, recognizing that his superstar status gave him leverage unavailable to most actors, Black or white.

Poitier secured a production deal with Columbia Pictures that gave him the power to choose his starring vehicles. Then, in 1969, Poitier became a founding owner, along with Paul Newman and Barbra Streisand, of First Artists, a new film studio owned and controlled by its superstar founders (Steve McQueen was added as an owner in 1971 and Dustin Hoffman in 1972). The premise of First Artists was that it would reach profitability by allowing its star owners complete creative control in exchange for agreeing to accept a fraction of their normal fees. First Artists, the brainchild of agent Freddie Fields and future Columbia Pictures president David Begelman, was not unlike United Artists, the studio formed in 1919 by Charlie Chaplin, Mary Pickford, Douglas Fairbanks, and D. W. Griffith.

First Artists was troubled from the start. In its ten-year existence, the company only produced fifteen films, the number that most studios produced in one year. The studio became embroiled in litigation with Dustin Hoffman, who balked at providing his exclusive services to a studio that would not pay him his quote. Steve McQueen and Paul Newman chose vehicles that were not commercial. Barbra Streisand, who was responsible for the studio's most successful pictures, *A Star Is Born* and *The Main Event*, was seemingly the only founder with strong commercial instincts.

Poitier's ownership stake in First Artists and his production deal with Columbia Pictures afforded him an unprecedented degree of creative control. He seized the opportunity to produce and direct films that were a radical departure from the roles that had won him acclaim in the previous decade. In 1972, Poitier made his directorial debut in *Buck and the Preacher*, a Western that subverted the tropes of the classic American genre, depicting white people as villains and Indigenous people as allies in Black people's struggle for agency over their own lives.

Buck and the Preacher stars Poitier as Buck, a guide responsible for leading a wagon train of newly emancipated Black people out West to pursue a better life. Harry Belafonte stars as the Preacher, a con man at odds with Buck until the two are compelled to join forces to combat a gang of white bounty hunters looking to kidnap the Black settlers and force them back into lives of subservience working the same plantations they had while enslaved. In contrast to Poitier's other films, *Buck and the Preacher* is clearly aimed at Black audiences. It does not have any scenes where Poitier's character ingratiates himself with or forgives white racists.

Poitier followed his directorial debut at Columbia Pictures with four films he directed and starred in for First Artists. He plays a familiar type in 1973's *A Warm December*: widower Dr. Matt Younger, who devotes his life to getting lifesaving medication to African countries. Unlike his earlier films, where his characters were saints who served to facilitate the growth of white characters, *A Warm December* centers on the doomed romance between Younger and an ambitious African diplomat named Catherine Oswandu that is cut short when Catherine develops a terminal illness.

Poitier's next three films for First Artists were *Uptown Saturday Night*, *Let's Do It Again*, and *A Piece of the Action*, rollicking comedies featuring everyday Black people and set in the Black community. The films, released in 1974, 1975, and 1977, respectively, showcased the bus drivers, laborers, street sweepers, schoolteachers, hustlers, and ordinary people whom Poitier knew were missing from Hollywood's depiction of Black life. Poitier plays a blue-collar steel mill worker in *Uptown Saturday Night* who devises an elaborate plan to recover a stolen winning lottery ticket. *Let's Do It Again* features Poitier and Bill Cosby as friends who attempt to rig a boxing match to raise money for their lodge. In *A Piece of the Action*, Poitier plays a retired thief pressed into volunteering for a youth center.

Bill Cosby, the now-disgraced comedian, was Poitier's costar in all three films, alongside all-star casts of Black actors like Harry Belafonte, Richard Pryor, and Calvin Lockhart. Although they were derided by white writers in outlets like *The New York Times* as "limited-interest ghetto pictures," the films were hits with Black audiences. We need look no further than the fact that one of the most prominent rappers of the 1990s, the Notorious B.I.G., took his stage name Biggie Smalls from the name of the character Calvin Lockhart plays in *Let's Do It Again*.

Poitier used the control over content he enjoyed as a producer and co-owner of a studio to broaden the depiction of Black people beyond mere dramatic devices that held up a mirror to white society's racism. On a personal level, he added director and producer to his role as an actor in the film business, an insurance policy against changing public tastes.

One year before Poitier's directorial debut in *Buck and the Preacher*, a prolific polymath burst onto the scene with a film so original, so uncompromising, and so *successful* that it spawned an entire film genre. That film was *Sweet Sweetback's Baadasssss Song*, written, directed, produced by, and starring Melvin Van Peebles.

Van Peebles was a truly astonishing man whose career could be several movies in itself. Van Peebles was born in Chicago in 1932 and grew up in the suburb of Phoenix, Illinois. He originally attended historically Black West Virginia State University before transferring to Ohio Wesleyan University through the ROTC program. Upon graduation at age twenty in 1953, Van Peebles joined the US Air Force, serving as a navigator on B-47 bombers for three years.

Once Van Peebles was discharged from the air force, he pursued jobs with commercial airlines, but despite the established career pipeline between the US Air Force and commercial aviation, Van Peebles was rejected. No commercial airline would hire a Black veteran, regardless of his qualifications or military record. It took nearly ten years and a Supreme Court decision before a domestic airline hired a Black pilot in 1964.

After being rebuffed by the airlines, Van Peebles moved with his wife to Mexico City and supported himself by painting portraits. They then relocated to San Francisco, where he worked at the post office and as a cable car operator. According to film critic Mel Gussow, while working as an operator, Van Peebles "wrote the text for a picture book about cable cars, and when it was published in 1957, he was fired." Van Peebles sued the cable car company without success, and then, undeterred by his lack of formal training, turned his attention to filmmaking.

Van Peebles directed several short films and tried to parlay those shorts into opportunities in Hollywood but was once again stymied by racism. The only studio jobs available to Black people in 1957 were as elevator operators. Van Peebles refused to accept the limitations imposed on Black people in the United States by rigid segregation and moved to the Netherlands to study astronomy on the G.I. Bill. Van Peebles's wife tired of a life of peripatetic penury and divorced him.

Van Peebles moved again, this time to Paris, where Black Americans like Josephine Baker, Richard Wright, and James Baldwin had flocked before him in search of artistic freedom and basic human dignity. Although Van Peebles self-deprecatingly claimed that he supported himself in Paris by busking on the street and keeping company with wealthy women, his creative output during his time in Paris was astonishing. Over the course of about a decade, Van Peebles edited a humor magazine and wrote a "volume of short stories and five novels that were published in French," as *The New York Times* noted. In 1967, Van Peebles took advantage of a French government subsidy for works written in French to adapt his novel *La Permission* into his first feature film, *The Story of a Three-Day Pass*, about the racism faced by a Black soldier and his white girlfriend.

Van Peebles entered the film into the 1967 San Francisco International Film Festival as a French delegate. When the film won the Critics' Choice Award, Hollywood was finally willing to offer him something other than a menial job. Columbia Pictures hired Van Peebles to direct *Watermelon Man*, the tale of a white bigot who wakes up one morning to discover that he has become a Black man overnight. The film was inspired both by Franz Kafka's *The Metamorphosis* and John Howard Griffin's bestselling 1961 memoir *Black Like Me*, chronicling the racism Griffin experienced when he traveled the segregated South disguised as a Black man.

Columbia wanted to hire a white actor and put him in blackface, but Van Peebles convinced the studio to hire Black comedian Godfrey Cambridge, reasoning that the character was Black for most of the movie. Van Peebles and the producers clashed over creative decisions during production, culminating in Van Peebles "forgetting" to film an alternative ending to the film where the main character wakes up and finds that he had merely dreamed that he had become a Black man. A horrified producer told Van Peebles that he had made the film with a "Black point of view."

When *Watermelon Man* was a hit despite its Black point of view, Columbia Pictures offered Van Peebles a three-picture deal. Van Peebles had other ideas. His experience making *Watermelon Man* taught him that to work in the Hollywood studio system, he would have to "deal in compromise" and strive for "consensus." Van Peebles decided to make his next film independently.

Van Peebles repeatedly showed that he refused to be constrained by the limits American society imposed on Black people. He said that he aimed to make a "victorious film" showing Black people getting "the Man's foot out of all of our Black asses." Van Peebles knew that Hollywood would run screaming in the other direction, and applied his same rule-breaking approach to the making of *Sweetback*.

In his memoir, Van Peebles gleefully recounts the onanistic inspiration for his script: a tale of a sex worker turned revolutionary, killing cops and ending up a fugitive on the run from the law. To make such a subversive picture, Van Peebles had to be the writer, director, producer, and star. He leveraged relationships at Columbia Pictures to get the film-processing lab services and equipment on a deferred basis. Van Peebles threw the unions off his trail by claiming he was making a porn film and recruited his Black production manager and director of photography from porn productions in the Valley. The film, though hardly pornographic, contains a lot of onscreen sex, not all of which was simulated. Van Peebles claimed that he contracted an STD during production, "applied for workmen's compensation, and got it."

The resulting film was unlike anything Hollywood had seen before. The hero, who only has six lines of dialogue, struck a literal blow against the pervasive police brutality inflicted on Black people. Sweetback outwits the cops and ends the film bloody but unbowed, having eluded capture and made it across the border.

Sweet Sweetback's Baadasssss Song contained too much sex for the MPAA, which slapped it with an X rating (the equivalent of today's NC-17). Van Peebles cannily turned that into a marketing hook, using the tagline "Rated X by an All-White Jury." Thanks to the X rating, "only two theaters in the entire United States would take it—a bingo house called the Grand Circus in Detroit and a little theater in Atlanta, Georgia." *Sweetback* made more the first night than those theaters typically made in an entire week.

Once the film broke records at those two theaters, genre distributor Cinemation Industries opened it wide, where it went on to earn $15.2 million at the box office. The success of *Sweet Sweetback's Baadasssss Song* spawned an entire genre of films that came to be known as Blaxploitation. These films had sex, action, and killer soundtracks like *Sweetback*, but without the systemic critique of racism and corruption and the sly subversion of gender roles that distinguished Van Peebles's film.

With the notable exceptions of *Shaft* and *Super Fly*, helmed by Gordon Parks and Gordon Parks Jr., respectively, most Blaxploitation films were written and/or directed by white men and financed by mostly white Hollywood studios. It was yet another example of the white-run entertainment industry co-opting and imitating what it could not control. Blaxploitation films offered Black audiences the vicarious thrill of triumphing over the most visible perpetrators of Black oppression—mobsters and drug dealers—rather than the incendiary critique of racist systems embedded in *Sweetback* that made that film required viewing for members of the Black Panther Party.

Audience appetite for repetitive Blaxploitation tropes waned after a few years, but the example set by Melvin Van Peebles with *Sweetback* would go on to inspire independent Black filmmakers like Robert Townsend and Spike Lee a generation later, leading to a renaissance of Black cinema. Although their approaches and subject matter were vastly different, Sidney Poitier and Melvin Van Peebles demonstrated that Black control of the development, financing, and production of film, and the resulting ownership of the intellectual property, led to movies with a range of Black stories, populated by Black characters who were full human beings with flaws, warmth, and rich inner lives. Each man proved that there was money to be made making films for the Black audience, not just the white gaze, a lesson that Hollywood seems to need to relearn every twenty years.

EIGHT

HIP HOP: THE MOTOWN REMIX

The 1972 election of Richard Nixon represented a definitive backlash against the civil rights and anti-war activism of the 1960s. By the mid-seventies, the combination of a federal government hostile to civil rights and a downturn in the American economy had a particularly devastating effect on New York City, with reverberations that profoundly impacted Black music.

In the 1960s, New York was a noble example of a municipal government that tried to serve all its residents. Its liberal mayor, John Lindsay, expanded the city's generous social safety net. The City University of New York (CUNY), with its free tuition, had long been famous for offering a world-class education to poor and working-class New Yorkers. But by the end of the 1960s, the city's luck began to run out, with the country's economic depression hitting New York hard. According to historian Michael Beyea Reagan, between 1969 and

1976, New York City lost "half a million jobs [and] 11,000 housing units between 1970–1975. [B]y the end of the '70s, [New York City] had lost close to one million residents."

When New York City came perilously close to declaring bankruptcy after being unable to meet its bond obligations, bankers forced the city to radically cut its budget by sharply reducing the municipal workforce and slashing programs that benefited middle- and working-class New Yorkers, like after-school programs and the free CUNY tuition.

White flight contributed to much of New York City's population loss, and by the time of the 1975 fiscal crisis, Black and Brown New Yorkers were trapped in a diminished, dirty, and dangerous city, with avenues of upward mobility via academics or arts education slashed. Cuts to arts education in New York City predated the national trend by twenty years.

Yet Black people in America are nothing if not resilient. Black youth responded to the hardships brought on by fiscal austerity by making the subways and streets their canvas and turning turntables and vinyl records into instruments, in the process transforming American music and youth culture.

Clive Campbell came to the Bronx from Jamaica with his family in 1967. After a childhood in a suburban area of Jamaica called Franklin Town, the dirt, concrete, and cold was a "rude awakening" for twelve-year-old Campbell. Campbell found America to be a far cry from the placid images he had consumed from American media exports like *Dennis the Menace* and *Petticoat Junction*.

Although Campbell was initially teased for his "country" dress and manner, he gained stature in high school for his track and field prowess, earning the nickname Hercules, later shortened to "Herc."

Around this time, Herc joined a graffiti crew called the Ex-Vandals, using the tag "Kool" and becoming known as Kool Herc.

On August 11, 1973, Kool Herc's younger sister hosted a "back to school" party in the rec room of their apartment building at 1520 Sedgwick Avenue in the Bronx. The Campbell family had recently moved to this new building on the west side after being burned out of their building in the East Bronx. Although Kool Herc had been deejaying for some time using his father's powerful stereo equipment, the August 11 party marked the first time that he used a technique that would become the foundation of Hip Hop music. Using two turntables and a mixer, Herc took two copies of the same record and extended the percussive danceable sections of the same songs—or the "breaks"—to rev up the dancers and keep the party going strong.

Other DJs began the practice of extending the breaks, but Kool Herc dominated the early Hip Hop party circuit. Not only had he pioneered the technique, but he had *power.* When battling other DJs like DJ Smokey, Herc was able to "blow them out" with his massive sound system.

As the Rock & Roll Hall of Fame acknowledged, there is no question that Kool Herc "transformed the two turntables into a single instrument and began making new material from other people's records." Yet Herc and his contemporaries viewed this groundbreaking innovation mainly as a way to have the best parties, not as a new musical genre to be recorded and sold. Kool Herc worked with MC Coke La Rock, and together they shouted out partygoers, working the crowd in the tradition of dancehall "toasting" from Herc's native Jamaica. As Hip Hop evolved, the emphasis shifted from the DJs to MCs. That evolution, combined with the fact that Kool Herc didn't record, meant that "for years he remained relatively unknown."

Kool Herc, the "Father of Hip Hop," was belatedly celebrated when he was inducted into the Rock & Roll Hall of Fame in 2023 to coincide with Hip Hop's fiftieth anniversary. The person widely acknowledged as the "Mother of Hip Hop," Sylvia Robinson—the visionary who recognized that the combination of turntable wizardry and rapping MCs was the stuff of hit records—only made it into the Rock & Roll Hall of Fame in 2022, beating Kool Herc by a mere twelve months.

The cofounder of Sugar Hill Records and the mastermind behind the Sugarhill Gang, Sylvia Robinson had a life story that could be a limited series. Born Sylvia Vanderpool in Harlem in 1935, she began her career in the music business as a fourteen-year-old singer under the moniker Little Sylvia. In the late 1950s, Sylvia took guitar lessons from session player Mickey Baker, ultimately forming the duo Mickey & Sylvia with him. "Love Is Strange," Mickey & Sylvia's 1957 song, hit #11 on the *Billboard* pop chart.

The duo broke up the next year, but Sylvia continued to work in the music business. In 1960, she produced "You Talk Too Much" by Joe Jones, which reached #3 on the *Billboard* pop chart. According to author Dan Charnas, that feat would have made Robinson "the first Black and female independent producer to have a top-ten pop hit—if she had gotten credit for the record."

Robinson followed up the next year by producing "It's Gonna Work Out Fine" for Ike & Tina Turner. Robinson said that she taught the tune to Tina and even played guitar on the record, but that Ike stole credit.

These back-to-back experiences disgusted Sylvia so much that she quit the music business in 1962 and moved to Paris. Two years later, she married Joe Robinson, who convinced her to give the music business another shot—but as a label owner rather than performer. In 1966, the couple founded All Platinum Records, headquartered at their home in suburban Englewood, New Jersey.

All Platinum signed the male R & B group the Moments (later known as Ray, Goodman & Brown), who scored a hit in 1970 with "Love on a Two-Way Street." The song, cowritten by Robinson, went to #1 R & B and #3 on the pop chart in *Billboard*. All Platinum also had success in 1975 with Shirley & Company's "Shame, Shame, Shame," a tune written by Robinson that went to #1 R & B and #12 on the *Billboard* pop chart.

But All Platinum's biggest hit was the 1973 record "Pillow Talk," written, produced, and performed by Robinson, who released the song under her first name, Sylvia. Robinson originally intended the song for soul legend Al Green, but he rejected the song for being too suggestive.

The lyrics of "Pillow Talk" evoke All Platinum's earlier hit "Love on a Two-Way Street," with lines like "You can't find love on a one-way street." The clever word play is backed by a track that has been described as "intoxicating" "bedroom funk."

"Pillow Talk" predated Donna Summer's 1975 smash "Love to Love You Baby," which featured sixteen minutes of simulated orgasms over a disco beat, by two years. The combination of lyrics that left nothing to the imagination and a mid-tempo earworm proved irresistible. "Pillow Talk" shot to #1 on the *Billboard* R & B chart and #3 on its Hot 100 chart. "Pillow Talk" marked Sylvia's third reinvention as a performer in the music business, from child star and half of the early R & B duo Mickey & Sylvia to sultry proto-disco songstress.

By the mid-1970s, Sylvia and Joe Robinson's All Platinum Records had filed for bankruptcy, and she and her husband formed a new label, Sugar Hill Records. Over this same period, the deejaying technique introduced by Kool Herc and MC Coke La Rock had become widespread, with DJs mixing records and MCs rapping over the extended breaks in parties throughout New York City. As popular as "two turntables and a microphone" had become among Black and Latino partygoers, no one viewed it as more than a technique to motivate dancers, an ephemeral performance to be experienced.

Journalist Alan Light described Sylvia Robinson as the "visionary" who understood that "rap was viable as recorded music." In 1979, Robinson heard Lovebug Starski rapping over records at a party in her native Harlem. As she put it, "a spirit said to me, 'put a concept like that on record and it will be the biggest thing you ever had.'" Robinson promptly went back to Englewood to look for her own MCs to record.

Using her son as a talent scout, Robinson auditioned three different rappers: Guy "Master Gee" O'Brien, Henry Lee "Big Bank Hank" Jackson, and "Wonder Mike" Wright. As reported in *The Guardian*, Hank "auditioned in front of the pizza parlor where he worked," while Master Gee and Wonder Mike "rapped in [Robinson's] car."

When Robinson was unable to decide among the three MCs, she decided to put them together, boy-band style, into a group she dubbed the Sugarhill Gang. From there, she meticulously crafted the record that would put Hip Hop on the map across the nation. She chose the disco hit "Good Times" by Chic as the backing track.

Chic, comprised of guitarist Nile Rodgers and bassist Bernard Edwards, cowrote the infectious "Good Times," which was released on June 4, 1979, and was #1 on the Billboard Hot 100 by August 18. The Sugarhill Gang's record "Rapper's Delight" was released just over two months later on September 16, 1979.

Rodgers was initially unhappy with the blatant rip-off of his song, but quickly settled with the group when he and Edwards were given songwriting credit and a share of the copyright ownership. Although the copyright dispute over Hip Hop's first hit record was settled amicably, it presaged the thorny legal issues inherent in this nascent art form that were absent from other musical genres. Jazz musicians frequently quoted other compositions in their improvisations, but Hip Hop relied much more heavily on preexisting works. The ubiquity and extent of borrowing in Hip Hop was understandable, given that the genre was originally conceived as a hype mechanism for live parties.

In theory, the problem could be resolved by licensing the underlying track or by using multiple samples to create a "collage," rendering the original songs unrecognizable (as Public Enemy's producers, the Hank Shocklee–led Bomb Squad, did). In practice, Hip Hop artists and producers often simply failed to get permission, resulting in expensive copyright claims that required artists to surrender a significant percentage of the copyright interest (and the mechanical royalty income that accompanied it) to the writers and publishers of the original compositions.

The economic impact on Hip Hop artists was profound. Copyright interest in a song is typically divided as 50 percent to the writer/publisher of the lyrics and 50 percent to the writer/publisher of the music, with mechanical royalty income divided the same way. Most record contracts in the 1980s and 1990s contained what is known as a "controlled composition clause," which required artists to accept three-fourths of the then-prevailing statutory mechanical rate on any song they recorded that they wrote or cowrote. Record contracts also customarily capped the total amount of mechanical royalties to an amount equal to ten times the three-fourths rate.

By way of example, in 1980, the statutory mechanical short song rate was 4 cents, but the typical recording contract capped the total amount of mechanicals payable per album sold to 30 cents (10 × 3 cents). If a Hip Hop artist had twelve songs on their album, the amount of mechanicals payable for each song would be reduced to 2.5 cents per song. If samples were used for the music for all twelve songs, the artist would be required to pay out 2 of that 2.5 cents, since third-party publishers were not likely to accept three-fourths of the statutory rate or abide by the cap. This could leave the artist with a total of 6 cents in mechanical royalties for an entire album of songwriting.

The fact that Hip Hop music, by definition, was built on a foundation of preexisting compositions deprived Hip Hop artists of an important income stream *and* full creative control of their output. Publishers of sampled compositions could either impose onerous financial terms that eviscerated an artist's record royalties or simply refuse to grant permission altogether.

At Hip Hop's beginnings, song lyrics reflected the genre's origins as music designed to hype a party. Early Hip Hop hits like "Making Cash Money" by Busy Bee and "Real Rocking Groove" by Chapter III were full of innocuous rhymes extolling the MC's skills on the mic. Hip Hop took a turn with the July 1982 release of "The Message" by Grandmaster Flash & the Furious Five.

Once again, Sylvia Robinson was responsible for the first Hip Hop record to unsparingly depict the harsh realities of Black urban life, overcoming the reticence of the artists themselves. "The Message," written by Melle Mel and Duke Bootee, contains verse after verse that describes the ugliness and desperation of daily inner-city life, punctuated by a chorus that was both a plea and a warning: "Don't push me 'cause I'm close to the edge."

"The Message" peaked at #4 on *Billboard*'s Black music chart. It never cracked the Top 10 on *Billboard*'s Hot 100, but it had a lasting impact. The song was #51 on *Rolling Stone*'s list of the 500 Greatest Songs of All Time, and the Library of Congress added "The Message" to the National Recording Registry in 2002, its first year of eligibility.

The importance of "The Message" goes beyond sales figures or critical acclaim. It marked the beginning of focus on the MC, rather than the DJ, in Hip Hop music. "The Message" also marked the maturation of a genre with lyrics to match. In 1983, Furious Five member Melle Mel followed up "The Message" with "White Lines," a cautionary tale about the dangers of crack and cocaine, set to an infectious bass line. "The Message" and "White Lines" encouraged other MCs to pen lyrics that offered unsparing accounts of Black urban life that led Public Enemy's Chuck D to dub Hip Hop "Black America's CNN" a few years later.

By the mid-1980s, tastes in Hip Hop changed, and the Sugar Hill sound was left behind. The label became virtually dormant, and it filed for bankruptcy in 1985. Sylvia Robinson did not live to see her pivotal role in Hip Hop recognized by the Rock & Roll Hall of Fame. She died of congestive heart failure in 2011.

Although Hip Hop's first label did not survive, by the late 1980s, Hip Hop's cultural dominance and staying power was undeniable. In contrast to the aspirational, smooth R & B of the Motown sound or the Afrofuturist funk of Parliament-Funkadelic, Hip Hop's lyrics were raw and unapologetic, unafraid to show the bravado, the pain, and sometimes the ugliness of Black inner-city life. There were cautionary tales, like Slick Rick's 1989 hit "Children's Story," and revolutionary anthems, like Public Enemy's 1989 smash "Fight the Power," featured in Spike Lee's classic film *Do the Right Thing*. But there were also misogynistic lyrics that reduced Black women to "bitches" and "hoes," lyrics about explicit sex unmoored from romance, and tales of violence, both between rival drug dealers or gang members and the kind meted out by racist police officers.

Black people asserting their freedom, even if only musically, has always been treated as a threat to be extinguished. Rap's popularity and ubiquity led in short order to moral panic, just as rock and roll and jazz had before it. As legal scholar Mathieu Deflem noted, moral panics are always a struggle for cultural power. The Parents Music Resource Center (PMRC), formed in the mid-1980s to wage a campaign against popular music, was no different.

The PMRC was founded by a bipartisan group of politically connected white women, including Tipper Gore (at the time, the wife of then Senator Al Gore) and Susan Baker (wife of George H. W. Bush's chief of staff James Baker). According to the organization's lore, Tipper Gore overheard her daughter listening to Prince's song "Darling Nikki" and was horrified that her eleven-year-old daughter had been exposed to lyrics describing the titular Nikki as a "sex fiend" whom the singer met "masturbating to a magazine."

In 1985, pre–internet and cellphone, American teenagers did not have porn accessible at the touch of a button. Then as now, white parents labored under the illusion of their children's innocence and stopped at nothing to maintain that illusion. Still, the most shocking thing about the lyrics of "Darling Nikki" is the description of a woman asserting her sexual agency and right to pleasure.

Nonetheless, the song spurred this pearl-clutching gaggle of Washington wives to spring into action. They formed the PMRC with the purported goal of "informing" parents. The PMRC requested that the Recording Industry Association of America (RIAA) impose a ratings system similar to the one that the MPAA used for films, and to "reconsider contracts with artists who displayed sex or violence during shows or on record." The RIAA caved immediately and proposed a warning label in August 1985, which the PMRC rejected as not going far enough.

The PMRC leveraged their members' connections and secured a Senate hearing on obscenity in popular music in September 1985. PMRC members testified about the "filthy fifteen," which included artists like Madonna, Cyndi Lauper, Sheena Easton (no doubt for the Prince-penned hit "Sugar Walls"), and Rick James's protégés the Mary Jane Girls.

By November 1985, the PMRC had extracted an agreement from the RIAA to require record labeling stickers that initially read PARENTAL GUIDANCE: EXPLICIT LYRICS. That victory did not mark the end of the PMRC's campaign against popular music. After initially focusing on rock and metal, by the late 1980s, the PMRC, like the rest of white mainstream authority, turned its attention to Hip Hop, whose influence was too big to be ignored.

Sex was not the only topic that outraged mainstream society. West Coast "gangsta rap" was attacked for its scathing commentaries on police brutality with deliberately provocative titles. N.W.A released "Fuck tha Police" in 1988, and in response, police attempted to shut down their concerts. "Cop Killer," Ice-T's 1992 song with his group Body Count, generated a widespread furious response. Law enforcement groups around the country called for a "boycott of all Time Warner products" and threatened to have their pension funds divest from all of the company's stock. Both Republican and Democratic politicians denounced the song, calling it "vile," "destructive," and "ugly." The political campaign culminated in President George

H. W. Bush decrying it as "sick." Once Ice-T had been singled out by a sitting president, as *Rolling Stone* reported, the FBI added him to its "National Threat List, and the IRS audited his taxes twice." Ice-T capitulated under the weight of the relentless attacks and removed "Cop Killer" from the track list of Body Count's album. In the ultimate irony, by 2000, Ice-T had remade himself in the public imagination as streetwise NYPD Detective Fin Tutuola on *Law & Order: Special Victims Unit*, a role he plays to this day.

Violent Hip Hop lyrics brought societal opprobrium, and then the sexual content of Hip Hop lyrics brought even greater scrutiny, given rap's rising popularity with white teenagers. Since Black men were the ones writing and performing these suggestive lyrics, it raised the specter of these same Black men having sex with young white women—white supremacist America's most existential fear.

No early Hip Hop artist faced the long arm of the law, both civilly and criminally, more than a pugnacious son of Caribbean immigrants from Miami, Florida. Luther Campbell was born on December 22, 1960, in Miami Beach. The Miami Beach of 1960 was rigidly segregated. Black people were prohibited from staying in Miami Beach hotels even if they were performing there. According to Campbell, Black people couldn't even *be* in Miami Beach unless they were working for white people.

Miami's history as a resort town can be traced to the arrival of white businesswoman Julia Tuttle to South Florida in 1891, making her the only woman to found what would become a major American city. Tuttle purchased the rundown Fort Dallas, a former plantation that had been taken over by the US military during its battles with the Indigenous Seminole tribe in the early nineteenth century and then abandoned after the Civil War. According to historian

Andrew K. Frank, Tuttle "lured Henry Flagler, who brought the East Coast Railroad and built the Royal Palm Hotel" on Tuttle's Fort Dallas property.

Flagler's construction crew razed all preexisting structures, destroying evidence of the Indigenous Tequesta community who had lived in Miami for four thousand years, the missionaries who came to try to convert them, and the enslaved Africans who toiled in the plantations built on the land once the Indigenous had been killed or displaced.

Flagler's development transformed Miami into a luxury resort destination, and as a result, Miami powerbrokers shunted Black people across the railroad tracks to the Overtown neighborhood. Despite the fact that many homes in Overtown were wooden shacks without electricity or running water, Black people built their own business community there, with banks, restaurants, and clubs, just as they had in Gary, Indiana, and Detroit. Campbell recounts that, like so many other thriving Black communities in municipalities all over the country, in the 1950s Overtown was "destroyed, intentionally, to make way for white development." The route of Interstate 95 was deliberately shifted west to run through the heart of Overtown.

The city of Miami built projects in a white neighborhood north of Overtown called Liberty City to house the displaced Black people. Campbell's father refused to move into the projects and bought a house for his family of seven in the part of Liberty City that was still white.

By Campbell's own account, he was an indifferent student with a passion for football. Although there were no Pop Warner youth football teams in Miami's Black communities in the late 1960s, Campbell was recruited to join a team by one of the many white coaches then scouting Black neighborhoods in search of players who could give their teams a competitive edge. Campbell quit football in his junior year of high school, and without the prospect of a football scholarship, college was out of the question. He graduated from high school unsure of what to do next, but his mother insisted that he leave the house for eight hours every day and find gainful employment.

Campbell combined work as a cook at a local hospital with an internship at radio station 99JAMZ. He also began deejaying at parties at local high schools with a crew he dubbed the "Ghetto Style DJs." From 1978 to 1979, Campbell graduated to promoting his own parties at a local roller rink under the moniker Pac Jam Teen Disco.

In May 1980, Miami was rocked by an uprising that erupted after the acquittal of four Dade County police officers who beat a man named Arthur McDuffie to death after a routine traffic stop and tried to cover it up to look like a motorcycle accident. To add insult to injury, McDuffie was a community pillar—a former marine and an insurance agent.

According to the *Miami Herald*, the Miami rebellion left "18 people dead, 400 injured and property damage in excess of $100 million." Although the federal government earmarked funds to rebuild, none of that money reached the Black communities of Overtown, Liberty City, or Brownsville.

The Miami riots and their aftermath had an impact on young Luther Campbell, now known professionally as Luke Skyywalker. Campbell saw that the same cycle of destruction and disinvestment had plagued the Black community in Miami for nearly one hundred years. This spurred him to open his own club, Pac Jam II, rather than renting out a business for a few nights per week and promoting parties.

As a club owner and DJ, Luke realized that he had the power to "break," or popularize, records regionally. He branched out into concert promotion and began bringing rap artists to Miami for promotional concerts to help them raise awareness and drive record sales in the Southeast region. While running Pac Jam II, Campbell met a West Coast group comprised of three air force members stationed in Riverside, California—David Hobbs, Christopher Wong Won, and Yuri Vielot—who called themselves 2 Live Crew.

In the mid-1980s, the major labels wanted nothing to do with Hip Hop, with independent labels like Sugar Hill, Profile Records, and Tommy Boy Records dominating the genre. The people who ran these labels may have had a love for the genre, but they replicated the business practices of the indie labels who recorded early rock-and-roll and R & B artists: paying tiny advances, acquiring their artists' publishing rights, and being slow to pay royalties. 2 Live Crew claimed that Macola Records, the tiny label they were signed to, wasn't paying them royalties.

Campbell decided to try to get them a deal with another label. When he was unsuccessful, he simply decided to start his own label. Luke came up with the concept for their first single, "Throw the 'D,'" released in January 1986, which peaked at #6 on the Billboard Hot 100 chart.

2 Live Crew's sound was grounded in the uniquely South Floridian amalgam of Latin, Caribbean, and R & B sounds that came to be known as "Miami bass." While it was tremendously popular in Miami, Campbell recognized that the group would need a gimmick if it was going to stand out from all the New York Hip Hop artists that defined the genre.

By this time, Campbell had joined the group as hype man,

as well as serving as 2 Live Crew's manager and label owner. He and the group members decided that their lyrics should be both funny and sexually explicit, in the tradition of Rudy Ray Moore, aka Dolemite. Given the shared cultural context, Luke was sure that Black audiences would get the joke. He didn't account for Hip Hop's increasing popularity with white teenagers. When 2 Live Crew released their raunchy first album, *The 2 Live Crew Is What We Are*, in July 1986, he got letters from a Parent Teacher Association in Birmingham, Alabama, complaining that kids were "getting a hold of [their] songs."

In response to these complaints—and the arrest of a record store owner in Florida for selling their first album to a fourteen-year-old girl—Campbell decided to make a clean version *and* an explicit version of the group's second album, *Move Somethin'*. Although the explicit version bore a PMRC warning sticker, that did not protect Luther Campbell and 2 Live Crew from the wrath of a white society determined to protect the imagined innocence of their teenagers.

In June 1988, a plainclothes police officer went into Take Home the Hits, an Alexander City, Alabama, record store, and requested a copy of *Move Somethin'*. He purchased it and returned thirty minutes later "with a detective and uniformed officers in tow," who arrested the store owner for selling pornography.

Campbell realized that 2 Live Crew was violating both societal and business taboos. He reflected that "Black-owned businesses were allowed to thrive in America as long as they stayed in their place," only catering to Black people. In Campbell's opinion, Berry Gordy and Motown were able to cross over to reach all of America "by making Motown and its acts squeaky-clean and as respectable as possible." In contrast, Hip Hop did not moderate Black culture but attracted a white audience in spite (or perhaps because) of it. That made it a threat to the status quo.

As Hip Hop began to broaden its popularity, major labels began to make deals to either acquire, or at a minimum distribute, the independent labels that specialized in Hip Hop. The involvement of major labels gave the societal arbiters of respectability ways to pressure artists if their music was deemed too violent or too explicit, such as by threatening the labels and their parent companies with boycotts or divestment, as happened with Ice-T's "Cop Killer."

Campbell was well aware of the increased scrutiny on Hip Hop in general, and 2 Live Crew in particular, and decided to defy the likes of the Moral Majority and Focus on the Family by making their next album, *As Nasty as They Wanna Be*, as explicit as possible. He assumed that as an independent, self-distributed label, he was immune from the usual pressure tactics that major labels exerted on their musicians. Campbell didn't imagine that his opponents, unable to use economic pressure, would resort to criminal law to silence him.

Crusading right-wing attorney Jack Thompson put a target on Luther Campbell's and 2 Live Crew's backs. Thompson was unabashed about his determination to "[drive the] Miami rap entrepreneur and his group, 2 Live Crew, out of business," as the *Los Angeles Times* reported; Thompson accused them of "peddling obscenity to children."

Thompson, the Coral Gables, Florida, attorney waging a one-man war on obscenity, had unsuccessfully campaigned to unseat Dade County attorney (and future US attorney general) Janet Reno in 1988. He was incensed that Campbell had recorded a song supporting Reno in that campaign. Luke was convinced that Thompson's anti-smut campaign against 2 Live Crew was just petty political retaliation.

Regardless of Thompson's motivation, he was successful in getting to Florida Governor Bob Martinez. Martinez tried to convince his attorney general to prosecute Campbell and 2 Live Crew under state Racketeer Influenced and Corrupt Organizations statutes, better known as RICO laws, that were typically used to prosecute mobsters and drug dealers. The attorney general demurred but sent information about the potential case to counties around the state to see if there were any takers. Broward County Sheriff Nick Navarro took the bait.

Navarro was as publicity-hungry as Jack Thompson and already had a taste of fame from his appearances on the show *Cops*. There was no question that the prosecution of a platinum-selling rap group would raise Navarro's profile. He swore out an affidavit, transcribed the album's lyrics, and prevailed on his motion requesting that the Broward County Circuit Court issue a finding of probable cause that the album was obscene.

Armed with that order, Navarro's deputies fanned out around the county, threatening record stores with prosecution if they sold *As Nasty as They Wanna Be*. Campbell hired noted First Amendment litigator Bruce Rogow to go on the offensive. Rogow filed a case against Navarro in federal court, alleging that the sheriff had engaged in an unconstitutional prior restraint in violation of the group's First Amendment rights, and seeking a declaration that the album *As Nasty as They Wanna Be* was not obscene.

Navarro's only evidence was the album itself, but the plaintiffs introduced three expert witnesses to testify about the album's artistic merit: Gregory Baker, a music journalist from Florida alternative newspaper *New Times*; John Leland, then a music critic at *New York Newsday*; and Carlton Long, a Rhodes scholar and Columbia University political science professor. Despite the imbalance in the evidence presented, the district court judge relied on his own assessment of community standards as a resident of Broward County and found that *As Nasty as They Wanna Be* was obscene.

As soon as the district court issued its ruling, seven other Florida counties commenced criminal obscenity proceedings against Campbell and 2 Live Crew. Campbell appealed to the U.S. Court of Appeals for the Eleventh Circuit, which reversed the lower court's decision. The circuit court held that the district court had misapplied the long-standing test for determining if a work is obscene, laid out in the 1973 Supreme Court case of *Miller v. California*. According to the Eleventh Circuit, the district court erred by failing to assess whether the work had any "serious artistic, scientific, literary, or political value." The appeals court further clarified that this "was not a question to be decided by contemporary community standards."

Unfortunately, victory in the obscenity case was not the end of 2 Live Crew's legal battles over their music. Surprisingly, their next dispute arose from a song on the non-explicit companion album *As Clean as They Wanna Be*. The album was designed to blunt criticism of *As Nasty as They Wanna Be* by simultaneously offering an alternative that was appropriate for minors. Little did Campbell and 2 Live Crew know that the album would give rise to a landmark case that would define an important aspect of copyright law for a generation to come.

One of the songs on that album, "Pretty Woman," used the same melody as the 1964 Roy Orbison hit "Oh Pretty Woman." 2 Live Crew had initially asked to license the song from Orbison's publisher, Acuff-Rose Music. When Acuff-Rose turned them down, 2 Live Crew decided to use it anyway, crediting Orbison and his cowriters. Acuff-Rose did not assert a claim against Campbell and 2 Live Crew when the album was released in early summer of 1989, but filed suit one year later, after the album had sold 250,000 units.

In response to the suit, Campbell and 2 Live Crew asserted that their song was legally permissible "fair use" and moved to have judgment granted in their favor. Fair use is a legally recognized exception to the exclusive rights granted to authors under the copyright law. The doctrine allows creators to incorporate copyrighted material into their new works without the permission of the copyright holder. Whether or not the use of copyrighted material in a new work is fair use depends on four factors that are enumerated in the statute (17 U.S. Code § 107):

1. The purpose and character of the use, including whether such use is of a commercial nature or is for nonprofit purposes;

2. The nature of the copyrighted work;

3. The amount and substantiality of the portion used in relation to the copyrighted work as a whole; and

4. The effect of the use upon the potential market for or value of the copyrighted work.

Fair use was, and remains, a fact-specific inquiry. Up until this case, it had rarely been successfully invoked by Hip Hop songwriters. In a musical genre *built* on the incorporation of preexisting works, this had not only financial but substantive implications. Third parties could deny permission, necessitating a departure from the creative direction that a Hip Hop artist intended, or, if denied late enough in the process, keep a song from hitting the market altogether.

The major labels that distributed much of Hip Hop were risk-averse and insisted on clearance of all samples interpolated in the

Hip Hop songs they released. Label executives knew that the wrong call on a question of fair use could expose their companies to costly lawsuits (and cost a label executive their job). Campbell, as the owner of an independent label, decided to take the risk.

Luther Campbell's argument was that 2 Live Crew's version of "Pretty Woman" was a parody that fit squarely within the parameters of fair use. The district court agreed and granted Campbell summary judgment, in effect ruling that there was no need for a trial and that Campbell was entitled to win as a matter of law. Acuff-Rose appealed to the US Court of Appeals for the Sixth Circuit, which reversed the district court. The appellate court reasoned that even though 2 Live Crew's song was a parody of the Orbison original, its "admittedly commercial nature" rendered the 2 Live Crew song presumptively unfair.

Then Campbell appealed to the United States Supreme Court, which reversed the Sixth Circuit's decision and used 2 Live Crew's raunchy (if not explicit) parody of Orbison's rock classic to explicate the proper framework for analyzing when a use of copyrighted material in a new work constitutes "fair use." Justice David Souter rejected the Sixth Circuit's contention that the commercial nature of "Pretty Woman" was dispositive. Souter said that a finding of fair use hinges on "whether and to what extent the new work is transformative." Importantly, Justice Souter stated that "whether a parody is in good taste or bad does not and should not matter to fair use."

Campbell v. Acuff-Rose Music marked the first time that the Supreme Court treated Hip Hop writers and performers as *artists* capable of creating nuanced and sophisticated work that commented on the copyrighted work that they sampled. Justice Souter described 2 Live Crew's song as a "comment on the naiveté of the original of an earlier day, as a rejection of its sentiment that ignores the ugliness of street life and the debasement that it signifies."

The importance of *Campbell* cannot be overstated. It was the high court's definitive statement on fair use in the copyright law, cited in literally hundreds of cases. While some legal commentators say it may have been limited by the Supreme Court's recent decision in *Andy Warhol Foundation for the Visual Arts, Inc. v. Goldsmith*, the court took pains to distinguish *Warhol*, which concerned two portraits of Prince used for the same commercial purpose, from *Campbell*, a parody case where the two songs were aimed at different audiences.

Campbell v. Acuff-Rose Music was the high-water mark for Campbell and 2 Live Crew. The following year, Campbell's label, Luke Records, was forced into bankruptcy. The cost of years of legal battles, along with some dubious maneuvering by his former lawyer, resulted in Campbell losing the rights to his master recordings to his former lawyer. By the end of the bankruptcy proceeding, all that he retained from his empire was his home, his parents' home, his office in downtown Miami, his label name, and a Supreme Court victory that protects parodists to this day.

After some modestly successful solo albums and a foray into adult films, Luther Campbell retired from the entertainment business, turning his attention to coaching and sponsoring youth football in his beloved Liberty City neighborhood and even running for mayor of Miami in 2011. Still, his legacy as a fighter for the First Amendment rights of Hip Hop artists lives on.

Hip Hop today is the dominant musical genre, a multibillion-dollar business that is unmistakably and unapologetically Black. It influences youth culture globally, and many current Hip Hop artists follow the templates established by Sylvia Robinson and Luther

Campbell, learning from their mistakes to build successful companies that own or control their intellectual property and profit directly from the brands that they build. Technological advances in the first quarter of the twenty-first century have challenged those models, draining music IP of much of its value and making it tougher for an artist to build a brand that can be leveraged. Hip Hop has forced America to confront the reality and the complexity of the lives of people in the neighborhoods they bypass on the interstate. Hip Hop's most important contribution to the culture was to simply insist on the humanity of *all* Black people.

NINE

SPIKE TO OPRAH TO TYLER: REMAKING BLACK IMAGES THROUGH THE POWER OF OWNERSHIP

New York City summers have always been sticky and stinky. With eight million people crammed into just over three hundred square miles, how could they not be? New Yorkers have long been accustomed to the heat and smells of summers in the city, of the asphalt softened by day after day of ninety-degree temperatures, of the acrid, heat-heightened urine and sweat smells lurking in every alleyway and stairwell. With over two million people commuting by subway every day, New Yorkers have become adept at the delicate dance of standing just close enough to the edge of the subway platform to push their way into the next crowded subway car, but not so close that they risk being shoved onto the tracks by the horde of impatient commuters at their backs.

During the summer of 1977, all of that was accompanied by an overarching sense of dread. Two years after the city's near-default, New York was in crisis. As PBS's *American Experience* described the city in "The Night New York's Lights Went Out," austerity had forced "dramatic cuts in social services—including hospital and library closures and massive layoffs of firefighters, police, public school teachers, and sanitation workers." Crime had exploded over the preceding decade. The murder rate had doubled, burglaries had tripled, and the robbery rate had increased tenfold. New Yorkers were increasingly reckoning with escalating deprivation and violence.

The fear that permeated the city that summer, though, was largely due to the threat posed by a serial killer targeting young white women in the outer boroughs. The murderer, who dubbed himself Son of Sam, had evaded capture for a year, despite a killing spree that had left six people dead and seven injured. Son of Sam taunted law enforcement by leaving "rambling handwritten notes near the bodies of his victims," and in June 1977, he escalated his perverse PR campaign by sending a four-page letter to famed *New York Daily News* columnist Jimmy Breslin.

The city may have been grimy and broken in the summer of 1977, yet Black and Brown New Yorkers were not. An ever-resourceful bunch, they took wrenches and pried fire hydrants open, unleashing ice-cold geysers to relieve delighted children and teenagers. They turned their blocks into youth centers, with DJs jacking electricity from streetlights to power outdoor parties. The financially strapped city had no resources for summer youth employment, so one enterprising college student named Spike Lee decided to take the Super 8 camera he had been gifted out into the New York City streets, filming the dancers doing the hustle at those block parties. When he returned to Morehouse College that fall as a junior, Lee declared mass communications as his major and cut his footage into a short film he dubbed *Last Hustle in Brooklyn*.

Choosing a career as a filmmaker in 1977 as a Black American was a pure expression of faith, defined as hope over experience. By the late 1970s, the Blaxploitation boom was petering out. Black audiences had grown tired of being fed the same tropes over and over again—Black superstuds battling the Mob or the Man while bedding a bevy of beautiful women. These weren't the films that inspired Spike Lee. He had been "weaned on, not just art, but purer forms of art" by his schoolteacher mother and jazz musician father.

On the other side of the country during the 1970s, a group of young film students looked to Blaxploitation as an example of what *not* to do. The Black film movement that came to be known as the "LA Rebellion" was a direct outgrowth of the Civil Rights Movement and the Watts Rebellion. According to the editors of *L.A. Rebellion: Creating a New Black Cinema*, the comprehensive book about this cinematic movement, the social upheaval of the time prodded elite institutions like UCLA to "create opportunities for increasing numbers of Black students . . . while also providing a critical framework for social critique." From the late 1960s to the mid-1980s, a group of Black students studied film at UCLA under the tutelage of Elyseo Taylor, a Black filmmaker and the first African American faculty member at the UCLA School of Theater, Film and Television, and Teshome Gabriel, an Ethiopian-born cinema scholar who replaced Taylor after he was denied tenure. As critic Clyde Taylor noted, they envisioned creating an independent Black cinema that featured humanistic portrayals of "Black people in full flight as beings-for-themselves instead of fantasy beings for others."

Yet those Black filmmakers faced the same obstacles that had confronted earlier generations of Black filmmakers. As film professor Chuck Kleinhans observed, film is an "industrial art form" that requires expensive equipment and a legion of skilled performers and craftspeople to produce. Those "economic realities were bracketed" in film school, where the equipment was provided and fellow students could crew for one another for free.

Once these UCLA film students completed their films, they ran headlong into the indifference of a mainstream film industry that had little interest in films depicting 360 degrees of Black humanity. It didn't help that their films had more in common with European neorealism and rejected the "assimilationism" of earlier Black films. Although the Black film students at UCLA were making films for a Black audience, during the 1970s, they had difficulty convincing the gatekeepers that there was a Black audience for their films. One notable exception was filmmaker Jamaa Fanaka, whose more consciously commercial features—*Welcome Home Brother Charles*, *Emma Mae*, and *Penitentiary*—were all released theatrically during the 1970s.

The Black students at UCLA during this period included luminaries like Charles Burnett, Julie Dash, and Haile Gerima, but the group dubbed the "LA Rebellion" by film critic Clyde Taylor numbered fifty filmmakers "who were involved in over 100 films." Despite their prodigious output, as noted by the editors of *L.A. Rebellion*, "of the first seventy-three films and videos identified as LA Rebellion titles . . . only twenty-eight (39 percent) have ever been in distribution."

Back on the East Coast, aspiring filmmaker Spike Lee was blissfully unaware of these dismal percentages, but he was hardly naive about the entrenched racism of the film industry. Unlike UCLA, NYU had not instituted any program to increase the ranks of filmmakers of color, despite being smack in the middle of the most diverse city in the country. When Spike Lee and cinematographer Ernest Dickerson matriculated in NYU's MFA film program in 1979, they were the only Black students in their class.

Lee got an early taste of how institutionalized and unthinking the racism in the film business was during his time as a graduate student at NYU. He received negative feedback for his student film *The Answer*, which centered on a Black writer hired to direct a fifty-million-dollar remake of *The Birth of a Nation*. Lee doesn't specify, but apparently the august arbiters of "cinema" on the NYU faculty at the time could not abide any takedown of the film that they and other white cinephiles had uncritically dubbed a masterpiece, rather than an artful piece of virulently anti-Black propaganda.

Undeterred by the narrow-minded reaction to his critique of a cinema "classic," Spike Lee went on to win the Student Academy Award in 1983 for his thesis film, *Joe's Bed-Stuy Barbershop: We Cut Heads*, which featured his classmates Ernest Dickerson as director of photography and Ang Lee as assistant director.

Armed with an MFA from one of the most prestigious film schools in the country and a Student Academy Award, Lee set out to write and direct his first feature. But the film industry of the early 1980s was an inhospitable place for a Black independent filmmaker.

The era of gritty urban dramas like *The French Connection* and *Taxi Driver* had largely passed, and the wave of Blaxploitation films had crested in the late 1970s. In their place were high-concept comedies like *Trading Places* and *Risky Business*, musicals like *Flashdance* and the *Saturday Night Fever* sequel *Staying Alive*, and sci-fi like *Return of the Jedi*, the third installment of the *Star Wars* franchise.

In 1984, Spike began preproduction for his first feature after graduation, titled *The Messenger*, based on his original screenplay. The planned film centered on a bike messenger who becomes the head of his household after his mother's unexpected death from a heart attack. Spike had assembled a crew and lined up Giancarlo Esposito and Laurence Fishburne to star. As Courtland Milloy recounted in *The Washington Post*, on the eve of production, Lee "learned that there was no money for the project" and had to "pull the plug."

Although Spike was devastated at the time, in hindsight he says that it was a "godsend that the film didn't get made," because the scope of the film, with stunts and car chases, was more than he was equipped to handle at the time. The project ended up losing about $50,000, but rather than give up, Lee realized that he needed to reduce the scale of his next film to "three-four people in a room."

In October 1984, three months after *The Messenger* fell apart, Spike came up with the title and the premise for his next film. *She's Gotta Have It* would feature a female main character and would explore the double standard about how women who enjoy sex are judged. Lee gave himself two months to research his subject matter, working with some women friends to devise a twenty-plus-question survey on women's attitudes about sex to inform the characterization of his heroine, Nola Darling. After finishing his research in the fall, Lee completed his script at the end of December 1984, with the goal of shooting in the summer of 1985.

As a writer/director making an independent film, Lee was in the position to own 100 percent of the film's copyright if it was made outside of the studio system. He also stood to reap a significant upside if he could get it distributed theatrically on a meaningful number of screens around the country. Initially, he planned to finance a significant portion of his low-six-figure budget through grants from entities like the National Endowment for the Arts (NEA), the American Film Institute (AFI), and the Jerome Foundation. As Lee went from preparation to preproduction, he quickly realized that he would have to supplement any grants he received with significant investments from individual investors. After being disappointed by *The Messenger* producer's failure to raise the requisite financing, Lee was unwilling to delegate the fundraising task and took it upon himself.

From the vantage point of his incredible four-decade career, it is tempting to assume that fundraising was easy, but Lee's contemporaneous journal makes clear it was anything but. His electricity and his phone were nearly cut off several times, and he was constantly cutting deals with vendors like film labs and equipment rental houses to ensure that production and postproduction were not delayed. Once *She's Gotta Have It* was completed at the end of 1985, Lee began screening it for distributors with the help of producer's representative and independent film champion John Pierson.

In the mid-1980s, before they became specialty wings of major studios, several independent companies existed that were in the business of distributing modestly budgeted independent films. Spike screened *She's Gotta Have It* for three such companies—Samuel Goldwyn Films, Island Pictures, and Circle Films—ultimately entering into a distribution deal with Island.

The film had its world premiere at the San Francisco International Film Festival on March 28, 1986, an eventful screening that was disrupted by a forty-minute blackout. Two months later, *She's*

Gotta Have It had its international premiere during the Directors' Fortnight section of the Cannes Film Festival.

The white critics at Cannes gave voice to conventional wisdom and doubted "that [*She's Gotta Have It*] had much of a future outside the relatively confined world of arts festivals and private screenings," which reflected their insular ignorance. Spike knew there was a "vast [B]lack audience out there that's been longing, craving, for an intelligent [B]lack film," and when *She's Gotta Have It* opened theatrically on August 8, 1986, showings were met by long lines of young Black people eager to see themselves reflected onscreen. Spike's modestly budgeted debut feature film—financed by folks like his grandmother Zimmie Shelton, Nelson George, and John Pierson, among others— went on to gross $7 million at the domestic box office. *She's Gotta Have It* ignited a new Black film movement, and as Nelson George correctly observed, the film threw "down a gauntlet at those Black filmmakers awaiting the blessings of cinema's great white fathers."

The next year, actor turned writer/director Robert Townsend picked up that gauntlet and maxed out his credit cards to cowrite, direct, produce, and star in *Hollywood Shuffle*. The Chicago-born-and-raised Townsend had his film debut in a small role in the 1975 classic Black film *Cooley High*, directed by Michael Schultz, which Townsend said had "changed [his] life" by showing him that films created by Black people could "paint with that brush of truly being human."

In the twelve years since *Cooley High*, Townsend had grown increasingly frustrated by the stereotypical, one-dimensional roles offered to Black actors in Hollywood. Townsend decided to take matters into his own hands and satirize Hollywood's myopic view of Black people. He cowrote the *Hollywood Shuffle* script with Keenen Ivory Wayans and made the film on a mere $100,000 budget. Samuel

Goldwyn acquired distribution rights, and the film went on to gross $5.2 million in domestic box office receipts.

In the film business, people often say that one is an outlier and two is a trend. The back-to-back successes of *She's Gotta Have It* and *Hollywood Shuffle* could not be ignored, even by studio executives indifferent or even hostile to the idea of presenting multifaceted images of Black people onscreen. Those two films proved once again that there was money to be made in films that showed the authentic lives and perspectives of Black people, particularly when made for a fraction of the budget of the average Hollywood film. Studios began tentatively pursuing Black filmmakers in the hopes of snapping up unique Black stories and collecting the more than ten-to-one return on investment of those two films.

The increase in Black films in the marketplace was gradual. Spike Lee's sophomore feature, *School Daze*, a musical set during homecoming at a fictional historically Black college, was released in 1988. Spike's blistering and brilliant *Do the Right Thing* was released in 1989. The rollicking 1990 teen comedy *House Party*, written and directed by Reginald Hudlin and produced by his brother Warrington Hudlin, earned $26 million at the box office on a $2.5 million budget.

But 1991 was the apex for Black film. That year, the studios released a bumper crop of films helmed by Black directors, including Julie Dash's *Daughters of the Dust*, the first feature directed by a Black woman to receive a theatrical release. The phenomenon was so pronounced that it led to a *New York Times Magazine* cover story titled "They've Gotta Have Us." The common thread uniting films as disparate as Spike Lee's *Jungle Fever*, Dash's *Daughters of the Dust*, Matty Rich's *Straight Out of Brooklyn*, and John Singleton's runaway hit debut feature *Boyz n the Hood* is that all the films were based on original screenplays these Black directors wrote.

These filmmakers gained much-needed leverage in the asymmetrical negotiation with distributors by independently developing their original intellectual property. Instead of pitching to rooms full of people with no knowledge or understanding of Black life in the hopes of securing screenwriting fees at an early stage, they were able to force distributors to say yes or no to the films as written, with them as directors to oversee the vision. Rather than risk being strung along in a lengthy development process, taking notes from executives who might water down their script to make it palatable to the mythical "mainstream audience"—or worse still, forfeit ownership of their original ideas without being able to make a film—these pioneers invested in themselves.

Twenty Black-themed films were released in the United States in 1991, out of a total of 140 theatrical releases, representing approximately 14 percent of all US films released that year. The next year saw a dramatic drop, with only ten films released domestically in 1992 that were either written or directed by a Black filmmaker. Of those ten, only two—Ernest Dickerson's *Juice* (cowritten with Black screenwriter Gerard Brown) and Spike Lee's *Malcolm X*—were also the product of a writer-director.

The long road to making *Malcolm X* was paved with many of the obstacles that had long bedeviled Black film. From the moment that *The Autobiography of Malcolm X* was published posthumously in October 1965, a mere eight months after Malcolm X was tragically assassinated in the Audubon Ballroom, Hollywood had been trying to adapt Malcolm's powerful story for the screen.

Producer Marvin Worth had acquired the rights to the autobiography shortly after Malcolm's death. For years, Worth tried without success to develop a feature script that would be both true to Malcolm's legacy and palatable to a Hollywood studio. Worth had produced an Oscar-nominated documentary about Malcolm X, but he went through several feature scripts that never got made. By 1990, Worth had lined up Warner Bros. to distribute a feature film and was in talks with Denzel Washington to star and Norman Jewison to direct.

When word got out that a white director was in talks to tackle the life story of one of Black America's most revered leaders, Black people raised an outcry. Worth pivoted to Spike Lee, who had not been shy about his interest in directing the film.

Once Lee was attached, Warner Bros. balked at committing to the budget Lee's vision of the film required. Lee observed that, like other studios at the time, Warner Bros. believed that "white moviegoers here in America [were] not interested in films with Black subject matter." The studio's conviction that Black films only appealed to Black audiences imposed a ceiling on the amount of money they were willing to spend.

Thus, although the film was budgeted at $31–33 million, Warner Bros. refused to commit more than $18–20 million. They agreed to acquire only domestic distribution rights so that the producers could leverage foreign distribution rights for additional money. Producer Lawrence Gordon's Largo Entertainment acquired foreign distribution rights for $8 million, giving Spike a total budget of $26 million—$5 million less than the $31 million Lee considered the bare minimum necessary to realize his vision.

Spike entered into a negative pickup deal with Warner Bros., a financing arrangement where the studio purchases the movie from an independent producer for a fixed price at the end of production and does not face financial risk until then. Then the producer and the studio split net profits. Filmmakers typically secure a bank loan in the amount of the negative pickup price, and the studio and bank risk is insured by a completion guarantor, who agrees to step in and deliver a completed film to the studio if the director goes over budget or over schedule by a certain amount. On *Malcolm X*, the Completion Bond Company, founded in 1981 by a Black woman named Bette L. Smith, bonded the picture. As coproducer Preston Holmes observed, with a bond in place, Warner Bros. was "in a no-lose situation," since they didn't have to give Lee the additional financing that his script required but could simply sit back and watch the bond company either pay the overages or be the villain who wrested *Malcolm X* from Spike Lee.

Warner Bros. probably thought that Spike would cave and cut the budget; they assumed he would compromise and film the Mecca sequences in the Arizona desert. But they underestimated Lee's determination to give Malcolm X's life the epic treatment it deserved. Lee didn't budge, and neither did Warner Bros., leaving Completion Bond in a difficult position. Things came to a head when Lee returned from the 1992 Cannes Film Festival. *Malcolm X* was $5 million over budget, and neither Warner Bros. nor Completion Bond were willing to spend another dime.

Harkening back to his first film, Spike Lee turned to the Black community. With foreign and domestic distribution rights spoken for, Spike had nothing to offer investors. But he was no longer a struggling new film-school grad trying to keep the lights on. He was *Spike Lee*, and so was able to turn to a network of Black celebrities and philanthropists.

Spike stressed the importance of having Malcolm X's story told the *right way* on the big screen by a Black filmmaker. Explaining that he had already invested two-thirds of his fee into the film, Spike asked his friends and colleagues to make up the shortfall as a gift to the community, not an investment. In the end, Oprah Winfrey, Michael Jordan, Janet Jackson, Prince, Tracy Chapman, Bill Cosby, Magic Johnson, and philanthropist Peggy Cooper Cafritz contributed to covering the overage. *Malcolm X* opened in theaters on November 18, 1992. As Spike Lee said, "[W]e as a people have . . . to start coming up with financing." *Malcolm X* marked the second time he proved that we could.

By 1995, the wave of Black directors had receded. That was the year that much of America spent mesmerized by the spectacle of the double murder trial of football star turned actor and commercial pitchman O. J. Simpson. The trial began in January 1995 and continued into October. It is hard to fathom how much the televised trial consumed pop culture. The trial lawyers became household names, from prosecutors Marcia Clark and Christopher Darden to the defense lawyers: Johnnie Cochran, the legendary F. Lee Bailey, and the man who literally spawned the Kardashians, Robert Kardashian. *The Tonight Show with Jay Leno* had a recurring comedy segment called "The Dancing Itos," parodying presiding Judge Lance Ito.

While O.J. was awaiting his fate, former heavyweight champion Mike Tyson was finishing a three-year prison sentence after being convicted of raping an eighteen-year-old beauty pageant contestant. The year 1995 was when Republicans, having swept the 1994 midterms, began enacting their "Contract with America," a legislative agenda of draconian budget cuts primarily targeted to gut social safety-net programs that many Black Americans relied on.

In response to the one-two punch of the fall from grace of two high-profile Black men and a national political movement focused on scapegoating and punishing Black people, Nation of Islam leader Louis Farrakhan and former head of the NAACP Benjamin Chavis conceived of and organized the Million Man March. The march summoned Black men to convene on the National Mall in Washington, DC, on October 16, 1995, and pledge to "support their families, refrain from abusive behavior toward women and children . . . renounce violence except in self-defense," and commit to building up Black businesses and institutions.

The march was criticized for being patriarchal and excluding women. It was criticized because it was the brainchild of Minister Farrakhan, the notoriously anti-Semitic and homophobic head of the Nation of Islam. Yet there was no question that it was impactful. March leaders recruited a wide array of Black male civil rights and faith leaders to serve on the organizing committee. Speakers at the march included Rev. Jesse Jackson, Maya Angelou, Martin Luther King III, and Rosa Parks. In the end, the National Park Service estimated that 870,000 Black men heeded the call and came to the march.

In 1996, on the one-year anniversary of the Million Man March, the next Spike Lee Joint landed on 1,207 theater screens. *Get on the Bus*, written by Reggie Rock Bythewood and directed by Spike Lee, chronicled the fictional journey of a busload of Black men traveling from South Central LA to Washington, DC, for the Million Man March. The film's stars included Ossie Davis, Andre Braugher, Hill Harper, Harry Lennix, Bernie Mac, and Wendell Pierce.

Get on the Bus didn't merely dramatize the historic Million Man March; it embodied its principles in the way it was produced and financed. Reuben Cannon and his fellow producers struck a negative pickup deal with Columbia Pictures to acquire rights to the film for its budget of $2.4 million, contingent on the producers independently raising the financing from investors. Cannon's pitch to potential investors, all wealthy Black men, was: "If we are ever to be truly free and become a factor in this world, we must make a commitment to efforts like this."

Cannon successfully got fifteen Black men to invest either $100,000 or $200,000 to finance the film's production. Robert Guillaume, Danny Glover, Will Smith, Johnnie Cochran, Wesley Snipes, and Black Entertainment Television (BET) founder Robert L. Johnson were among the fifteen, which also included producer Cannon, writer Bythewood, and director Lee. Cannon crowed that the investors all recouped 100 percent of their original investment, together with 8 percent interest, "before one reel [of film] was shipped to theaters." He called *Get on the Bus* "a blueprint for how to make a movie," and nine years later Cannon had a front-row seat as a producer when another filmmaker used that blueprint to build a film and television empire.

In 2005, Tyler Perry was a playwright on the twenty-first-century chitlin circuit, producing plays for Black audiences in venues like Newark Symphony Hall in New Jersey or New York City's Beacon Theatre. His shows were tremendously popular in the Black community and virtually unknown outside of it. The recurring character of Madea was a major reason for the appeal of Perry's plays, and he built his audience by selling DVDs of his shows on his website.

When Perry decided to move into filmmaking, he chose to adapt his play *Diary of a Mad Black Woman* for the screen. The first studio executives that Perry approached didn't understand the play's success. They made comments like "Black people who go to church don't go to the movies" and tried to suggest script changes to make the film more palatable to white audiences. Perry refused to pander to the ignorance of studio executives or their idea of the "mainstream audience." He approached Lionsgate Studios head Jon Feltheimer with a novel proposal: Perry would finance 50 percent of the budget, retain the copyright in the film, and receive 50 percent of the profits. Lionsgate would be entitled to recoup its marketing costs and a 12.5 percent distribution fee (less than half of the customary 35 percent distribution fee that studios charge). When *Diary of a Mad Black Woman* opened on February 25, 2005, it went on to gross $50,633,099 at the domestic box office and became the first of a string of eleven lucrative "Madea" movies that Perry produced with Lionsgate over fourteen years.

Film was only the initial salvo in Perry's battle for Hollywood dominance. From sneaking into the National Association of Television Program Executives (NATPE) meetings when he worked at the host hotel for the NATPE conference, Perry learned that the magic formula for creating wealth in the television business was (1) to have a loyal audience; (2) to have a willing distributor; and (3) to produce one hundred episodes of a series. Perry made that his target. He shot ten episodes of his original television series *House of Payne* on his own dime and licensed them to the fledgling CW Network in 2006. TBS saw its success and offered Perry $200 million for the right to air the remaining ninety episodes of *House of Payne* in first-run syndication.

Perry parlayed his keen understanding of his Black audience and his refusal to cede ownership of his intellectual property into a billion-dollar fortune that allowed him to buy a 330-acre former Confederate and US military base, Fort McPherson, and turn it into a state-of-the-art studio complex that is larger than the Warner Bros. studio lot. In film, Perry was building on the foundation laid by Oscar

Micheaux and Spike Lee. In his television deals, Perry was leveraging the business model pioneered by a Cuban-born immigrant and his American wife, Desi Arnaz and Lucille Ball, and deployed with dizzying success by his mentor, Black billionaire Oprah Winfrey.

When *The Oprah Winfrey Show* had its nationwide debut on September 8, 1986, about one month after *She's Gotta Have It* opened in theaters, there was no reason to believe that Oprah Winfrey would become a billionaire and arbiter of culture, rather than just a successful talk show host.

In 1984, Winfrey was recruited from Baltimore to Chicago to host a thirty-minute local morning show called *AM Chicago*. Shortly after Oprah's arrival, it was expanded to an hour, and within months had become the #1 talk show in Chicago, displacing Phil Donahue.

Oprah Winfrey could have been content to continue in the mold of a traditional talk show host: highly paid, respected, with the power to shape the national conversation through the topics and guests on her show. Oprah certainly did that at a level not seen before, but she also became much more. She became a shaper of culture through the films, television series, and stage plays her production company, Harpo Studios, produced while building wealth that made her a billionaire.

Just before *The Oprah Winfrey Show* was slated to go national, she made a crucial decision that set her on the path to outsized influence and wealth. Oprah was torn between signing with ABC, which could pay to produce the show and keep it on the air while it found its footing, or signing with a syndication company, King World Productions, which would allow her to own the show but might yank her off the air in three months if her ratings were poor.

While she was wrestling with this decision, Oprah had a fateful conversation with film critic Roger Ebert, cohost of the weekly syndicated show *Siskel & Ebert At the Movies*. The two were discussing her choice over dinner, and Ebert urged her to take the risk and enter a deal with King World that would allow her to own her show.

To illustrate, Ebert took out a pen, grabbed a napkin, and wrote a figure down, representing what he made each week from *Siskel & Ebert At the Movies*. He told Oprah to double that, because he and Gene Siskel made the same amount. Ebert then told her to multiply that number by five, since her show aired five days a week. Lastly, he told Oprah to multiply the number by two, to account for what he was certain would be Oprah's higher ratings. According to Ebert, Oprah looked at the math for "ten seconds" and decided to sign with King World.

Thanks to that timely illustration of the economics of intellectual property ownership in television, Oprah signed the syndication contract, and King World remained the syndication company for the show from its national debut in 1986 through its acquisition by Viacom in 1999, until the show went off the air in 2011. Ownership of the show allowed Oprah to maximize her revenue and build her production company. Ownership allowed Oprah to leverage her fame to bring a wide array of Black stories to the screen, from *The Wedding*, a 1998 television movie based on the novel by Harlem Renaissance writer Dorothy West, to *Their Eyes Were Watching God*, a 2005 television movie based on Zora Neale Hurston's novel. Harpo was one of the production companies behind *When They See Us*, the harrowing docudrama about the Exonerated Five, and the documentary series *The 1619 Project*, ensuring that the history in Nikole Hannah-Jones's anthology of the same name reached an audience beyond readers of *The New York Times*.

It is important to understand that Oprah's deal with King World occurred toward the end of a period that provided a particularly favorable legal and technological environment for the business of television syndication. From 1971 to 1995, broadcast television was governed by a pair of Federal Communications Commission (FCC) rules: the Financial Interest Syndication Rule, known as the fin-syn rule, and the Prime Time Access Rule, specifically enacted to curtail the power of the Big Three broadcasters at the time: ABC, CBS, and NBC.

Regulators at the FCC began a study of the Big Three networks in 1959, out of concern that vertical integration in the television industry was choking competition and limiting the diversity of programming available to viewers. By 1968, the Big Three had profit shares in 60 percent of the programs that they licensed. The FCC study concluded that networks had used their monopsony power to obtain a financial interest in programs that they licensed and to deny exhibition for programs where the producer insisted upon retaining all syndication and merchandising rights and the profits from those rights.

In response, the FCC promulgated a pair of rules designed to curtail the television networks' abuse of their power. The fin-syn and Prime Time Access rules became effective on September 1, 1971. The fin-syn rule prohibited networks from (1) obtaining syndication rights or profit shares in any program not produced by them and (2) domestically syndicating or "retaining profit shares from domestic syndication" of any program they produced.

The Prime Time Access Rule was designed to create space in the schedule for non-network-controlled programming by limiting network affiliate stations in the top fifty US markets to no more than three hours of programming between 7 and 11 p.m. (6 to 10 p.m. in the Central Time Zone). The stated goal of the rules was to increase program diversity and competition in the television industry.

The fin-syn and Prime Time Access rules governed the television industry for nearly a quarter century, despite staunch and persistent opposition from the television networks, making it possible for a few lucky and tenacious independent producers to build fortunes. The rules withstood an early legal challenge in *Mt. Mansfield Television, Inc. v. FCC.* Despite that loss, the networks continued to push the FCC for repeal of the rule. They nearly succeeded in 1983, but thanks to lobbying by powerful independent Hollywood producers, actor-turned-president Ronald Reagan kept the rules—a rare instance of his administration being *in favor* of government regulation.

One early beneficiary of the new rule was local Chicago DJ and television newsman Don Cornelius. Cornelius, born on the South Side of Chicago in 1936, had a lifelong interest in a career in broadcasting. After high school, he served in the marines during the Korean War and then took a job selling insurance to support his young family. In 1966, Cornelius took a three-day broadcasting course, which led to work as a part-time DJ at Chicago radio station WVON, as well as work as a sports anchor on a local TV program targeting a Black audience.

In 1970, Don Cornelius took $400 of his own money and shot a pilot for a music program patterned after the show he had been producing for local high schools. The series, which he called *Soul Train,* was similar in format to the popular *American Bandstand,* except that *Soul Train* showcased Black music exclusively, and the audience and dancers were all young Black people. *Soul Train* debuted on a local Chicago station in 1970. One year later, Cornelius moved the show to LA and started the process of syndicating it, just as the fin-syn rules were going into effect.

It was a tough slog to get stations interested in carrying such an unapologetically Black program, but Cornelius was able to get Johnson Products Company, the maker of the Afro Sheen and Ultra Sheen lines of Black haircare products, to sign on as a major sponsor, marking the first time that a Black-owned company sponsored a national television program. Over time, Cornelius attracted sponsors like Coca-Cola and McDonald's, eventually partnering with Tribune Entertainment for syndication in the 1980s.

Soul Train became Saturday-morning viewing for generations of Black and white teenagers who eagerly tuned in to see their favorite Black artists and learn the coolest dance moves on what Cornelius dubbed the "hippest trip in America." *Soul Train* became one of the longest-running syndicated shows on television, with an impressive thirty-five-year run from 1971 to 2006. As Kenny Gamble, one half of Gamble and Huff, the duo credited with creating the Philly soul sound, said, "*Soul Train* created an outlet for [B]lack artists that never would have been if it hadn't been for Cornelius."

Don Cornelius's cultural impact was undeniable, but his impact among Black businesspeople was just as profound. As a business dominated by the Big Three networks and major advertisers, television was particularly impenetrable for Black producers. Cornelius was a trailblazer who proved there was a profitable audience for Black culture, and that the money existed *within the Black community* to support it on a national scale. NPR stated, "*Soul Train* was the *first* Black-owned, nationally syndicated TV franchise" (emphasis added), making Don Cornelius "the television analogue to [B]lack . . . business entrepreneurs like Berry Gordy and the precursor to . . . mogul Bob Johnson."

Arguably, there is a direct line from Don Cornelius to Oprah Winfrey. Both started with local shows in Chicago that went on to national syndicated success. *Soul Train* demonstrated that there was an audience for unapologetically Black culture. Oprah, of course, did not position herself as an arbiter of Black culture, but through her show she redefined the mainstream to include Black culture. This was most evident with Oprah's Book Club, which, by leveraging Oprah's personal brand to mint bestselling authors, single-handedly changed the publishing business.

When Oprah chose *Song of Solomon* as her second book club pick in 1996, Toni Morrison was already a Nobel Prize–winning tenured professor at Princeton University. Oprah's imprimatur turned a literary superstar into a *commercial* superstar, propelling the dense, lyrical *Song of Solomon* to the bestseller list nineteen years after its initial publication, constituting what scholar John Young called a "dramatic example of the merger between canonicity and commercialism."

Both Don Cornelius and Oprah Winfrey offer pointed examples of how Black people use the *power* conferred by intellectual property ownership. In our capitalist society, those with a foundational understanding of intellectual property law understand that ownership of intellectual property rights is a vehicle for building wealth. For Black creators, it is even more. It is a way to create space in the culture for other Black creators, both to show that there is a powerful Black audience and to prove the appeal of Black art to white audiences.

Oprah wielded her power not only to introduce mainstream white audiences to Toni Morrison, Maya Angelou, Pearl Cleage, and Edwidge Danticat but to give another Black television producer the tools, and later the platform, to help him become a billionaire.

Tyler Perry first appeared on *The Oprah Winfrey Show* in 2001, four years before the film adaptation of his play *Diary of a Mad Black Woman* introduced film audiences to Madea. According to Perry,

Oprah "offered [him] a secret . . . the importance of 'writing your own checks' and being fully in control."

Perry took that advice to heart when he entered into a deal with TBS for *House of Payne* in 2006. Perry structured the deals for his subsequent series in a similar fashion, building a library of intellectual property that included more than "1,200 episodes of television by 2020."

Unfortunately, the window for any television producer, let alone a Black one, was already closing by the time Tyler Perry made his TBS deal. Technological advances that enabled the digitization of music had already upended the music business, with Napster in 1999 and iTunes in 2001. In 2006, neither networks nor television producers fully understood how a pivot to streaming in 2008 by a plucky mail-order DVD rental business named Netflix would remake the entire film and television business.

TEN

NOT LIKE US:
WHEN THE BOTS TAKE OVER

The biggest pop music phenomenon of 2024 was the monster hit "Not Like Us," Kendrick Lamar's death blow in his escalating musical beef with Drake that had transfixed fans of both artists since April of that year. The long-simmering conflict actually began more than a decade before, starting with Kendrick's verse on Big Sean's 2013 hit "Control," where Kendrick called out twelve rappers by name, including Drake. Drake responded with coded barbs in his September 2013 track "The Language," which many Hip Hop heads interpreted as aimed at Kendrick.

The two traded subtle and not-so-subtle jabs over the next decade, all while cementing their positions at the pinnacle of Hip Hop. Kendrick favored socially conscious and introspective lyrics and in 2018 won a Pulitzer Prize for his 2017 album, *Damn*, securing his stature as every Blerd's favorite rapper. Drake, meanwhile, scaled the heights of pop stardom, breaking *Billboard* records for the most top-ten Billboard Hot 100 hits, while being named #1 on that same magazine's Top R&B/Hip-Hop Artists of the 21st Century list.

The escalation of the competition between the two began innocuously enough: with a J. Cole line on Drake's October 2023 song "First Person Shooter." In it, J. Cole raps about the "big three" in Hip Hop, whom Cole identifies as Drake, Kendrick, and himself. In March 2024, Kendrick shot back on a song with Future and Metro Boomin, "Like That," spitting with controlled fury, "Motherf—k the big three, n—ga, it's just big me."

From that point, it was on. On April 5, 2024, J. Cole released a diss track called "7 Minute Drill," only to quickly pull it and issue a public apology. Perhaps J. Cole realized that there was little upside in picking a fight with a Pulitzer Prize winner.

Drake had no such reservations. On April 13, 2024, Drake released "Push Ups," a scathing track that lampooned Kendrick's height; implied that Kendrick was being exploited by his label, Top Dawg Entertainment (TDE); and stated that there were many artists who were more successful than Kendrick. Six days later, Drake dropped another song, "Taylor Made Freestyle," mocking Kendrick's collaboration with Taylor Swift. Drake made the mistake of incorporating an AI-generated sample by Tupac Shakur in the song and immediately received a cease-and-desist letter from the Shakur estate, forcing Drake to pull the track.

Just under two weeks later, on April 30, 2024, Kendrick entered the fray again with "Euphoria"—using a deceptively smooth intro, courtesy of a sample of the Teddy Pendergrass ballad "You're My Latest, My Greatest Inspiration"—to call Drake a "habitual liar" and "a lame" who lacked a commitment to fatherhood. Four days later, Kendrick dropped another diss track, "6:16 in LA." Drake responded immediately with "Family Matters," the harshest entry in the battle up to that point. Drake's lyrics accused Kendrick of infidelity and spousal abuse and suggested that producer (and former TDE co-head) Dave Free was actually the father of one of Kendrick's children.

One day later, on May 4, 2024, Kendrick released two diss tracks. "Meet the Grahams" went through every member of Drake's family and included an accusation that Drake had a secret daughter he had not acknowledged. But it was "Not Like Us," rapped over a catchy beat by DJ Mustard, that was the nail in the coffin. In four minutes and thirty-three seconds, Kendrick adroitly destroyed Drake's reputation—accusing him of being a pedophile and contextualizing Drake's pop stardom as the product of a person not from the culture who worked solely to profit from it. In Kendrick's eyes, Drake's worst sin was that he "was not a colleague, but a f—kin' colonizer."

After the release of "Not Like Us," there was no question who had won the battle. Kendrick followed up the release with a Juneteenth concert in LA attended by LeBron James, Russell Westbrook, Ayo Edebiri, and LaKeith Stanfield, where the crowd sang along as Kendrick performed the song five times in a row. As of this writing, "Not Like Us," which won 2025 Grammys for Record of the Year and Song of the Year (along with Grammys for Best Rap Performance, Best Rap Song, and Best Music Video!), has been streamed more than 1.6 billion times, more than all the tracks Drake released in the battle *combined*.

The Drake/Kendrick battle was epic, but it was hardly the only storied beef in a genre famous for them. Sadly, those sometimes spilled over into the streets. The most tragic, of course, was the one between Tupac and Biggie that started not with a song, but with a shooting.

On November 30, 1994, Tupac arrived at Manhattan's Quad Studios for a recording session and was confronted by two armed men who robbed him and shot him multiple times. Tupac was convinced that his former friend, rapper the Notorious B.I.G., aka "Biggie," and Sean "Puffy" Combs, the head of Biggie's label Bad Boy Records, were behind the robbery and attempted murder.

Biggie's release of the song "Who Shot Ya?" on February 21, 1995, didn't help matters, although Biggie was adamant that it had nothing to do with Tupac. Tupac responded a few months later with the June 1996 release of "Hit 'Em Up," with lyrics that directly threatened Biggie, Puffy, and the entire Junior M.A.F.I.A. and Bad Boy crews. The lyrics were so rough that Ice-T pleaded with Tupac not to release it.

Although both songs were hits, they inflamed, rather than resolved the beef between Tupac and Biggie. Tupac was shot in Las Vegas on September 7, 1996, and died from his injuries six days later. He was twenty-four years old. Six months later, on March 9, 1997, Biggie was shot and killed in a drive-by in Los Angeles, after a party hosted by *Vibe* magazine. He was twenty-four years old.

Fortunately, not every rap beef has ended in violence. The Nas/Jay-Z feud was sparked by Jay-Z's 2001 song "The Takeover," which bragged that Jay-Z and his Roc-A-Fella Records crew were taking over the rap game and attacked Nas as a "has-been" whose career was over. Nas responded with "Ether," a vicious Jay-Z takedown rife with homophobia. The consensus among fans was that Nas won the beef, although the two artists continued to trade insults on records for a few years before publicly burying the hatchet at a Jay-Z concert in 2005.

The tragic end to the Tupac/Biggie feud casts a long shadow, but rap beefs have historically been decided by the culture declaring a winner, consistent with the Black oral tradition of the dozens—the progenitor of rap beefs and rap battles. As Jay-Z himself said, his feud with Nas was "definitely going to bring out the best of me. . . . He's gonna put me on top of my game; I hope I do the same for him. . . . It's just verbal sparring. No one is fighting."

The dozens is an informal game in which two Black kids trade insults back and forth in front of an audience, typically centered on each other's family and mother in particular. The goal is to be increasingly funny and clever in your insults (as gauged by the crowd reaction) until you make the other person cry or fight, signaling victory. There is a clear direct line from the dozens to rap battles. Rap beefs are just rap battles memorialized on vinyl for an audience of Hip Hop fans, rather than just the kids on the corner.

White sociologists, folklorists, and linguists studied the dozens for most of the last century and documented how common the practice was among Black youth, from rural Mississippi to urban Philadelphia. Black novelists, from Zora Neale Hurston and Langston Hughes to Richard Wright and Chester Himes, depicted characters playing the dozens in their fiction. The dozens could be rhyming or non-rhyming, dirty or clean.

Rudy Ray Moore, aka Dolemite, was a performer and Hip Hop precursor who preserved the dozens on vinyl on his 1971 record *The Rudy Ray Moore House Party Album: The Dirty Dozens, Vol. 1*, which at least one Hip Hop pioneer, Big Daddy Kane, cited as an influence. Moore ended up recording a duet with Kane, "Big Daddy Kane vs. Dolemite," in 1990.

Like the dozens, the beef between Drake and Kendrick escalated with each round, going from anodyne boasts about who is the top rapper before rapidly devolving into accusations of domestic violence and pedophilia. Although Drake released "The Heart Part 6" in response to the accusations in "Not Like Us," it was simply no match for the massive appeal of "Not Like Us."

For Drake, the blows kept coming. Kendrick followed up his Juneteenth Pop Out concert with the release of the "Not Like Us" video on July 4, 2024, featuring a visual of an owl—the logo of Drake's label, OVO Sound—being pummeled in piñata form. Then on September 8, the NFL announced that Kendrick Lamar would be the featured performer at the 2025 Super Bowl halftime show.

That knockout blow should have decisively ended the beef, with Kendrick the winner by every metric, but then Drake made a move that was unprecedented in the history of rap beefs. On November 22, 2024, one day after Kendrick released his surprise album, *GNX*, Drake filed petitions in New York and Texas state courts accusing Universal Music Group (UMG) of engaging in an "elaborate scheme" to boost the streams and radio airplay of "Not Like Us" to manipulate the public into making it a massive hit.

Drake's petition accused UMG—ironically the label that releases not only Kendrick's music but Drake's—of engaging in old-fashioned "plugola," the practice of paying third-party promoters to get airplay for a record. Plugola is a practice that goes back to the early days of rock and roll, and there is nothing novel or surprising about the idea that a major label might hire independent promoters to boost a release by one of its top artists. Drake's other allegations related to streaming platforms—the way that most people consume music today. Drake alleged that UMG (1) had hired someone to create bots to stream "Not Like Us" and artificially boost the track's popularity; (2) had given Spotify a 30 percent discount on license fees for "Not Like Us;" and, most comically, (3) was behind the fact that when Apple Music listeners asked Siri to play Drake's *Certified Lover Boy* album, it would play "Not Like Us" instead, with its famous line calling Drake a "certified pedophile."

Drake ultimately withdrew the New York State court petition and filed a straightforward defamation claim in federal court, which was ultimately dismissed, but his original claims are illustrative of how much digitization and streaming has transformed the curation, consumption, and monetization of popular culture, with profound ramifications for Black (and all) artists. Prior to the transition from analog to digital, popularity could be judged, in part, by how many physical copies of an artist's music were sold. Even if a music fan only wanted two or three hit songs from a particular artist, they would have to buy the whole album, a physical CD that retailed for $16. If they just wanted one hit, they could purchase a CD single that sold for approximately $3. In either case, the artist was paid for the sale of each physical item embodying their performance. Record company accounting was (and is) anything but transparent, with manufacturing and packaging costs deducted from artists' royalties and a portion of their royalties held back in anticipation of returns of unsold merchandise by retailers. Still, artists stood to receive about $2.80 for each full-length CD and 52 cents for each CD single.

In the week of June 12, 1999, R & B singer Maxwell had the #4 song on the Billboard Hot 100 chart with "Fortunate," from the *Life* motion picture soundtrack. "Fortunate" was certified gold by the RIAA, ultimately selling eight hundred thousand copies. Although Maxwell did not write the song, assuming that his artist's royalty was approximately 17.5 percent, he stood to earn about $420,000 from the single alone.

A mere eleven days earlier, on June 1, 1999, a software service debuted that would upend the music business. Napster, the peer-to-peer music sharing service, allowed users to search indexes of recordings on other users' computers and copy those MP3 files, without payment to record companies, music publishers, or artists. The reaction of record labels to a technology that completely bypassed commercial channels to make the product that labels invested in and *owned* available for free was equal parts rage and panic. They refused to accept the inexorable forward march of technology and spent no time trying to negotiate a licensing deal with Napster to eliminate large-scale copyright infringement as an essential element of Napster's business model.

Instead, the labels sued Napster out of existence, forcing it to declare bankruptcy in the wake of the industry's win in *A&M Records, Inc. v. Napster, Inc.* It was a Pyrrhic victory. The labels pursued an aggressive litigation strategy, not only going after Napster but suing its individual users, whether they were teen boys or a single mother in suburban Minnesota. Their efforts backfired spectacularly. Young music fans viewed the labels as greedy and out of touch and came to view free file sharing as a way of sticking it to large corporations that were demonstrably hostile to their customers.

By the time that Napster filed for bankruptcy, it had an estimated 26.4 million users, and other peer-to-peer services, like LimeWire, Kazaa, and Grokster, had sprung up in its wake. With record industry revenue steadily declining, labels had no choice but to enter into a licensing deal with Apple, which debuted its iTunes store in April 2003 and the iPod MP3 player six months later in October 2003. At least Apple was offering to actually pay the labels for their music and could promise that its secure rights management system would prevent piracy.

Since Apple was primarily in the hardware business, it could afford to set music prices at the consumer-friendly rate of 99 cents per song, which successfully dissuaded music fans from purchasing physical copies of music completely. Apple insisted on retaining 30 of those 99 cents, leaving labels with 69 cents per download. Within eight years of its launch, Apple had sold three hundred million iPods, and sales of CDs had plummeted to $3.1 billion, from a 2000 high of $13.2 billion. In the decade after Napster introduced digital distribution to the public, the record industry saw its *overall* revenue drop by 50 percent, from $14.6 billion in 1999 to $7.1 billion in 2011.

Apple's success in reorienting music fans away from the thrill of assembling their own physical archive of music had consequences for the earning power of artists. By way of example, in June 2011, Nicki Minaj's "Super Bass," from her debut studio album *Pink Friday*, was in the top ten on the Billboard Hot 100 chart. "Super Bass" was a massive hit, certified diamond by the RIAA, with sales of ten million copies. But, as the industry's own figures show, only 43 percent of those sales were likely to have been physical copies. If we assume the same 17.5 percent royalty and a $3 retail price for the sale of physical copies, then Minaj stood to earn $2,257,000 from the sale of physical units. On the digital download sales, the royalty that artists received ranged from a low of 9 cents per download up to 50 percent of the label's receipts, or approximately 34 cents per download. Since Nicki Minaj was signed to Lil Wayne's production company, Young Money Entertainment, at the time, it is safe to assume that she received less than 50 percent for downloads. If she was paid 9 cents per download, she would have earned approximately $513,000 in royalties for downloads, or less than a quarter of what she earned on 1.4 million fewer sales.

Although the business model that Apple imposed on the sale of digital downloads was responsible for the wide discrepancy between physical and digital sales, it paled in comparison to the dramatic drop in royalty income artists experienced with the advent of streaming. In 2011, the same year that Nicki Minaj had an RIAA Diamond hit with "Super Bass," Spotify launched its music streaming service in the US. Spotify is credited with "saving" the music industry, and indeed, after years of steep decline, labels began to see their revenues rise by 2015. But the impact on the recording artists and songwriters who actually *made* the music was radically worse.

A deep dive into the Spotify licensing arrangement shows why. Spotify's marketing hook was to give consumers unlimited access to a library of one hundred million songs, with "access" being the key word. Unlike the iTunes model, music fans were not purchasing digital copies of recordings but were renting the right to listen to them on Spotify, subject to their payment of a monthly subscription fee, or on an ad-supported free basis. Spotify agreed to pay record labels and music publishers a percentage of its revenue as a license fee. Labels in turn paid their artists a percentage of those receipts, based on the individual artist's contractual royalty rate. On average, labels retain 70 percent of what they receive from Spotify.

In practice, this arrangement slashed the amount of money that the people who create the music that consumers come to Spotify *for* receive. As of this writing, labels receive between $3,500 and $5,000 for one million streams. An artist with a net 12 percent royalty rate would receive between $420 and $600. A superstar artist with a *billion* streams and a 22 percent royalty would receive between $770,000 and $1,100,000. If we use the RIAA equivalents and assume that 150 streams are the equivalent of the sale of one single, then one billion streams are the equivalent of a single with 6.6 million copies sold. Twenty-five years ago, a superstar who sold that many physical copies would have made approximately $3.9 million.

Streaming isn't going away, but these mathematical examples demonstrate that artists and songwriters today receive a fraction of their income from the principal way that the public consumes music. As of 2020, only 7,500 Spotify artists (0.09 percent of the total on the platform) received over $100,000 from streaming royalties. Even for that top 0.09 percent, a massive hit doesn't translate into significant income from the public's consumption of their recorded music. This puts pressure on artists to generate more money from touring, merchandising, endorsements, or ventures outside of music altogether.

The situation for songwriters is similar. The Copyright Royalty Tribunal in Washington, DC, sets the rates that music publishers and songwriters receive from streaming, but the complicated formula provides a way for streamers to pay less than the 2026 top-line rate of 15.3 percent of their revenue: by bundling the music service with other offerings.

Despite its position as the market leader in music streaming, Spotify struggled to attain profitability, only recording its first full year of profitability in 2024. The reasons are twofold: First, since Spotify was pursuing growth at the behest of Wall Street, it was hesitant to increase subscription prices; second, because of the asymmetrical power balance between Spotify and the three major companies that control 70 percent of recorded music, the major labels receive 70 percent of Spotify's revenue.

An investigation by journalist Liz Pelly revealed that Spotify has adopted some arguably questionable practices in pursuit of profit. In 2017, Spotify began a shadowy program called Perfect Fit Content

(PFC). PFC was generic music Spotify commissioned from stock music production houses to fill out its playlists in genres like jazz and classical music.

Although Spotify denies that it pushes PFC on listeners, Pelly found internal communications revealing that Spotify strategy executives were analyzing usage data to determine how to increase the usage of PFC content on their playlists. The use of PFC dilutes the percentage of streams of music by independent artists and reduces the amount of income that musicians and composers in these less commercial genres receive. Spotify also launched the Discovery Mode program where artists traded promotion in the program for an agreement to accept a lower royalty rate. Both of these practices exerted downward pressure on the income of musical artists.

Spotify's practices don't only affect artists. These practices also impact what audiences listen to and the very relationship that people have with music itself. As *New Yorker* reporter Kyle Chayka has pointed out: Over the last decade, Spotify, along with other tech platforms, has shifted from a "user-centered approach" to a "corporation-centered approach . . . optimized to extract profit."

It is a short distance from pushing playlists with stock music and extracting lower royalties from musicians in exchange for exposure to supplanting human musicians entirely. In 2023, Spotify founder and CEO Daniel Ek waxed enthusiastically about the possibilities of AI, saying that "the boom in AI generated content could be 'great culturally' and [would] allow Spotify to 'grow engagement and revenue.'"

This viewpoint makes sense for the technology companies who now dominate the distribution of recorded music. Their business models prioritize capturing and monetizing your attention—*not* selling you music, per se. In that business model, artists are seen as a cost to be minimized, rather than the makers of the product itself.

This portends a dystopian future for artists and audiences alike, one where all the value is drained out of intellectual property, giving humans little ability to become full-time musicians and where audiences are fed increasingly simple aural wallpaper to serve as background for their daily lives instead of brilliant artists with something to say. In September 2025, independent label Hallwood Media signed an AI R & B artist named Xania Monet to a $3 million deal. Monet was the creation of a Mississippi-based poet named Telisha Jones, who used Suno, an AI music generator, to set her lyrics to music. Monet's single "How Was I Supposed to Know?" reached #1 on the Billboard R&B Digital Song Sales chart. While there has been pushback from Black artists like Kehlani, the contrast between the reaction to Xania Monet and to FN Meka is chilling.

Given what we know, Drake can be forgiven for hoping that the success of Kendrick's "Not Like Us" was the result of audience manipulation, rather than superior skills. Black artists—all artists—need to be mindful, though, that we are living in an era dominated by charisma-free tech trillionaires looking to automate every skill they need but don't possess. We have already seen the way that social media platforms can accelerate America's proclivity toward cultural appropriation and erasure.

We only need to note the zeal with which Black history is being banned—how those in power seek to push Black people out of public life and deny the ways in which Black genius has made, and actually continues to make, this country great—to imagine that an effort to make Black art without Black people will not be far behind.

Before this country recognized the citizenship of Black people, an enslaved Black man used the knowledge he brought with him from Africa to protect Bostonians from smallpox. Black people took the Western religion thrust upon them in slavery, made it their own in hush harbors, and fashioned it into spirituals and the blues. Once emancipated, Black people wasted no time in patenting their innovations, many of which powered the Industrial Revolution, from streetlights to railroads. They built self-sufficient communities in the South and, after the Great Migration, in the North. Those communities inspired entrepreneurs who founded record companies that created the "sound of young America." When America took musical instruments out of schools, they raided their parents' record collections and created Hip Hop, which became the soundtrack for global youth.

The truth is Black creativity has always created community, inspired activists, and helped push the cause of freedom. The Black people in this country have lessons to teach us, if we are willing to learn. Following in their footsteps will ensure that we survive these challenging times because, in America, brilliant Black minds will *always* be free!

Acknowledgments

So many people supported me during the five-year journey of writing this book that listing them all would be impossible, but I will try.

First off, my indefatigable editor, Stephanie Frerich, who had patience with this harried first-time author who took forever to churn out each chapter. Stephanie combined exactly the right mix of pressure and encouragement to get me over the finish line. I am grateful to Dawn Davis, who initially acquired the book, and to my agent, Tanya McKinnon, who signed me on the strength of my blog, *Journal of the Plague Years*, before I even knew what I would write about.

I am deeply indebted to Lori Tharps, whose editorial support on the proposal gave me a roadmap for writing this book, and to Salamishah Tillet, who called me a writer when I was afraid to call myself one. I could not have written this book without the help of my magnificent research assistants, Chinyere Obi, Talya Whyte, and Nonso Elelleh. You each tracked down all the sources of information I needed, no matter how ancient or obscure, and always brought fresh insights to our weekly discussions.

I have been blessed to have incredible lifelong friends who have been my cheerleaders at every turn. Thank you to Jane Abernethy, Dayna Cunningham, Cheryl Hooks, Deb Langford, Robin Lynch, Susan Mobley, Gale Monk, Bethanne Moore, Bob Rothery, Ben

Schatz, Marcia Smith, Margaret Walton, and Lenore Washington. I love and am grateful for each of you.

Thank you to the S.O.B.s (South Orange Babes): Vivian Armstrong, Nan Bloom, Akua Lesesne, Miriam Norman, Nikki Livingston, Nikki Reininga, Sheri Spears, Valencia Yearwood, our dearly departed Tanya Gibson Clark (may she Rest in Power), and our newest S.O.B.s, Jackie Dorante and Jeanine Redd. We have created a sisterhood that has taken us all the way from the maternity ward to menopause. I couldn't have done it without you all!

My colleagues at Frankfurt Kurnit have modeled what it means to be lawyers who understand that compromising your integrity or humanity is incompatible with professional excellence. I have been privileged to practice alongside you for more than three decades.

Last, but far from least, I want to thank my family for their love, support, and most of all patience. Anthony, my husband of thirty-one years, gave me the idea for this book. My children, Marcus and Noelle, served as accountability partners and sounding boards. Most importantly, I have to thank my mother, Gwen. No one has ever had more faith in me than she has. I love you all to the moon and back.

Notes

INTRODUCTION

ix *FN Meka quickly amassed ten million followers on TikTok*: Murray Stassen, "Capitol Just Signed a Virtual Artist. He Has Over Ten Million Followers on TikTok," Music Business Worldwide, August 12, 2022, https://www.musicbusinessworldwide.com/capitol-records-just-signed-a-virtual-artist-fn-meka-he-has-over-10-million-followers-on-tiktok.

ix *FN Meka "rapped" about being the victim of police brutality*: Marc Tracy, "A 'Virtual Rapper' Was Fired. Questions About Art and Tech Remain," *The New York Times*, September 6, 2022, https://www.nytimes.com/2022/09/06/arts/music/fn-meka-virtual-ai-rap.html.

x *The blowback was heavily covered in* The New York Times: Joe Coscarelli, "Capitol Drops 'Virtual Rapper' FN Meka After Backlash over Stereotypes," *The New York Times*, August 23, 2022, https://www.nytimes.com/2022/08/23/arts/music/fn-meka-dropped-capitol-records.html.

x *Factory New label head Anthony Martini boasted that FN Meka represented a new frontier*: Stassen, "Capitol Just Signed a Virtual Artist."

x *Once the deal imploded*: Mankaprr Conteh, "So What the Hell Was FN Meka, Anyway?," *Rolling Stone*, August 31, 2022, https://www.rollingstone.com/music/music-features/fn-meka-controversy-ai-1234585293.

xii *player piano technology was supplanted by radio*: Carole E. Scott, "The History of the Radio Industry in the United States to 1940," Economic History Association, https://eh.net/encyclopedia/the-history-of-the-radio-industry-in-the-united-states-to-1940.

xii *It would become a vehicle for recording everything*: Clive Thompson, "How the Phonograph Changed Music Forever," *Smithsonian Magazine*, January 2016, https://www.smithsonianmag.com/arts-culture/phonograph-changed-music-forever-180957677.

xiii   *By the 1890s he had announced the invention of a projector and then opened kineto-graph parlors*: American Experience, "The Early History of Motion Pictures," PBS, https://www.pbs.org/wgbh/americanexperience/features/pickford-early-history-motion-pictures.

xiii   *By 1916, there were twenty-one thousand movie theaters*: Kat Eschner, "Movie Palaces Let Everyday Americans Be Royalty," *Smithsonian Magazine*, April 12, 2017, https://www.smithsonianmag.com/smart-news/movie-palaces-let-everyday-americans-be-royalty-180962824/.

xiii   *What followed less than two decades later was the formation of the modern Writers Guild of America (WGA)*: Hilary Swett, "The Screen Writers' Guild: An Early History of the Writers Guild of America," The Writers Guild Foundation, 2020, https://www.wgfoundation.org/screenwritersguild-history.

xiv   *The defining moment for the musicians' union, the American Federation of Musicians (AFM)*: Christopher Milazzo, "A Swan Song for Live Music?: Problems Facing the American Federation of Musicians in a Technological Age," *Hofstra Labor & Employment Law Journal* 13, no. 2 (1996): 4–6, https://scholarlycommons.law.hofstra.edu/hlelj/vol13/iss2/7.

xv   *From the carbon filament that allows light bulbs to last longer*: Thaddeus Morgan, "8 Black Inventors Who Made Daily Life Easier," HISTORY.com, February 20, 2019, https://www.history.com/articles/8-black-inventors-african-american.

xvii   *The story of Onesimus, a West African enslaved*: Erin Blakemore, "How an Enslaved African Man in Boston Helped Save Generations from Smallpox," HISTORY.com, February 1, 2019, https://www.history.com/articles/smallpox-vaccine-onesimus-slave-cotton-mather; Michael Harriot, host, *Drapetomaniax: Unshackled History*, season 1, episode 7, "Onesimus and the Great Vaccine Debate," OTHERtone, Sony Music Entertainment, and Queer Media, August 29, 2023, https://podcasts.apple.com/us/podcast/onesimus-the-great-vaccine-debate-featuring-damon/id1687096254?i=1000626069112.

xviii   *Although Onesimus was clearly responsible*: David S. Bernstein, ed., "The 100 Best Bostonians of All Time," *Boston* magazine, January 5, 2016, https://www.bostonmagazine.com/news/2016/01/05/100-best-bostonians.

xviii   *Although Eli Whitney received a patent*: Clay Thompson, "Ask Clay: Eli Whitney's Cotton Gin Owes a Lot to Sam and His Father," azcentral.com, November 11, 2016, https://www.azcentral.com/story/opinion/op-ed/claythompson/2016/11/11/ask-clay-eli-whitneys-cotton-gin-owes-lot-sam-and-his-father/93547662.

xviii   *there was an "explosion of patents awarded to Black people"*: Portia P. James, *The Real McCoy: Afro-American Invention and Innovation, 1619–1930*, exhibition records, Smithsonian Institution, May 1989–May 1990, https://sova.si.edu/record/acma.03-026.

xix *Yet outbreaks of racial violence and the imposition of Jim Crow*: Lisa D. Cook, "Violence and Economic Activity: Evidence from African American Patents, 1870–1940," *Journal of Economic Growth* 19, no. 2 (June 2014): 221–57, https://www.jstor.org/stable/44113425.

CHAPTER ONE: THE INTELLECTUAL PROPERTY OF PROPERTY

2 *American laws made the acquisition of intellectual property rights more accessible*: Keith Aoki, "Distributive and Syncretic Motives in Intellectual Property Law (with Special Reference to Coercion, Agency, and Development)," *UC Davis Law Review* 40 (March 2007): 739–40, https://lawreview.law.ucdavis.edu/archives/40/3/distributive-and-syncretic-motives-intellectual-property-law-special-reference.

3 *Those kidnapped from Africa came from diverse peoples with rich histories*: Patricia Carter Sluby (quoting Ivan Van Sertima, *Blacks in Science: Ancient and Modern*), from *The Inventive Spirit of African Americans: Patented Ingenuity* (Praeger, 2004), 2.

4 *In the colonial era, New York City was already a teeming metropolis*: "New York City," HISTORY.com, updated May 28, 2025, https://www.history.com/articles/new-york-city.

4 *After the Revolutionary War, New York City became the nation's first capital*: Sylviane A. Diouf, "New York City's Slave Market," New York Public Library, June 29, 2015, https://www.nypl.org/blog/2015/06/29/slave-market.

4 *Thomas L. Jennings was a free Black man born into this complicated city in 1791*: Frederick Douglass, "Obituary of Thomas L. Jennings," *The Anglo-African Magazine* 1 (April 1859): 126–28, cited in Jerry Mikorenda, "A Bold Man of Color," The Gotham Center for New York City History, January 21, 2016, https://www.gothamcenter.org/blog/a-bold-man-of-color-thomas-l-jennings-and-the-proceeds-of-a-patent.

5 *Later, Jennings opened his own tailor shop on the corner of Nassau Street*: Sluby, *The Inventive Spirit of African Americans*, 15–17.

5 *The attendees at the 1858 National Convention of People of Color cataloged the inventions of Black men*: Kara W. Swanson, PhD, JD, "Patent Law's Hidden Figures: Race, Memory and Invention of a Slave," draft presentation at Northwestern Legal History Colloquium, law.northwestern.edu, November 2019.

5 *Jennings hung his letters patent*: Emily Matchar, "The First African-American to Hold a Patent Invented 'Dry Scouring,'" *Smithsonian Magazine*, February 27,

2019, https://www.smithsonianmag.com/innovation/first-african-american -hold-patent-invented-dry-scouring-180971394.

5 *The patent laws in effect in the United States*: Mary Bellis, "Biography of Thomas Jennings, First African American Patent Holder," ThoughtCo, updated July 3, 2019, https://www.thoughtco.com/thomas-jennings-inventor-1991311.

6 *At the National Conventions, those assembled*: "Minutes and Proceedings of the Convention of Free People of Colour 1831, 1832," omeka.coloredconven tions.org.

6 *Jennings and his wife, Elizabeth, had five children*: Sluby, *The Inventive Spirit of African Americans*, 16.

6 *On July 16, 1854, Elizabeth Jennings*: Amy Hill Hearth, *Streetcar to Justice: How Elizabeth Jennings Won the Right to Ride in New York* (Greenwillow Books, 2018), 29.

7 *At the next stop*: Hearth, *Streetcar to Justice*, 36.

7 *The day after Elizabeth was assaulted*: Hearth, *Streetcar to Justice*, 49.

8 *For example, in the period after the Revolutionary War*: Gene Allen Smith, "Uncertain Americans: The Slippery Status of African American Soldiers and Civilians," National Park Service, https://www.nps.gov/articles/uncertain -americans.htm.

9 *One example is Henry Boyd*: Carter G. Woodson, *The Mis-Education of the Negro* (Wilder, 2016), chap. 15, Kindle.

9 *Still, Boyd felt compelled*: Patricia Carter Sluby, *The Entrepreneurial Spirit of African American Inventors* (Praeger, 2011), 11.

9 *Armed with legal protection*: Woodson, *The Mis-Education of the Negro*, chap. 15, Kindle.

10 *White envy of Boyd's economic success*: Carter G. Woodson, "The Negroes in Cincinnati Prior to the Civil War," *Journal of Negro History* 1, no. 1 (1933): 1–22, https://www.gutenberg.org/.

10 *Between 1833 and 1837*: Max Grivno, "Antebellum Mississippi," Mississippi History Now, July 2015, http://www.mshistorynow.mdah.ms.gov/issue/ante bellum-mississippi.

11 *Oscar J. E. Stuart was a lawyer*: Dorothy Cowser Yancy, "The Stuart Double Plow and Double Scraper: The Invention of a Slave," *Journal of Negro History* 69, no. 1 (Winter 1984): 50, https://www.jstor.org/stable/2717659.

11 *On November 24, 1857*: Brian L. Frye, "Invention of a Slave," *Syracuse Law Review* 68, no. 181 (2018): 191.

11 *notorious* Dred Scott *decision*: *Dred Scott v. Sandford*, 60 U.S. 373 (1857).

12 *Despite Stuart's extensive lobbying*: Frye, "Invention of a Slave," 199.

12 *Stuart's letter to Senator John Quitman*: Frye, "Invention of a Slave," 203.

12 *In January 1859*: Frye, "Invention of a Slave," 210.

13 *Senator Reid's bill went nowhere*: Frye, "Invention of a Slave," 207–208.

14 *Montgomery was born enslaved in Loudoun County, Virginia*: Frye, "Invention of a Slave," 210–11.

14 *The older Davis had been influenced*: Janet Sharp Hermann, *The Pursuit of a Dream* (University Press of Mississippi, 1999), loc. 89, Kindle.

14 *Inspired by Owen*: Hermann, *The Pursuit of a Dream*, loc. 209.

15 *Nonetheless, Montgomery made the most of this system*: Hermann, *The Pursuit of a Dream*, loc. 280.

15 *Montgomery and his wife, Mary Lewis Montgomery*: Hermann, *The Pursuit of a Dream*, loc. 290.

15 *Montgomery's talents were not limited to his skills*: Hermann, *The Pursuit of a Dream*, loc. 269.

16 *After the outbreak of the Civil War*: Frye, "Invention of a Slave," 225.

16 *After the Civil War ended*: National Archives, "The Freedmen's Bureau," last reviewed October 28, 2021, https://www.archives.gov/research/african-americans/freedmens-bureau.

16 *As part of that program*: Frye, "Invention of a Slave," 217.

17 *Once Mississippi law was amended in 1867*: Frye, "Invention of a Slave," 218.

17 *Montgomery's ad included*: Hermann, *The Pursuit of a Dream*, chap. 4.

18 *Although massive flooding*: Hermann, *The Pursuit of a Dream*, loc. 1682.

18 *Montgomery's success was due*: Frye, "Invention of a Slave," 219.

18 *Joseph Davis died in 1870, and his heirs*: Hermann, *The Pursuit of a Dream*, loc. 1968.

18 *Benjamin Montgomery lived at Brierfield, the former home of Jefferson Davis*: Hermann, *The Pursuit of a Dream*, loc. 2077.

19 *In 1874, former Confederate president Jefferson Davis*: Hermann, *The Pursuit of a Dream*, loc. 2655.

20 *In 1878, a Mississippi Supreme Court*: Hermann, *The Pursuit of a Dream*, loc. 2811.

20 *Like his father, Isaiah Montgomery*: Hermann, *The Pursuit of a Dream*, loc. 2821.

20 *Mound Bayou prospered*: Melissa Block and Elissa Nadworny, "Here's What's Become of a Historic All-Black Town in the Mississippi Delta," NPR, March 8, 2017, https://www.npr.org/2017/03/08/515814287/heres-whats-become-of-a-historic-all-black-town-in-the-mississippi-delta.

21 *Eli Whitney's famous cotton gin*: Keith Aoki, "Distributive and Syncretic Motives in Intellectual Property Law," *UC Davis Law Review* 40 (March 2007):

745–47, https://lawreview.law.ucdavis.edu/archives/40/3/distributive-and-syn cretic-motives-intellectual-property-law-special-reference.

22 *In 1887, Granville T. Woods*: "Granville T. Woods," Biography.com, updated May 4, 2021, https://www.biography.com/inventors/granville-t-woods.

22 *Elijah McCoy invented*: "Elijah McCoy," National Inventors Hall of Fame, https://www.invent.org/inductees/elijah-mccoy.

CHAPTER TWO: GOD AND THE DEVIL: GOSPEL MUSIC VERSUS THE BLUES

24 *Harry T. Burleigh was born with every privilege*: Jean E. Snyder, *Harry T. Burleigh: From the Spiritual to the Harlem Renaissance* (University of Illinois Press, 2016), 34.

26 *It may be difficult to imagine now*: Alain Locke, *The Negro and His Music* (The Associates in Negro Folk Education, 1936), 18.

26 *Throughout his childhood in Erie, Burleigh heard African American spirituals*: Snyder, *Harry T. Burleigh*, 42–44.

26 *After high school, he attended the National Conservatory of Music of America*: Snyder, *Harry T. Burleigh*, 65–68.

27 *According to Burleigh biographer*: Snyder, *Harry T. Burleigh*, 75.

27 *In 1893, Dvořák premiered his* New World *Symphony*: Snyder, *Harry T. Burleigh*, quoting *The New York Herald*, 84.

28 *Shortly after Dvořák's triumphant premiere*: Chris Albertson, *Bessie* (Yale University Press, 2003), 71.

28 *Bessie Smith was born in Chattanooga*: "Chickamauga: Animated Battle Map," American Battlefield Trust, Battlefields.org.

29 *By the time of Bessie Smith's birth*: "Read about the lynching of Ed Johnson in Chattanooga," Tennessee State Museum, TN4ME.org.

29 *a lynching so heinous that it led to the first and only trial in the Supreme Court*: United States v. Shipp, 203 U.S. 563 (1906).

29 *Turn-of-the-century Chattanooga*: Albertson, *Bessie*, 8–11.

30 *Of course, Black performers did not have access*: Thomas Riis, revised by Howard Rye, "Theater Owners' Booking Association," *Grove Dictionary of Jazz*, Grove Music Online, January 20, 2002, https://www.oxfordmusiconline.com /grovemusic/display/10.1093/gmo/9781561592630.001.0001/omo-97815 61592630-e-2000445700.

31 *Although Bessie Smith began performing*: Albertson, *Bessie*, 11–13.

31 *Spirituals, dating back to slavery*: Angela Y. Davis, *Blues Legacies and Black Feminism: Gertrude "Ma" Rainey, Bessie Smith, and Billie Holiday* (Pantheon Books, 1998), 4.

31   *The blues, by contrast*: Davis, *Blues Legacies and Black Feminism*, 8.

32   *When the Supreme Court agreed with piano manufacturers*: White-Smith Music Publishing Co. v. Apollo Co., 209 U.S. 1 (S. Ct. 1908).

33   *Harry Burleigh's stepfather*: Samuel A. Floyd Jr., "The Invisibility and Fame of Harry T. Burleigh: A Retrospect and Prospect," *Black Music Research Journal* 24, no. 2 (Autumn 2004): 182, 187.

33   *Burleigh's relationship with conservatory faculty member*: Snyder, *Harry T. Burleigh*, 267.

34   *The dispute landed in court, culminating in the Supreme Court case*: Herbert v. Shanley, 242 U.S. 591 (S. Ct. 1917).

34   *The popularity of the blues exploded when the record player*: Albertson, *Bessie*, 25.

35   *W. C. Handy was a songwriter, arranger, and bandleader*: Albertson, *Bessie*, 30.

35   *Nothing in Frank Walker's background*: "Frank Walker: A&R Man for Columbia," Bluegrass Messengers, http://www.bluegrassmessengers.com/frank-walker--a--r-man-for-columbia.aspx.

35   *On February 15, 1923*: Albertson, *Bessie*, 36.

36   *Unfortunately, Smith merely traded a small-time hustler for a bigger one*: Albertson, *Bessie*, 37.

36   *If Walker's one-sided, ruthless business dealings*: "Frank Walker," Bluegrass Messengers.

37   *In the spring of 1923, Columbia released*: Albertson, *Bessie*, 37.

37   *Bessie Smith was also a talented songwriter*: Robert Springer, "Folklore, Commercialism and Exploitation: Copyright in the Blues," *Popular Music* 26, no. 1 (2007): 36, https://www.jstor.org/stable/4500298.

37   *During her lifetime*: Gee v. CBS, Inc., 471 F. Supp. 600 (E.D. Pa. 1979), 619–21.

38   *Like most other blues women*: Davis, *Blues Legacies and Black Feminism*, 17–19.

39   *After eight years with the label*: Gee v. CBS, Inc., 621.

39   *Bessie Smith died in a tragic car accident*: Albertson, *Bessie*, 258–63.

39   *Although he made a great display of grief*: Albertson, *Bessie*, 277.

40   *In a meticulously detailed opinion*: Gee v. CBS, Inc., 618.

40   *In addition, Judge Becker wrote*: Gee v. CBS, Inc., 620.

40   *there was no evidence*: Gee v. CBS, Inc., 657.

41   *Judge Becker credited plaintiffs' allegations*: Gee v. CBS, Inc., 622.

CHAPTER THREE: THE POWER OF IMAGE: D. W. GRIFFITH AND OSCAR MICHEAUX AND THE CENSORSHIP FIGHT IN HOLLYWOOD

46   *The Birth of a Nation has been hailed as a masterpiece*: Stephen Werner, "'The Birth of a Nation' Sparked Decades of Racial Violence. This Jesuit Understood

Its Unholy Power," *America: The Jesuit Review*, February 19, 2021, https://www.americamagazine.org/arts-culture/2021/02/19/daniel-lord-birth-of-a-nation-racism-239956.

47 *When the film was released in 1915*: Tom Brook, "The Birth of a Nation: The Most Racist Movie Ever Made?," BBC, February 6, 2015, https://www.bbc.com/culture/article/20150206-the-most-racist-movie-ever-made.

47 *Film critics have paid scant attention*: Desmond Ang, "The Birth of a Nation: Media and Racial Hate," *American Economic Review* 113, no. 6 (June 2023): 1424–60, https://www.aeaweb.org/articles?id=10.1257/aer.20201867.

47 *The National Association for the Advancement of Colored People (NAACP) organized protests*: Richard Brody, "The Black Activist Who Fought Against D. W. Griffth's 'The Birth of a Nation,'" *The New Yorker*, February 6, 2017, https://www.newyorker.com/culture/richard-brody/the-black-activist-who-fought-against-d-w-griffiths-the-birth-of-a-nation.

48 *After all, President Woodrow Wilson*: "The Rise and Fall of Jim Crow: Jim Crow Stories—D. W. Griffith's *The Birth of a Nation*," Thirteen: PBS, https://www.thirteen.org/wnet/jimcrow/stories_events_birth.html.

51 *Griffith was born in a suburb*: "D. W. Griffith, 73, Film Pioneer, Dies," UPI Archives, United Press, July 23, 1948, https://www.upi.com/Archives/1948/07/23/DW-Griffith-73-film-pioneer-dies/1121532273956.

51 *This makes Oscar Micheaux's ascent*: "Oscar Micheaux," NAACP, https://naacp.org/find-resources/history-explained/civil-rights-leaders/oscar-micheaux.

52 *In addition, as filmmaker and professor Bob Pondillo notes*: Bob Pondillo, "*Mutual Film Corp. v. Industrial Commission of Ohio* (1915)," *First Amendment Encyclopedia*, Free Speech Center at Middle Tennessee State University, 2009 (revised 2024), https://firstamendment.mtsu.edu/article/mutual-film-corp-v-industrial-commission-of-ohio/.

52 *State film censorship boards were one important mechanism*: *Mutual Film Corporation v. Industrial Commission of Ohio*, 236 U.S. 230 (1915), 242.

53 *Although Black people's effort to condemn*: David Rylance, "Breech Birth: The Receptions to D. W. Griffith's 'Birth of a Nation,'" *Australasian Journal of American Studies* 24, no. 2 (2005): 1, 15–16.

53 *Black protests against*: Anna Siomopoulos, "The Birth of Black Cinema: Race, Reception, and Oscar Micheaux's 'Within Our Gates,'" *The Moving Image: The Journal of the Association of Moving Image Archivists* 6, no. 2 (2006): 111.

53 The Birth of a Nation *was not only a box office smash*: "How a Racist Film Helped the Ku Klux Klan Grow for Generations," *The Economist*, March 27,

2021, https://www.economist.com/graphic-detail/2021/03/27/how-a-racist
-film-helped-the-ku-klux-klan-grow-for-generations.

54 *Black Illinois State Senator*: Ellen C. Scott, "Black 'Censor,' White Liberties:
Civil Rights and Illinois's 1917 Film Law," *American Quarterly* 64, no. 2 (June
2012): 220, https://www.jstor.org/stable/23273515.

54 *Similar laws were passed soon*: Scott, "Black 'Censor,' White Liberties," 237.

54 *In 1920, when Micheaux released* Within Our Gates: W. Fitzhugh Brundage,
"Why I'll Watch Oscar Micheaux's *Within Our Gates* Until I Wear It Out,"
The Newsmagazine, American Historical Association (AHA), September 1,
2010, https://www.historians.org/perspectives-article/why-ill-watch-oscar-mi
cheauxs-within-our-gates-until-i-wear-it-out-september-2010.

54 *In addition, separate scandals*: Gregory D. Black, "Hollywood Censored: The
Production Code Administration and the Hollywood Film Industry, 1930–
1940," *Film History* 3, no. 3 (1989): 167–89, https://www.jstor.org/stable
/3814976.

55 *The Hollywood Production Code contained only two mentions of race*: Olga J.
Martin, *Hollywood's Movie Commandments 56: A Handbook for Motion Picture Writers and Reviewers* (H. W. Wilson Company, 1937), https://babel.ha
thitrust.org/cgi/pt?id=uc1.$b276078&seq=7&q1=White+slavery.

56 *The early experience of auteur Fritz Lang*: Black, "Hollywood Censored," 185.

56 *Although as an independent filmmaker*: Donald Bogle, "No Business Like Micheaux Business: 'B' . . . for Black." *Film Comment* 21, no. 5 (1985): 31–34,
http://www.jstor.org/stable/43452116.

57 *one notable instance of prosecution under the law was detailed in the 1952 Supreme
Court case*: Beauharnais v. Illinois, 343 U.S. 250 (1952).

57 *Ironically, that same year*: Joseph Burstyn, Inc. v. Wilson, 343 U.S. 495 (1952).

58 *it was supplanted by the Motion Picture Association of America (MPAA) rating
system*: Matt Goldberg, "The Hays Code: A History of Hollywood's Self-
Censorship and Its Influence on Film," *Backstage*, September 17, 2024, https://
www.backstage.com/magazine/article/hays-code-rules-history-77748.

59 The Birth of a Nation *was protected by copyright*: Epoch Producing Co. v. Killiam
Shows, Inc., 522 F. 2d 737 (2nd Cir. 1975).

59 *Although Paul Robeson's debut film*, Body and Soul: Race Films Series, *Body
and Soul*, Eastman Museum, https://www.eastman.org/event/film-screenings
/body-and-soul.

60 *Despite the formidable obstacles*: Monica Drake, Overlooked, "Oscar Micheaux," *The New York Times*, January 31, 2019, https://www.nytimes.com
/interactive/2019/obituaries/oscar-micheaux-overlooked.html.

CHAPTER FOUR: JAZZ AND THE FIRST WAR ON DRUGS

61   *In May 1947*: Farah Jasmine Griffin, *If You Can't Be Free, Be a Mystery: In Search of Billie Holiday* (Ballantine Books, 2002), 40.

61   *The Earle Theatre was*: "Earle Theatre," Cinema Treasures, https://cinematrea sures.org/theaters/1806.

61   *Billie Holiday was at the height of her fame*: Griffin, *If You Can't Be Free, Be a Mystery*, 24.

62   *"Strange Fruit" catapulted Billie Holiday to stardom*: "Billie Holliday: The Long Night of Lady Day—About Billie Holiday's Life and Career," PBS, June 8, 2006, https://www.pbs.org/wnet/americanmasters/billie-holiday-about-the -singer/68.

62   *Billie Holiday had often said*: John Szwed, *Billie Holiday: The Musician and the Myth* (Viking, 2015), 108.

62   *None of this mattered to the federal agents*: Billie Holiday with William Dufty, *Lady Sings the Blues: The 50th Anniversary Edition* (Harlem Moon, 2006), 140–42.

62   *Although much of her memoir*: Griffin, *If You Can't Be Free, Be a Mystery*, 42.

63   *Even then, the typical royalty rate*: Felix Contreras, "Royalties Elusive for Many Jazz Greats," NPR, April 20, 2005, https://www.npr.org/2005/04/20 /4608713/royalties-elusive-for-many-jazz-greats.

63   *As a result, when Billie Holiday died*: Elizabeth Blair, "Encore: Billie Holiday's Grave," NPR, July 13, 2019, https://www.npr.org/2019/07/13/741391152 /encore-billie-holidays-grave.

64   *Due to their convictions and incarcerations*: Robin D. G. Kelley, *Thelonious Monk: The Life and Times of an American Original* (Free Press, 2010), 59.

64   *During the 1920s, Harlem became a mecca for Black artists*: PBS Learning Media, "Harlem in the 1920s: The African Americans," https://ca.pbslearningmedia .org/resource/mr13.socst.us.harlem1920s/harlem-in-the-1920s/.

64   *As detailed in the legislative history of the cabaret card law*: Proceedings of the Board of Aldermen, Municipal Assembly of the City of New York, Recommendation No. 10, December 7, 1926.

64   *The original legislation addressed permanent staff*: "Police Department, Rules Governing Cabarets," *The City Record*, vol. LXIX, no. 20540, January 9, 1941.

65   *In 1941, the union covering bartenders and hotel and restaurant workers*: *Friedman v. Valentine*, 177 Misc. 437 (New York S. Ct. 1941), 441.

66   *The NYPD of the 1940s*: Arthur Browne, "A History of Blacks in NYPD Blue: It All Started with Samuel Battle," *New York Daily News*, June 11, 2015, https://www.nydailynews.com/2015/06/11/a-history-of-blacks-in-nypd -blue-it-all-started-with-samuel-battle.

66 *The criminalization of a range of recreational drugs*: Laura Smith, "How a Racist Hate-Monger Masterminded America's War on Drugs," *Timeline*, February 28, 2018, https://medium.com/timeline/harry-anslinger-racist-war-on-drugs-prison-industrial-complex-fb5cbc281189.

67 *Anslinger's efforts were successful*: Brooke Gladstone, host, *On the Media*, "The Man Who Declared War On Drugs," WNYC Studios, April 13, 2017, https://www.wnycstudios.org/podcasts/otm/segments/man-who-declared-war-drugs.

67 *After the Civil War, male doctors*: "A Social History of America's Most Popular Drugs," *Frontline*, PBS, https://www.pbs.org/wgbh/pages/frontline/shows/drugs/buyers/socialhistory.html.

67 *Once drug use crossed class and racial lines*: Gladstone, "The Man Who Declared War on Drugs."

67 *At its birth in the early twentieth century*: Maureen Anderson, "The White Reception of Jazz in America," *African American Review* 38, no. 1 (2004): 135–36, https://doi.org/10.2307/1512237.

68 *At least one Black musician, James Reese Europe*: James Reese Europe, "A Negro Explains Jazz," in *Keeping Time: Readings in Jazz History*, ed. Robert Walser (Oxford University Press, 1999).

68 *Unfortunately, Europe's passionate defense*: Anderson, "The White Reception of Jazz in America," 141–42.

69 *Even the white critics*: LeRoi Jones (Amiri Baraka), "Jazz and the White Critic," in *Black Music* (Akashi Classics, 2002).

69 *Harry Anslinger, the viciously racist*: Johann Hari, "The Hunting of Billie Holiday," *Politico Magazine*, January 17, 2015, https://www.politico.com/magazine/story/2015/01/drug-war-the-hunting-of-billie-holiday-114298.

69 *Monk was harassed*: Kelley, *Thelonious Monk*, 139, 155, 253–54.

70 *Billie Holiday first performed*: Szwed, *Billie Holiday*, 154.

71 *Certain facts about the authorship*: Szwed, *Billie Holiday*, 158.

71 *Holiday's account in her memoir*: Holiday with Dufty, *Lady Sings the Blues*, 93.

71 *Once "Strange Fruit" was added*: Szwed, *Billie Holiday*, 159.

72 *Meeropol, not content with earning 100 percent of the copyright*: Szwed, *Billie Holiday*, 161.

73 *As Frank Sinatra said*: David Hajdu, "Who Loves You?," *The Nation*, September 10, 2015, https://www.thenation.com/article/archive/who-loves-you.

73 *In this century*: Will Layman, "Billie Holiday at 100: Still an Inspiration," PopMatters, April 7, 2015, https://www.popmatters.com/192087-billie-holiday-at-100-2495543690.html.

74 *He composed several songs*: Lewis Porter, "What Thelonious Monk's Most Famous Composition Owes to Dizzy Gillespie," WBGO, May 25, 2021, https://www.wbgo.org/music/2021-05-25/what-thelonious-monks-most -famous-composition-owes-to-dizzy-gillespie.

74 *Monk grew up in the San Juan Hill neighborhood*: Kelley, *Thelonious Monk*, 26.

74 *Monk's musical education*: Kelley, *Thelonious Monk*, 27.

74 *When Monk returned to New York*: Kelley, *Thelonious Monk*, 57.

75 *Even though Black musicians*: Kelley, *Thelonious Monk*, 57.

75 *Against this backdrop*: Kelley, *Thelonious Monk*, 70.

76 *Lacking any publishing connections*: Kelley, *Thelonious Monk*, 94.

76 *Over the summer of 1943*: Kelley, *Thelonious Monk*, 87–88.

76 *The composition languished*: Kelley, *Thelonious Monk*, 101.

77 *Stung by these early experiences*: Noal Cohen and Michael Fitzgerald, *Rat Race Blues: The Musical Life of Gigi Gryce* (Current Research in Jazz, 2014).

78 *Although New York State passed*: Rothman's Roadmap to the Right of Publicity, https://rightofpublicityroadmap.com.

78 *For years after her premature death*: Griffin, *If You Can't Be Free, Be a Mystery*, 150.

CHAPTER FIVE: HAIL, HAIL, ROCK AND ROLL

81 *The Rock & Roll Hall of Fame is*: Ben Sisario, "'We're Making Progress.' How the Rock Hall of Fame Is Trying to Evolve," *The New York Times*, November 1, 2023, https://www.nytimes.com/2023/11/01/arts/music/rock -and-roll-hall-of-fame-john-sykes.html.

81 *The Rock Hall was also founded by a team dominated*: CSU Center for Public History and Digital Humanities, "Rock and Roll Hall of Fame and Museum: Why Is the Rock Hall in Cleveland?" Cleveland Historical, https://cleveland historical.org/items/show/704.

82 *Conversely, everyone knows that rhythm and blues*: Ashley Kahn, "Jerry Wexler: The Man Who Invented Rhythm & Blues," *Rolling Stone*, August 15, 2008, https://www.rollingstone.com/music/music-news/jerry-wexler-the-man -who-invented-rhythm-blues-245859.

83 *The sound of Black R & B music is ineffable*: Wesley Morris, "Music," in *The 1619 Project: A New Origin Story*, ed. Nikole Hannah-Jones, Caitlin Roper, Ilena Silverman, and Jake Silverstein (One World, 2021).

83 *As Danyel Smith said*: Danyel Smith, *Shine Bright: A Very Personal History of Black Women in Pop* (Rock Lit 101, 2022).

84 *Cotton Plant, Arkansas*: "Cotton Plant (Woodruff County)," Encyclopedia of Arkansas, https://encyclopediaofarkansas.net/entries/cotton-plant-wood ruff-county-2551/.

84 *Cotton Plant became a thriving cultural center*: Encyclopedia of Arkansas, "Cotton Plant."

85 *Rosetta, known as Rosa in her youth*: Gayle F. Wald, *Shout, Sister, Shout! The Untold Story of Rock-and-Roll Trailblazer Sister Rosetta Tharpe* (Beacon Press, 2007), 14.

85 *COGIC was the first Black Baptist denomination*: Anthea Butler, "Church Mothers and Migration in the Church of God in Christ," in *Religion in the American South: Protestants and Others in History and Culture*, Beth Barton Schweiger and Donald G. Mathews, eds. (The University of North Carolina Press, 2004), 313–14.

85 *COGIC embodied a paradox*: Wald, *Shout, Sister, Shout!*, 15.

86 *In the aftermath of the Civil War*: James R. Grossman, *Chicago, Black Southerners, and the Great Migration* (University of Chicago Press, 1989), loc. 617, Kindle.

86 *According to historian James Grossman*: Grossman, *Chicago, Black Southerners, and the Great Migration*, loc. 617, Kindle.

87 *Around the country—from New York City to Monticello, Mississippi*: "For Action on Race Riot Peril," *The New York Times*, October 15, 1919, https://www .nytimes.com/1919/10/05/archives/for-action-on-race-riot-peril-radical-pro paganda-among-negroes.html.

87 *On July 27, 1919, a riot broke out*: "Red Summer: The Race Riots of 1919," The National WWI Museum and Memorial, https://www.theworldwar.org/learn /about-wwi/red-summer.

87 *By far, the single deadliest event*: John Hill, "UA Little Rock Researchers Uncover Forgotten African American History in Arkansas," University News Archive/UA Little Rock, July 23, 2020, https://ualr.edu/news-archive/2020 -07-23/researchers-uncover-forgotten-african-american-history.

88 *The Red Summer of 1919 was characterized*: W. E. B. DuBois, "Returning Soldiers," *The Crisis* 18, no. 1 (May 1919), dchsny.org.

88 *The Black population of Chicago grew by 50 percent*: Michael W. Harris, *The Rise of Gospel Blues: The Music of Thomas Andrew Dorsey in the Urban Church* (Oxford University Press, 1992), chap. 6, Kindle.

88 *These churches were dedicated*: Harris, *The Rise of Gospel Blues*, chap. 6, Kindle.

89 *Chicago in the 1920s was fertile ground*: Wald, *Shout, Sister, Shout!*, 21–24.

89 *Thomas A. Dorsey was born in 1899*: Harris, *The Rise of Gospel Blues*, chap. 1.

90 *Despite their education*: Harris, *The Rise of Gospel Blues*, chap. 2.

90 *By the age of eleven, Thomas was disenchanted*: Harris, *The Rise of Gospel Blues*, chap. 2.

90 *Dorsey supplemented his on-the-job training*: Harris, *The Rise of the Gospel Blues*, chap. 2.

91 *As Lucy Chaudhuri explained*: Lucy Chaudhuri, "What Is Blues Music?," Classical Music, *BBC Music Magazine*, November 28, 2022, https://www.classical-music.com/articles/blues-music.

91 *Blues was the music of Black working people*: Harris, *The Rise of Gospel Blues*, chap. 4.

91 *Chicago was second only to New York*: Harris, *The Rise of Gospel Blues*, chap. 3.

91 *By October 1920*: Harris, *The Rise of Gospel Blues*, chap. 3.

91 *Unfortunately, Dorsey suffered a mental health crisis*: Harris, *The Rise of Gospel Blues*, chap. 4.

92 *While Dorsey was making another run*: Wald, *Shout, Sister, Shout!*, 21.

92 *Since Rosetta was raised*: Wald, *Shout, Sister, Shout!*, 22–24.

93 *Rosetta's formal education ended*: Wald, *Shout, Sister, Shout!*, 26.

93 *While Tharpe was soaking up musical technique*: Wald, *Shout, Sister, Shout!*, 24.

93 *The blues explosion that began*: Harris, *The Rise of Gospel Blues*, chap. 4.

93 *This allowed unscrupulous record companies*: Harris, *The Rise of Gospel Blues*, chap. 4.

93 *The only way around this was to deliver artists*: Harris, *The Rise of Gospel Blues*, chap. 4.

94 *Dorsey became a cog in this machine*: Harris, *The Rise of Gospel Blues*, chap. 4.

94 *Mayo's CMPC hired Dorsey*: Harris, *The Rise of Gospel Blues*, chap. 4.

94 *In 1925, Dorsey married*: Harris, *The Rise of Gospel Blues*, chap. 5.

94 *In 1928, Dorsey cowrote*: Harris, *The Rise of Gospel Blues*, chap. 6.

94 *The record sold seven million*: Associated Press, "Thomas Dorsey, Father of Gospel Music, Dies at 93," *The Washington Post*, January 24, 1993, https://www.washingtonpost.com/archive/local/1993/01/25/thomas-dorsey-father-of-gospel-music-dies-at-93/d4778588-dc68-4dbc-9819-891253fe7e15/.

94 *As Michael W. Harris elucidates*: Harris, *The Rise of Gospel Blues*, chap. 5.

95 *At nineteen years old*: Wald, *Shout, Sister, Shout!*, 28.

95 *Although Sister Rosetta Tharpe's fame*: Wald, *Shout, Sister, Shout!*, 31.

96 *The Cotton Club was infamous*: "The Cotton Club," Harlem Is . . . , https://www.harlem-is.org/clubs/the-cotton-club.

96 *In his memoir,* The Big Sea: Langston Hughes, *The Big Sea* (Hill & Wang, 1940), 224.

96 *When Sister Rosetta booked her engagement*: Wald, *Shout, Sister, Shout!*, 31–36.

97   *The success of Sister Rosetta's Decca recordings*: Wald, *Shout, Sister, Shout!*, 38–39.

97   *These engagements solidified Sister Rosetta's appeal to a secular audience*: Wald, *Shout, Sister, Shout!*, 40-42.

98   *In February 1941*: Wald, *Shout, Sister, Shout!*, 50.

98   *The Savoy was not just any venue*: "The Savoy Ballroom, Harlem, New York, 1930," *Harlem World*, October 27, 2014, https://www.harlemworldmagazine .com/the-savoy-ballroom-harlem-new-york-1930/.

99   *Once Tharpe began a regular engagement*: Wald, *Shout, Sister, Shout!*, 52–53.

100   *Still, the fame was surely rewarding*: Wald, *Shout, Sister, Shout!*, 55–58.

100   *On the song*: Paul Kucharski, "Resonators Explained," Acoustic Finger Style, September 2004, https://acousticfingerstyle.com/ResonatorsExplained.htm.

100   *"Strange Things" eerily presages*: "Watch the Hot Guitar Solos of Sister Rosetta Tharpe, 'America's First Gospel Rock Star,'" Open Culture, November 27, 2019, https://www.openculture.com/2019/11/the-hot-guitar-solos-of-sister -rosetta-tharpe.html.

100   *The record that was so clearly ahead of its time*: "Inductee Insights: Sister Rosetta Tharpe," posted September 12, 2018, by Rock & Roll Hall of Fame, YouTube, https://www.youtube.com/watch?v=XwSiieNFBXI.

101   *In 1945, when Tharpe was about to play*: Charles White, *The Life and Times of Little Richard: The Authorized Biography* (Omnibus Press, 1984), 26.

101   *By all accounts*: Jessica Diaz-Hurtado, "Forebears: Sister Rosetta Tharpe, the Godmother of Rock 'n' Roll," NPR, August 24, 2017, https://www.npr .org/2017/08/24/544226085/forebears-sister-rosetta-tharpe-the-godmother -of-rock-n-roll.

101   *The duo of Sister Rosetta and Marie Knight continued*: Wald, *Shout, Sister, Shout!*, 68.

101   *A decade after its initial release*: Peter Guralnick, "This is Daddy-O Dewey Phillips," Memphis Music Hall of Fame, https://memphismusichalloffame .com/inductee/deweyphillips.

102   *Every member of the famous "Million-Dollar Quartet"*: Wald, *Shout, Sister, Shout!*, 58.

102   *In the late 1950s, rock and roll exploded*: Wald, *Shout, Sister, Shout!*, 109.

102   *In this climate, Sister Rosetta Tharpe's star*: Wald, *Shout, Sister, Shout!*, 105.

103   *In April 1957*: Wald, *Shout, Sister, Shout!*, 117.

103   *British fans associated early pre-bebop jazz*: Wald, *Shout, Sister, Shout!*, 120.

103   *The darkest manifestation of this view of Black music*: Jack Hamilton, *Just Around Midnight: Rock and Roll and the Racial Imagination* (Harvard University Press, 2016), 104.

104   *The more benign strain of white fascination*: Hamilton, *Just Around Midnight*, 67–68.

105   *Dorsey established his own publishing company*: "Thomas Dorsey," TeachRock, https://teachrock.org/people/dorsey-thomas.

105   *writing and/or publishing one thousand*: "From Riots to Renaissance: Dorsey's Gospel," DuSable to Obama: Chicago's Black Metropolis, WTTW, https://www.wttw.com/dusable-to-obama/dorseys-gospel.

106   *After her death, white rock musicians*: Wald, *Shout, Sister, Shout!*, 63.

CHAPTER SIX: THE SOUND OF YOUNG AMERICA: THE RISE OF BLACK LABELS VEE-JAY RECORDS AND MOTOWN RECORDS

108   *When the U.S. Steel Corporation decided*: Gary Public Library and Rebecca Shrum, "The Experience of Manual Laborers: At the Bottom of the Rail in Gary," Discover Indiana, https://discoverindianahistory.org/items/show/604?tour=60&index=4.

108   *When Gary was founded, the Black population*: Ruth Needleman, "Gary 1919: An Untold Story of Racial Solidarity from Gary's History," *Portside*, https://portside.org/node/21078/printable/print.

109   *Despite this auspicious beginning*: Neil Betten and Raymond A. Mohl, "The Evolution of Racism in an Industrial City, 1906–1940: A Case Study of Gary, Indiana." *The Journal of Negro History* 59, no. 1 (1974): 54–57, https://doi.org/10.2307/2717140.

109   *Yet like Black people throughout the US*: Indiana Historical Society, "Vivian Carter and Vee-Jay Records," *Traces of Indiana and Midwestern History* 23, no. 1 (Winter 2011), 48, 49.

109   *born in Tunica, Mississippi*: Robert L. Campbell, Tom Kelly, Bob Marovich, Robert Pruter, Robert Stallworth, "Vee-Jay: The Early Years," Clemson University, campber.people.clemson.edu, July 4, 2020, https://campber.people.clemson.edu/veejay.html.

109   *Following her graduation in 1939*: Indiana Historical Society, "Vivian Carter and Vee-Jay Records," 48.

110   *Carter called herself*: Louise Hillery, "Vivian Carter," Indiana History Blog, July 5, 2018, https://blog.history.in.gov/tag/vivian-carter.

110   *Vivian was following a trail*: Doug Galloway and Eileen Kowalski, "Milton Gabler," *Variety*, July 29, 2001, https://variety.com/2001/scene/people-news/milton-gabler-1117850437.

110   *Once Vivian and Jimmy started Vee-Jay*: Indiana Historical Society, "Vivian Carter and Vee-Jay Records," 49–52.

111 *Vee-Jay's third Spaniels record*: Robert Pruter, *Doowop: The Chicago Scene* (University of Illinois Press, 1996).

111 *The McGuire Sisters' cover*: *Indiana's 200: The People Who Shaped the Hoosier State*, ed. James E. St. Clair and Linda Gugin (Indiana Historical Society Press, 2015), 54.

111 *For example, in 1956*: Cary O'Dell, "Tutti Frutti—Little Richard (1955)," Library of Congress, https://www.loc.gov/static/programs/national-recording -preservation-board/documents/TuttiFrutti.pdf.

111 *The fate of the song "Hound Dog"*: Haben Kelati, "Blues Singer 'Big Mama' Thornton Had a Hit with 'Hound Dog.' Then Elvis Came Along," *The Washington Post*, February 24, 2021, https://www.washingtonpost.com/lifestyle/kidspost /blues-singer-big-mama-thornton-had-a-hit-with-hound-dog-then-elvis -came-along/2021/02/23/60c36a04-6764-11eb-8468-21bc48f07fe5_story .html.

112 *What distinguished Elvis's cover*: Robert Hilburn, "From the Man Who Would Be King," *The Los Angeles Times*, February 6, 2005, https://www.latimes.com /archives/la-xpm-2005-feb-06-ca-presley6-story.html.

112 *The Spaniels never received a dime*: Indiana Historical Society, "Vivian Carter and Vee-Jay Records," 52.

112 *Take Little Richard's smash hit*: White, *The Life and Times of Little Richard*, 77.

113 *Vee-Jay used the money and credibility*: Mike Callahan, "The Vee-Jay Story," Both Sides Now Publications, December 19, 2006, https://www.bsnpubs .com/veejay/veejaystory1.html.

113 *By 1954, Vee-Jay had moved*: Indiana Historical Society, "Vivian Carter and Vee-Jay Records, 49–54.

114 *Like many independent labels*: Campbell et al., "Vee-Jay: The Early Years."

114 *Vee-Jay's roster included*: Indiana Historical Society, "Vivian Carter and Vee-Jay Records," 56.

114 *In 1961, Vee-Jay signed*: Indiana Historical Society, "Vivian Carter and Vee-Jay Records," 52–54.

115 *Vivian Carter blamed Ewart Abner's "unorthodox" accounting*: Indiana Historical Society, "Vivian Carter and Vee-Jay Records," 52.

115 *By the time of the Beatles' signing*: Alex Bagirov, "The History of the Beatles' Record Releases on Vee-Jay Records, 1963–1987," sponsored by *The Anthology of the Beatles Records*, http://www.dermon.com/Beatles/Veejay.htm.

116 *In August 1963*: Bagirov, "The History of the Beatles' Record Releases."

116 *By the end of 1963*: Bagirov, "The History of the Beatles' Record Releases."

117 *Not to be outdone*: Bagirov, "The History of the Beatles' Record Releases."

117   *Vee-Jay fought back in court*: Indiana Historical Society, "Vivian Carter and Vee-Jay Records," 54.

117   *Undeterred, EMI returned*: Bagirov, "The History of the Beatles' Record Releases."

117   *Losing the Beatles*: Indiana Historical Society, "Vivian Carter and Vee-Jay Records," 55.

118   *Similar to Gary, Indiana*: Emily Fisher, "Migration Has Been a Thorn in the Historical Story of Detroit's Black Population," Detroit Is It, February 18, 2021, https://detroitisit.com/migration-detroits-black-population-history/.

118   *By 1930, the Black population had tripled*: Ken Coleman, "The People and Places of Black Bottom, Detroit," National Endowment for the Humanities, *Humanities* 42, no. 4 (Fall 2021), https://www.neh.gov/article/people-and-places-black-bottom-detroit.

119   *Like most Black Detroiters*: Nelson George, *Where Did Our Love Go?: The Rise and Fall of the Motown Sound* (St. Martin's Press, 1985), 1.

119   *When a lightning strike*: George, *Where Did Our Love Go?*, 5–6.

120   *Berry Gordy Jr., the seventh of Berry Gordy Sr.*: Berry Gordy, *To Be Loved: The Music, the Magic, the Memories of Motown* (Warner Books, 1994), 22–24.

120   *opening a jazz record store*: George, *Where Did Our Love Go?*, 17.

120   *getting married*: Gordy, *To Be Loved*, 70.

120   *The Flame Show Bar booked*: Gordy, *To Be Loved*, 74.

120   *Gordy's first big break*: George, *Where Did Our Love Go?*, 20–21.

121   *Gordy's experiences as a songwriter*: Gordy, *To Be Loved*, 96–97.

122   *Gordy did agree to produce*: George, *Where Did Our Love Go?*, 22.

122   *Before his break with Jackie Wilson*: Smokey Robinson with David Ritz, *Smokey: Inside My Life* (McGraw Hill, 1989), 69–70.

122   *Although the Matadors failed to impress*: Gordy, *To Be Loved*, 91.

122   *Gordy yanked Smokey and the Matadors*: Robinson, *Smokey*, 72.

123   *Berry Gordy's frustration with a publishing company's refusal*: Gordy, *To Be Loved*, 103.

123   *Similarly, after receiving a producer's royalty check*: George, *Where Did Our Love Go?*, 27.

124   *Gordy was, however*: Gordy, *To Be Loved*, 105–108.

124   *With that, Berry Gordy launched*: Gordy, *To Be Loved*, 111–12.

124   *Giant distributors often took advantage*: George, *Where Did Our Love Go?*, 25.

125   *Incidents like these made it clear*: Gordy, *To Be Loved*, 118.

125   *Gordy set up several corporations*: George, *Where Did Our Love Go?*, 28.

125   *As Gordy tells it*: Gordy, *To Be Loved*, 123.

126   *While Berry Gordy didn't make much*: George, *Where Did Our Love Go?*, 31.

127   *Berry Gordy instituted specific business practices at Motown*: George, *Where Did Our Love Go?*, 29.

127   *Gordy instituted a quality control department*: Gordy, *To Be Loved*, 151.

127   *earlier by future Temptations hitmaker*: George, *Where Did Our Love Go?*, 42.

128   *The final key to Motown's cultural and chart dominance*: George, *Where Did Our Love Go?*, 45.

128   *The first Motortown Revue*: George, *Where Did Our Love Go?*, 87.

129   *As Nelson George observed*: George, *Where Did Our Love Go?*, 53.

129   *From the Blues craze of the 1920s*: George, *Where Did Our Love Go?*, 51–52.

CHAPTER SEVEN: FROM *SIR* TO *SWEETBACK*: SIDNEY POITIER AND MELVIN VAN PEEBLES, PIONEERS IN MODERN BLACK FILM

132   *The gruesome murder of fourteen-year-old Emmett Till*: Dianne Gallagher, Sara Smart, and Emma Tucker, "Woman Whose Accusation Led to the Lynching of Emmett Till Has Died at 88, Coroner Says," CNN, April 28, 2023, https://www.cnn.com/2023/04/27/us/carolyn-bryant-donham-emmett-till.

132   *A few months later*: "Emmett Till's Death Inspired a Movement," National Museum of African American History & Culture, Smithsonian, https://nmaahc.si.edu/explore/stories/emmett-tills-death-inspired-movement.

132   *In the aftermath of World War II*: Mary L. Dudziak, *Cold War Civil Rights: Race and the Image of American Democracy*, 25th Anniversary Edition (Princeton University Press, 2025), 79–80.

133   *After the war in 1948, the government won a landmark antitrust case*: *United States v. Paramount*, 334 U.S. 131 (S. Ct. 1948).

133   *This court-ordered divestment*: Alexandra Gil, "Breaking the Studios: Antitrust and the Motion Picture Industry," *NY Journal of Law & Liberty* 3, no. 83 (2008): 120, https://www.law.nyu.edu/sites/default/files/ECM_PRO_060965.pdf.

134   *Stanley Kramer was one such independent producer*: Rick Lyman, "Stanley Kramer, Filmmaker with Social Bent, Dies at 87," *The New York Times*, February 21, 2001, https://www.nytimes.com/2001/02/21/movies/stanley-kramer-filmmaker-with-social-bent-dies-at-87.html.

134   *Although the film received strong reviews*: Adrienne Wartts, "James Edwards (1918–1970)," Black Past, December 25, 2008, https://blackpast.org/african-american-history/edwards-james-1918-1970/.

135   *Poitier, by his own account*: Sidney Poitier, *The Measure of a Man* (Harper Collins, 2000), 56–63.

135   *Throughout the decade*: Poitier, *The Measure of a Man*, 101.

135 *In Kramer's 1958 drama* The Defiant Ones: Poitier, *The Measure of a Man*, 102.

136 *The year before* The Defiant Ones *was released*: "The Little Rock Nine," National Museum of African American History & Culture, Smithsonian, https://nmaahc.si.edu/explore/stories/little-rock-nine.

136 *When Poitier starred in the film adaptation*: Sidney Poitier, *This Life* (Ballantine Books, 1980), 237.

137 *As a contemporaneous review*: James Powers, "Review: Lilies of the Field," *The Hollywood Reporter*, July 23, 1963.

138 *Poitier noted that his win was a milestone*: Poitier, *This Life*, 333–34.

138 *The NAACP's sustained public campaign*: Mark Harris, *Pictures at a Revolution: Five Movies and the Birth of the New Hollywood* (Penguin, 2008), 56.

138 *As film historian and journalist Mark Harris noted*: Harris, *Pictures at a Revolution*, 58.

139 *On March 7, 1965, civil rights marchers*: "1965 Selma to Montgomery March Fast Facts," CNN, February 25, 2025, https://www.cnn.com/2013/09/15/us/1965-selma-to-montgomery-march-fast-facts.

139 *Poitier and Belafonte not only attended*: Joan Walsh, "49 Years Ago, Harry Belafonte Hosted the Tonight Show—and It Was Amazing," *The Nation*, February 16, 2017, https://www.thenation.com/article/archive/49-years-ago-harry-belafonte-hosted-the-tonight-show-and-it-was-amazing/.

140 *in exchange for accepting a fixed fee*: Harris, *Pictures at a Revolution*, 84.

140 *the picture eventually grossed $27 million*: "To Sir, with Love—Production & Contact Info," IMDbPro, accessed February 1, 2026, https://pro.imdb.com/title/tt0062376.

140 *The white filmmaking team*: Harris, *Pictures at a Revolution*, 141.

141 *According to Steve Ryfle's essay*: Steve Ryfle, "Desegregating Hollywood: The Impact and Legacy of 'In the Heat of the Night,'" *Cineaste* 42, no. 4 (2017): 4–8, https://www.jstor.org/stable/i26356777.

141 *Even in 1967, reviewers noted*: Roger Ebert, "Review: *Guess Who's Coming to Dinner*," *Chicago Sun-Times*, January 25, 1968, https://www.rogerebert.com/reviews/guess-whos-coming-to-dinner-1968.

142 *$57 million at the box office*: "Guess Who's Coming to Dinner—Production & Contact Info," IMDbPro, accessed February 1, 2026, https://pro.imdb.com/title/tt0061735.

142 *In the aftermath of the assassination*: Jessica I. Elfenbein, Thomas L. Hollowak, Elizabeth M. Nix, eds., host, *Holy Week: The Story of a Revolution Undone*, *The Atlantic*, March 14, 2023, https://www.theatlantic.com/podcasts/holy-week/; Jessica I. Elfenbein, Thomas L. Hollowak, Elizabeth M. Nix, eds., *Baltimore '68: Riots and Rebirth in an American City* (Temple University Press, 2011).

143   *Their move enraged "dictatorial" Mayor Richard Daley*: Ron Elving, "Chicago '68 Recalls a Democratic Convention and a Political Moment Like No Other," NPR, August 12, 2024, https://www.npr.org/2024/08/11/nx-s1-5068593 /chicago-68-democratic-national-convention.

143   *Eight of the protest leaders were indicted*: Elving, "Chicago '68."

143   *As a consequence, Black audiences began to abandon Poitier*: Poitier, *This Life*, 331.

144   *First Artists was troubled from the start*: Pamela G. Hollie, "First Artists Star-Crossed Child of the 1960's," *The New York Times*, December 23, 1979, https://www.nytimes.com/1979/12/23/archives/first-artistsstarcrossed-child -of-the-1960s-at-a-glance-first.html.

145   *The films, released in 1974, 1975, and 1977*: Poitier, *This Life*, 332–33.

146   *Although they were derided by white writers*: Hollie, "First Artists Star-Crossed Child of the 1960's."

146   *Van Peebles was a truly astonishing man*: Douglas Martin, "Melvin Van Peebles, Champion of New Black Cinema, Dies at 89," *The New York Times*, September 22, 2021, https://www.nytimes.com/2021/09/22/movies/melvin-van -peebles-champion-of-new-black-cinema-dies-at-89.html.

147   *It took nearly ten years and a Supreme Court decision*: Miguel Ortiz, "This Air Force Veteran Fought for Commercial Airlines to Hire Black Pilots," We Are the Mighty, February 8, 2023, https://www.wearethemighty.com/articles /this-air-force-veteran-fought-for-commercial-airlines-to-hire-black-pilots.

147   *According to film critic Mel Gussow*: Melvin Van Peebles, *Sweet Sweetback's Baadasssss Song: A Guerilla Filmmaking Manifesto* (Grand Central Publishing, 2008), loc. 89, Kindle.

147   *Van Peebles directed several short films*: Van Peebles, *Sweet Sweetback's Baadasssss Song*, loc. 89.

147   *Van Peebles moved again, this time to Paris*: Martin, "Melvin Van Peebles, Champion of New Black Cinema."

148   *Columbia wanted to hire a white actor and put him in blackface*: Van Peebles, *Sweet Sweetback's Baadasssss Song*, loc. 121.

149   *A horrified producer*: Van Peebles, *Sweet Sweetback's Baadasssss Song*, loc. 121.

149   *His experience making* Watermelon Man *taught him*: Van Peebles, *Sweet Sweetback's Baadasssss Song*, loc. 129.

149   *Van Peebles repeatedly showed*: Van Peebles, *Sweet Sweetback's Baadasssss Song*, loc. 560.

149   *In his memoir, Van Peebles gleefully recounted*: Van Peebles, *Sweet Sweetback's Baadasssss Song*, loc. 750–51.

149   *Van Peebles claimed*: Van Peebles, *Sweet Sweetback's Baadasssss Song*, loc. 131.

150   Sweet Sweetback's Baadasssss Song *contained too much sex for the MPAA*: Van Peebles, *Sweet Sweetback's Baadasssss Song*, loc. 131.

CHAPTER EIGHT: HIP HOP: THE MOTOWN REMIX

153   *In the 1960s, New York was a noble example of a municipal government that tried*: Michael Beyea Reagan, "A Crisis Without Keynes: The 1975 New York City Fiscal Crisis Revisited," The Gotham Center for New York City History, August 12, 2021, https://www.gothamcenter.org/blog/a-crisis-without-keynes -the-1975-new-york-city-fiscal-crisis-revisited.

154   *When New York City came perilously close to declaring bankruptcy*: Reagan, "A Crisis Without Keynes."

154   *Cuts to arts education*: "History of New York City Arts Education," Arthur Miller Foundation, September 1, 2015, https://arthurmillerfoundation.org /history-of-new-york-city-arts-education/.

154   *Clive Campbell came to the Bronx from Jamaica*: Terry Gross, host, *Fresh Air*, "Fresh Air Celebrates 50 Years of Hip-Hop: DJ Kool Herc," NPR, August 28, 2023, https://www.npr.org/2023/08/28/1195667940/fresh-air-celebrates-50-years-of -hip-hop-dj-kool-herc.

154   *Although Campbell was initially teased*: "DJ Kool Herc," Rock & Roll Hall of Fame, https://rockhall.com/inductees/dj-kool-herc.

155   *Herc joined a graffiti crew*: Caleb Hardy, "Who Is DJ Kool Herc? The 'Founding Father of Hip-Hop,'" *HotNewHipHop*, June 3, 2023, https://www.hotnew hiphop.com/685328-dj-kool-herc-hip-hop.

155   *On August 11, 1973, Kool Herc's younger sister*: Gross, "DJ Kool Herc."

155   *Other DJs began the practice of extending the breaks*: David Browne, "Kool Herc and the History (and Mystery) of Hip-Hop's First Day," *Rolling Stone*, August 11, 2023, https://www.rollingstone.com/music/music-features/kool-herc -hip-hop-50-august-11-1973-1234802035/.

155   *As the Rock & Roll Hall of Fame acknowledged*: "DJ Kool Herc," Rock & Roll Hall of Fame.

155   *As Hip Hop evolved*: Gross, "DJ Kool Herc."

156   *The cofounder of Sugar Hill Records*: "Sylvia Robinson," Rock & Roll Hall of Fame, https://rockhall.com/inductees/sylvia-robinson.

156   *Robinson followed up the next year*: Stephanie Phillips, "Sylvia Robinson's Legacy as 'The Mother of Hip Hop,'" She Shreds Media, February 6, 2019, https://sheshreds.com/sylvia-robinson.

156   *These back-to-back experiences disgusted Sylvia*: "Sylvia Robinson," Rock & Roll Hall of Fame.

157 *The clever word play*: Sylvia Robinson, *Pillow Talk*, In Sheep's Clothing, https://insheepsclothinghifi.com/album/pillow-talk.

158 *Journalist Alan Light described Sylvia Robinson as the "visionary"*: "Sylvia Robinson," Rock & Roll Hall of Fame.

158 *Using her son as a talent scout*: Dave Simpson, "Sugarhill Gang: How We Made Rapper's Delight," *The Guardian*, May 2, 2017, https://www.theguardian.com/music/2017/may/02/sugarhill-gang-how-we-made-rappers-delight-interview.

158 *Chic, comprised of guitarist Nile Rodgers*: Andrew Berman, "Chic's 'Good Times' Reverberates Across the Village, and the World," *Off the Grid: Village Preservation*, August 18, 2023, https://www.villagepreservation.org/2023/08/18/chics-good-times-reverberates-across-the-village-and-the-world.

160 *Once again, Sylvia Robinson was responsible*: Rich Bunnell, "'The Message'—Grandmaster Flash and the Furious Five (1982)," Library of Congress, www.loc.gov/static/programs/national-recording-preservation-board/documents/TheMessage.pdf.

161 *"The Message" and "White Lines" encouraged*: "Chuck D's Series on Hip-Hop: Fighting Power and Changing the World," Thirteen: PBS, July 17, 2023, https://www.thirteen.org/blog-post/chuck-d-tv-series-hip-hop/.

162 *As legal scholar Mathieu Deflem noted*: Mathieu Deflem, "Popular Culture and Social Control: The Moral Panic on Music Labeling," *American Journal of Criminal Justice* 45, no. 1 (2020): 3.

162 *The PMRC was founded by a bipartisan group*: Deflem, "Popular Culture and Social Control," 4.

162 *Nonetheless, the song spurred this pearl-clutching gaggle*: Deflem, "Popular Culture and Social Control," 5.

163 *"Cop Killer," Ice-T's 1992 song*: Kory Grow, "Ice-T and the Controversial History of Body Count's 'Cop Killer': 'Maybe You Should Be Scared,'" *Rolling Stone*, November 24, 2023, https://www.rollingstone.com/music/music-news/body-count-cop-killer-ice-t-book-excerpt-1234876409.

164 *According to Campbell, Black people couldn't*: Luther Campbell, *The Book of Luke: My Fight for Truth, Justice and Liberty City* (Amistad, 2015), 5.

164 *Miami's history as a resort town*: "Women's History Month: 'Mother of Miami' Julia Tuttle Remains Only Woman to Found Major U.S. City," CBS Miami, March 4, 2022, https://www.cbsnews.com/miami/news/womens-history-month-mother-of-miami-julia-tuttle; Andrew K. Frank, "Florida's Historical Amnesia and the Real History of Miami," *The Florida Bookshelf*, September 20, 2017, https://floridapress.blog/2017/09/20/floridas-historical-amnesia-and-the-real-history-of-miami.

165   *Flagler's construction crew razed*: Frank, "Florida's Historical Amnesia and the Real History of Miami."

165   *Campbell recounts that*: Campbell, *The Book of Luke*, 7–8.

165   *Campbell's father refused*: Campbell, *The Book of Luke*, 10.

165   *By Campbell's own account*: Campbell, *The Book of Luke*, 17–19.

166   *Campbell combined work as a cook*: Campbell, *The Book of Luke*, 43.

166   *In May 1980, Miami was rocked*: C. Isaiah Smalls II, "'A Seminal Moment.' Levine Cava Unveils Historical Marker for Arthur McDuffie," *Miami Herald*, February 24, 2024, https://www.miamiherald.com/news/local/community/miami-dade/article285839016.html.

166   *According to the* Miami Herald: Smalls, "'A Seminal Moment.'"

166   *Although the federal government*: Campbell, *The Book of Luke*, 57.

166   *The Miami riots and their aftermath*: Campbell, *The Book of Luke*, 68.

167   *As a club owner and DJ*: Campbell, *The Book of Luke*, 76–78.

167   *In the mid-1980s, the major labels*: Campbell, *The Book of Luke*, 78–82.

167   *By this time, Campbell had joined the group*: Campbell, *The Book of Luke*, 110–11.

168   *In Campbell's opinion, Berry Gordy*: Campbell, *The Book of Luke*, 115.

169   *Campbell was well aware of the increased scrutiny on Hip Hop*: Campbell, *The Book of Luke*, 145.

169   *Crusading right-wing attorney Jack Thompson*: Chuck Philips, "The 'Batman' Who Took On Rap: Obscenity: Lawyer Jack Thompson Put His Practice on Hold to Concentrate on Driving 2 Live Crew Out of Business. In Southern Florida, He Is Loved and Loathed," *Los Angeles Times*, June 18, 1990, https://www.latimes.com/archives/la-xpm-1990-06-18-ca-87-story.html.

169   *Thompson, the Coral Gables, Florida, attorney*: Campbell, *The Book of Luke*, 152.

170   *Regardless of Thompson's motivation*: Campbell, *The Book of Luke*, 153.

170   *Navarro was as publicity-hungry*: Skyywalker Records, inc. v. Navarro, 739 F. Supp. 578 (S.D. Fla. 1990).

170   *Navarro's only evidence*: Luke Records, inc. v. Navarro, 960 F.2d 134 (11th Cir. 1992).

171   *the 1973 Supreme Court case*: Miller v. California, 413 U.S. 15 (S. Ct. 1973).

171   *According to the Eleventh Circuit*: Luke Records, inc. v. Navarro, quoting Pope v. Illinois, 481 U.S. 497 (S. Ct. 1987), at 500.

171   *One of the songs on that album, "Pretty Woman"*: Campbell v. Acuff-Rose Music, inc., 510 U.S. 569 (S. Ct. 1994).

172   *Whether or not the use of copyrighted material*: 17 U.S. Code § 107.

173   *Luther Campbell's argument was that 2 Live Crew's version*: Campbell, 510 U.S. at 574.

173   *Then Campbell appealed to the United States Supreme Court*: Campbell, 510 U.S. at 579.

173   *Importantly, Justice Souter*: Campbell, 510 U.S. at 582.

173   Campbell v. Acuff-Rose Music *marked the first time*: Campbell, 510 U.S. at 583.

174   *While some legal commentators say*: Andy Warhol Foundation for the Visual Arts, Inc. v. Goldsmith, 598 U.S. 508 (S. Ct. 2023).

174   Campbell v. Acuff-Rose Music *was the high-water mark*: Campbell, *The Book of Luke*, 224–28.

CHAPTER NINE: SPIKE TO OPRAH TO TYLER: REMAKING BLACK IMAGES THROUGH THE POWER OF OWNERSHIP

178   *austerity had forced "dramatic cuts"*: Kristin Butler, "The Night New York's Lights Went Out," *American Experience*, PBS, July 15, 2021 https://www.pbs .org/wgbh/americanexperience/features/night-new-yorks-lights-went-out.

178   *The fear that permeated the city that summer*: Samira Asma-Sadeque, "Inside the Terror That Gripped New York City During the 'Son of Sam' Killings," *People*, June 22, 2024, https://people.com/son-of-sam-stalks-new-york-read -people-cover-story-8666846.

178   *The financially strapped city had no resources*: Spike Lee with Ralph Wiley, *By Any Means Necessary: The Trials and Tribulations of the Making of* Malcolm X . . . (Hyperion, 1992), 7–8.

179   *These weren't the films that inspired Spike Lee*: Lee with Wiley, *By Any Means Necessary*, 7.

179   *On the other side of the country*: Allyson Nadia Field, Jan-Christopher Horak, and Jacqueline Najuma Stewart, eds., *L.A. Rebellion: Creating a New Black Cinema* (University of California Press, 2015), 5.

179   *As critic Clyde Taylor noted*: Field, Horak, and Stewart, *L.A. Rebellion*, xxi.

180   *Yet those Black filmmakers faced*: Chuck Kleinhans, "Threads and Nets," in *L.A. Rebellion*, ed. Field, Horak, and Stewart, 58.

180   *Once these UCLA film students completed their films*: Field, Horak, and Stewart, *L.A. Rebellion*, 4.

180   *One notable exception*: Field, Horak, and Stewart, *L.A. Rebellion*, 30–32.

180   *The Black students at UCLA during this period*: Field, Horak, and Stewart, *L.A. Rebellion*, xxv.

180   *Despite their prodigious output*: Field, Horak, and Stewart, *L.A. Rebellion*, 39.

181   *When Spike Lee and cinematographer Ernest Dickerson matriculated*: Spike Lee, *Spike Lee's Gotta Have It: Inside Guerrilla Filmmaking* (Fireside, 1987), 32.

181   *He received negative feedback*: Lee, *Spike Lee's Gotta Have It*, 33.

181 *Undeterred by the narrow-minded reaction*: Danny Djeljosevic, "Oeuvre: Spike Lee: Joe's Bed-Stuy Barbershop: We Cut Heads," Spectrum Culture, March 15, 2012, https://spectrumculture.com/2012/03/15/oeuvre-spike-lee -joes-bed-stuy-barbershop-we-cut-heads.

182 *In 1984, Spike began preproduction*: Courtland Milloy, "The Message of Spike Lee's 'Messenger,'" *The Washington Post*, June 12, 1991, https://www.washing tonpost.com/archive/local/1991/06/13/the-message-of-spike-lees-messen ger/7e94218a-4a7c-4f3f-8fc8-17c9f1a1fc87.

182 *Although Spike was devastated at the time*: Charles Barfield, "'The Messenger': Spike Lee Describes Pulling the Plug on Unproduced 1984 Film as 'a Complete Disaster,'" The Playlist, January 8, 2021, https://theplaylist.net/spike -lee-the-messenger-disaster-20210108.

182 *In October 1984, three months after* The Messenger *fell apart*: Lee, *Spike Lee's Gotta Have It*, 66.

182 *After finishing his research in the fall*: Lee, *Spike Lee's Gotta Have It*, 68.

183 *Initially, he planned to finance*: Lee, *Spike Lee's Gotta Have It*, 128.

183 *His electricity and his phone were nearly cut off*: Lee, *Spike Lee's Gotta Have It*, 216, 229, 244.

184 *The white critics at Cannes gave voice*: Michael Dobbs, "Cannes' Fearless Filmmakers," *The Washington Post*, May 13, 1986, https://www.washingtonpost .com/archive/lifestyle/1986/05/14/cannes-fearless-filmmakers/692fb0b7 -a167-4a2b-bd71-5864d64b1624/.

184 *Spike knew there was a "vast [B]lack audience"*: Lee, *Spike Lee's Gotta Have It*, 61.

184 She's Gotta Have It *ignited a new Black film movement*: Interview by Nelson George in Lee, *Spike Lee's Gotta Have It*, 15.

184 *The next year, actor turned writer/director Robert Townsend*: Susan King, "How 'Cooley High' Changed the Landscape for Black Films in 1975," *Los Angeles Times*, July 6, 2019, https://www.latimes.com/entertainment/movies/la-et -mn-cooley-high-tribute-20190706-story.html.

184 *Samuel Goldwyn acquired distribution rights*: Robert Townsend, director and producer, *Hollywood Shuffle*, The Samuel Goldwyn Company and Metro-Goldwyn-Mayer, March 20, 1987, IMDbPro, https://pro.imdb.com/title /tt0093200.

185 *But 1991 was the apex for Black film*: Karen Grigsby Bates, "They've Gotta Have Us," *The New York Times Magazine*, July 14, 1991, https://www.nytimes .com/1991/07/14/magazine/theyve-gotta-have-us.html.

186 *The next year saw a dramatic drop, with only ten films released domestically in 1992*: "1992 Has Been a So-So Year for Black Films," *Orlando Sentinel*, September 13,

1992, https://www.orlandosentinel.com/1992/09/13/1992-has-been-a-so-so
-year-for-black-films.

186   *Producer Marvin Worth had acquired the rights*: Lee with Wiley, *By Any Means Necessary*, 9.

187   *Once Lee was attached, Warner Bros. balked*: Lee with Wiley, *By Any Means Necessary*, 11–12.

187   *Thus, although the film was budgeted*: Lee with Wiley, *By Any Means Necessary*, 31.

188   *As coproducer Preston Holmes observed*: Lee with Wiley, *By Any Means Necessary*, 112.

189   *Explaining that he had already invested two-thirds of his fee*: Lee with Wiley, *By Any Means Necessary*, 165.

189   *As Spike Lee said*: Lee with Wiley, *By Any Means Necessary*, 12.

189   *In response to the one-two punch*: "Million Man March," HISTORY.com, updated March 2, 2025, https://www.history.com/this-day-in-history/october
-16/million-man-march-1995.

190   *The March was criticized for being patriarchal*: "Million Man March," HISTORY.com.

190   Get on the Bus *didn't merely dramatize*: Judy Brennan, "The 'Bus' Stopped Here," *Los Angeles Times*, October 16, 1996, https://www.latimes.com/archives/la-xpm-1996-10-16-ca-54227-story.html.

191   *Cannon successfully got fifteen Black men*: Brennan, "The 'Bus' Stopped Here."

191   *In 2005, Tyler Perry was a playwright*: Shaheem Reid, "Tyler Perry's 'Mad Black Woman' Was No Overnight Success," MTV, March 17, 2005, http://www.mtv.com/news/1498236/tyler-perrys-mad-black-woman-was-no-overnight-success.

191   *When Perry decided to move into filmmaking*: Madeline Berg, "From 'Poor as Hell' to Billionaire: How Tyler Perry Changed Show Business Forever," *Forbes*, updated April 30, 2022, https://www.forbes.com/sites/maddieberg
/2020/09/01/from-poor-as-hell-to-billionaire-how-tyler-perry-changed
-show-business-forever.

192   *When* Diary of a Mad Black Woman: Darren Grant, director, Tyler Perry, writer, *Diary of a Mad Black Woman*, Lionsgate, Box Office Mojo by IMDbPro, February 25, 2005, https://www.boxofficemojo.com/title/tt0422093.

192   *Film was only the initial salvo*: Berg, "From 'Poor as Hell.'"

193   *In 1984, Winfrey was recruited from Baltimore*: Roger Ebert, "How I Gave Oprah Her Start," RogerEbert.com, December 19, 2012, https://www.rogerebert.com/roger-ebert/how-i-gave-oprah-her-start.

195   *Regulators at the FCC began a study*: Robert W. Crandall, "The Economic Effect of Television-Network Program 'Ownership,'" *The Journal of Law &*

Economics 14, no. 2 (1971): 385–412, http://www.jstor.org/stable/724952, 389–92.

195 *In response, the FCC promulgated*: Crandall, "The Economic Effect of Television-Network Program 'Ownership,'" 392.

196 *The fin-syn rules governed the television industry*: Jennifer González, "Syndication Regulation and TV's Big Three: Broadcasting Regulations and 1970s Television," Library of Congress Blogs: *In Custodia Legis*: Law Librarians of Congress, January 31, 2023, https://blogs.loc.gov/law/2023/01/syndication -regulation-and-tvs-big-three-broadcasting-regulations-and-1970s-televi sion.

196 *They nearly succeeded in 1983*: Matthew McAllister, "The Financial Interest and Syndication Rules," Museum of Broadcast Communications, https:// pages.stern.nyu.edu/~wgreene/entertainmentandmedia/FIN-SYN-RULES .pdf.

196 *One early beneficiary of the new rule*: James C. McKinley Jr., "Don Cornelius, 'Soul Train' Creator, Is Dead at 75," *The New York Times*, February 1, 2012, https://www.nytimes.com/2012/02/02/arts/music/don-cornelius-soul-train -creator-is-dead-at-75.html.

197 *It was a tough slog*: "'Soul Train' Host Don Cornelius Dead of Suicide," Associated Press, February 1, 2012, https://www.mprnews.org/story/2012/02/01 /don-cornelius.

197 *As Kenny Gamble, one half of Gamble and Huff, the duo credited with creating the Philly soul sound, said*: McKinley, "Don Cornelius."

197 *NPR stated, "Soul Train was the* first": Dan Charnas, "Why Don Cornelius Matters," *The Record*, NPR, February 1, 2012, https://www.npr.org/sections /therecord/2012/02/01/146225653/why-don-cornelius-matters.

198 *When Oprah chose* Song of Solomon: John Young, "Toni Morrison, Oprah Winfrey, and Postmodern Popular Audiences," *African American Review* 35, no. 2 (2001): 181, https://doi.org/10.2307/2903252.

198 *According to Perry, Oprah*: Berg, "From 'Poor as Hell.'"

CHAPTER TEN: NOT LIKE US: WHEN THE BOTS TAKE OVER

202 *Drake, meanwhile, scaled the heights of pop stardom*: Xander Zellner, "Here Are All the Hot 100 Records That Drake Has (and Hasn't) Broken," *Billboard*, July 18, 2025, https://www.billboard.com/lists/drake-hot-100-records/; Trevor Anderson, "Drake Is No. 1 on Billboard's Top R&B/Hip-Hop Artists of the 21st Century Chart," *Billboard*, August 26, 2025, https://www.billboard.com /lists/drake-top-rb-hip-hop-artists-21st-century-chart.

202   *The escalation of the competition*: Eliza Thompson, "A Complete Timeline of Kendrick Lamar and Drake's Feud: 'Not Like Us,' Super Bowl and More," updated October 9, 2025, https://www.usmagazine.com/entertainment/news /kendrick-lamar-and-drakes-feud-a-complete-timeline.

202   *Drake had no such reservations*: Thompson, "A Complete Timeline."

203   *In Kendrick's eyes, Drake's worst sin*: Kendrick Duckworth (Lamar), writer, Mustard, producer, "Not Like Us," Interscope Records, May 4, 2024.

203   *As of this writing, "Not Like Us"*: "Kendrick Lamar—Spotify Top Songs," Kworb, updated January 1, 2026, https://kworb.net/spotify/artist/2YZyLoL 8N0Wb9xBt1NhZWg_songs.html.

204   *On November 30, 1994*: "Tupac Shakur Dies," HISTORY.com, updated May 27, 2025, https://www.history.com/this-day-in-history/september-13 /tupac-shakur-dies.

204   *The lyrics were so rough*: Ice-T and Douglas Century, *Ice: A Memoir of Gangster Life and Redemption—from South Central to Hollywood* (One World/Ballantine Books, 2011), 139–140.

204   *The Nas/Jay-Z feud was sparked*: "What's Beef?: Diving into the Feud Between Jay-Z and Nas," Foxy99, updated December 2, 2023, https://foxy99 .com/2023/11/29/whats-beef-diving-in-to-the-feud-between-jay-z-and -nas/.

205   *The tragic end to the Tupac/Biggie feud casts a long shadow*: Elijah Wald, *Talking 'Bout Your Mama: The Dozens, Snaps, and the Deep Roots of Rap* (Oxford University Press, 2014), 194.

205   *The dozens is an informal game*: Wald, *Talking 'Bout Your Mama*, 11.

205   *White sociologists, folklorists, and linguists*: Wald, *Talking 'Bout Your Mama*, 65–68.

205   *Rudy Ray Moore, aka Dolemite*: Wald, *Talking 'Bout Your Mama*, 110–12.

206   *That knockout blow should have*: Ben Sisario, "Drake Accuses Universal Music of Boosting a Kendrick Lamar Song," *The New York Times*, November 26, 2024.

206   *Drake's petition accused UMG*: Ayana Archie, "Drake Accuses Universal Music Group and Spotify of Unfairly Promoting Kendrick Lamar's 'Not Like Us,'" NPR, November 26, 2024, https://www.npr.org/2024/11/26/nx-s1-5206303 /drake-kendrick-lamar-umg-spotify.

207   *In the week of June 12, 1999*: "Maxwell," *Billboard*, https://www.billboard.com /artist/maxwell/chart-history/bsi.

208   *Instead, the labels sued Napster out of existence*: *A&M Records, Inc. v. Napster, Inc.*, 239 F.3d 1004 (9th Cir. 2001).

208   *The labels pursued an aggressive litigation strategy*: Larry Wayte, *Pay for Play: How the Music Industry Works, Where the Money Goes, and Why* (University of Oregon Libraries, 2023), 112

208   *By the time that Napster filed for bankruptcy*: Wayte, *Pay for Play*, 112–13.

209   *Within eight years of its launch*: Cited in Peter Tschmuck, *The Economics of Music*, 2nd ed., (Agenda Publishing, 2021), https://doi.org/10.1017/9781788214292.

209   *In the decade after Napster*: Jem Aswad, "Inside the Multi-Billion Dollar Battle Royale over Music-Streaming Royalties," *Variety Australia*, July 29, 2022, https://au.variety.com/2022/digital/news/streaming-royalties-music-biz-dsps-spotify-4575.

211   *Streaming isn't going away*: Tanner J. Kramp, "Rage Against the Machine: Why the Music Modernization Act Is but the First Step in Musicians' Battle to Reclaim the Value of Their Works," *Boston College Law Review* 64, no. 1 (2023): 221–22, https://bclawreview.bc.edu/articles/2239.

211   *The situation for songwriters is similar*: Royalty Rates, 37 CFR 385.11, Code of Federal Regulations, https://www.ecfr.gov/current/title-37/chapter-III/subchapter-E/part-385/subpart-B/section-385.11.

211   *Despite its position as the market leader*: Liz Pelly, "The Ghosts in the Machine," *Harper's Magazine*, January 2025, https://harpers.org/archive/2025/01/the-ghosts-in-the-machine-liz-pelly-spotify-musicians, 5.

211   *An investigation by journalist Liz Pelly*: Pelly, "The Ghosts in the Machine," 3.

212   *Although Spotify denies that it pushes PFC on listeners*: Pelly, "The Ghosts in the Machine," 6–7.

212   *As* New Yorker *reporter Kyle Chayka has pointed out*: Kyle Chayka, "Why I Finally Quit Spotify," *The New Yorker*, July 31, 2024, https://www.newyorker.com/culture/infinite-scroll/why-i-finally-quit-spotify.

212   *In 2023, Spotify founder*: Pelly, "The Ghosts in the Machine," 11.

213   *In September 2025, independent label Hallwood Media*: Doug Melville, "AI Singer Xania Monet Just Charted on Billboard, Signed $3 Million Deal. Is This the Future of Music?," *Forbes*, updated November 12, 2025, https://www.forbes.com/sites/dougmelville/2025/09/27/al-singer-xania-monet-just-charted-on-billboard-signed-3m-deal-is-this-the-future-of-music.

LISA E. DAVIS is one of the foremost entertainment attorneys in the country. She is chair of the entertainment group of Frankfurt Kurnit Klein & Selz, representing clients in the film, television, publishing, music, theater, and sports industries. Davis has been ranked as a New York–area Super Lawyer since 2007. She is recognized in *Who's Who Legal* 2024; *Best Lawyers in America* 2023–2025; *The Hollywood Reporter*'s Power Lawyers 2025, 2024, 2023, 2021, and 2020 lists of New York's Top 20 Entertainment Attorneys; *Variety*'s Legal Impact Report; and more. A graduate of Harvard College and New York University School of Law, Davis clerked for the Honorable Constance Baker Motley. Davis also writes a political blog titled *Journal of the Plague Years*. She practices law in New York and lives in New Jersey with her family.